illustrated Radio Premium catalog and price guide

including comic character, pulp hero, cereal, TV and other premiums

by Tom Tumbusch

Color Photography by Tom Schwartz

Over 2,000 illustrations of radio, cereal, comic characters, pulp and TV premiums including the rings, badges, decoders, secret code manuals and other amazing gadgets that thrilled two generations of kids from the early 30's to the middle 50's...the golden age of premium giveaways.

TOMART PUBLICATIONS
P.O. BOX 292102
DAYTON, OHIO 45429

To Evie Wilson, a premium lady.

    Prices listed are based on the author's experience and are presented as a guide for information purposes only. No one is obligated in any way to buy, sell, or trade according to these prices. Condition, rarity, demand and the reader's desire to own determine the actual price paid. No offer to buy or sell at the prices listed is intended or made. If there are any questions as to the prices listed, please direct them in writing to the author c/o Tomart Publications, P.O. Box 292102, Dayton, OH 45429. Buying and selling is conducted at the reader's risk. Neither the author or publisher assumes any liability for any losses suffered for use of, or any typographic errors contained in this book. All value estimates are presented in U.S. dollars. The dollar sign is omitted to avoid needless repetition.

    Tomart's *illustrated Radio Premium catalog and price guide* will be updated on a regular basis. If you wish to be notified when the supplements become available, send a self-addressed stamped envelope to Tomart Publications, P.O. Box 292102, Dayton, OH 45429.

    ©Copyright 1989, Thomas E. Tumbusch. All rights reserved, specifically, but not limited to, electronic or other data base entry or storage, in whole or in part, or further reproduction of any material contained herein. No further use of this material may be made without the expressed written permission of Tomart Publications, P.O. Box 292102, Dayton, OH 45429.

Library of Congress Catalog Card Number: 88-51079

ISBN: 0-914293-06-0   Printed in U.S.A.

ACKNOWLEDGEMENTS

It's a thrill to bring you this book . . . a return to yesteryear when premiums definitely were better. If you have as much fun with it as I had putting it together, the work will have all been worthwhile.

This volume supersedes all other lists and booklets. Minor modifications were necessary to a few code numbers used in the past because of unsuspected material found. This book contains nearly twice the information ever possible before, plus two sections of premiums in full color. All color items also appear in black and white in the proper sections. Enjoy matching up items you haven't seen before.

A book such as this represents the accumulated knowledge and discoveries of many people. Without their help this book wouldn't be possible. Special thanks are always in order to Harry, Tom and Jean Hall, Joe Sarno, Joel Allen, Jack Melcher (the guy who really got the hobby together), Gerry Kramer, Tom Claggett (the pioneering editor of The Premium Exchange), Joe Hehn, Ken Chapman, Bill Joppeck, Gerry Springer, Andy Anderson, Rich King, Larry Fait, John Quarterman, and George Hagenauer. Special contributors to this publication were Phil Vandrey, Art Lasky, Fred King, Bob Hencey, Michael Gronsky, Bernie Wernes, Don Coviello, Charles French, Randy Zbiciak, Leon Rue, John Snyder, John Hintz, Steven Boyd, Jack Melcher (he's worth two mentions), Bob Barrett, Jean Toll, Ron Schultz, Ted Hake, Dick Cummings, DeWayne Nall, Wayne Jagielski, Joe Young, Robert Brown, and especially Don Maris for his great Big D show.

My friendly companion in old radio Charles Sexton was always around to help proofread and advise as the book went together.

Ed Pragler and Jim Buchanan trusted me with some of their rarest items for color photography in Dayton - help above and beyond the norm. Thank you gentlemen.

Evie Wilson provided insight, information, and encouragement, but most of all, her understanding why premiums are important to American popular culture . . . and to the people who are interested in seeing this highly successful segment of American marketing history preserved.

Getting the manuscript ready and into print required another team of specialists. Tom Schwartz assisted by Fred Boomer and Terry Cavanaugh did the color photography. Warren Miller and Jim Tromley of Printing Preparations guided the color separations. Rick Lenhard, Jeanne Conners, and Pamela Owings at Boldruler provided their usual excellent service in getting the type set.

Last, but not least, my son Tom, for his contributions over the years; daughter Amy and Marilyn Scott, for having to contend with a guy who works weekends; and Rebecca Trissel who did the typing, proofing, suggested corrections, and provided the support when it was needed most.

Tom Tumbusch
October, 1988

TABLE OF CONTENTS

Dedication 2
Acknowledgements 3
Table of Contents 3-4
About the Author 5
Foreword 5
Market Report 5
What Is The "Rarest" Premium 6
"How it All Began" 6
White Hats, Black Hats And The Theater Of The Mind ... 7
And Now An Important Word From Our Sponsor 8
The Premium Creators 10
How To Find Radio Premiums 12
The Values In This Price Guide 13
Rarity 14
Condition 14
Be Sure To Listen Next Time For More Exciting Offers. .. 15
Premium Newsletter 15
Number Code System 15
Dating Radio Premiums 15
Admiral Byrd 17
Advertising Displays and Signs 17
Allen's Alley — See Fred Allen
American Eagle Defenders 19
Amos and Andy 19
Aunt Jenny's True-Life Stories 20
Armstrong of the SBI — See Jack Armstrong
Babe Ruth Boys' Club 21
Baby Snooks 21
Batman 23
Black Flame of the Amazon, The 23
Bobby Benson of the H-Bar-O 23
Breakfast Club—See Don McNeill
Buck Jones (Hoofbeats) 24
Buck Rogers in the 25th Century 25
Buster Brown Gang (Smilin' Ed's Gang) 27
Captain America 29
Captain Battle Boy's Brigade 29
Captain Gallant of the Foreign Legion 29
Captain Frank Hawks 29
Captain Marvel 31
Captain Midnight 33
Captain Tim Healy's Ivory Stamp Club 37
Captain Video 37
Casey, Crime Photographer 37
Cereal Boxes 38
Challenge of the Yukon, The — See Sgt. Preston
Chandu The Magician 44
Charlie McCarthy 44
Cinnamon Bear, The 45
Cisco Kid, The 45
Clara, Lu and Em 47
Counterspy 47
Cranky Crocodile 47
Davey Adams Shipmates Club (D.A.S.C.) 47
Death Valley Days 48
Detectives Black and Blue 48
Dick Daring, A Boy of Today 48
Dick Steel, Boy Police Reporter 48
Dick Tracy 57
Dizzy Dean Winners Club 59

Doc Savage	59
Don McNeill's Breakfast Club	59
Don Winslow of the Navy	60
Dorothy Hart, Sunbrite Jr. Nurse Corps	61
Duffy's Tavern	62
Edgar Bergen & Charlie McCarthy Show — See Charlie McCarthy	
Eddie Cantor	62
Ed Wynn, The Fire Chief	62
Ellery Queen	62
Fibber McGee and Molly	63
Flashgun Casey — See Casey Crime Photographer	
Flying Family - The Hutchinsons	63
Frank Buck	63
Fred Allen	64
Fu Manchu	64
Gabby Hayes	64
Gangbusters	65
Gene Autry's Melody Ranch	65
Goldbergs, The	65
Green Hornet, The	66
Green Lama, The	66
Gumps, The	66
Hermit's Cave, The	66
Hobby Lobby	66
Hoofbeats — See Buck Jones	
Hop Harrigan	67
Hopalong Cassidy	67
Howdy Doody	68
Howie Wing	71
Inspector Post	71
Jack Armstrong - The All-l-l-l American Boy	72
Jack Benny	75
Jack Westaway Under Sea Adventure Club	76
Jimmie Allen, Air Adventures of	76
Joe E. Brown Club	77
Junior Justice Society of America, The	77
Kate Smith	77
Kayo	78
Kukla, Fran and Ollie	78
Lassie	78
Lightning Jim (Meadow Gold Round-Up)	78
Little Orphan Annie — See Radio Orphan Annie	
Lone Ranger, The	79
Lone Wolf Tribe	86
Lum and Abner	86
Ma Perkins	86
Major Bowes Original Amateur Hour	87
Mandrake The Magician	87
Meadow Gold Round-Up—See Lightning Jim	
Melvin Purvis	88
Nick Carter, Master Detective	88

Og, Son of Fire	88
One Man's Family	89
Operator #5	89
Orphan Annie — See Radio Orphan Annie	
PEP Cereal Pins	89
Phantom Pilot Patrol	91
Popeye	91
Post Comic Rings	92
Quiz Kids	92
Radio Orphan Annie	92
Red Ryder	105
Renfrew of the Mounted	106
Rin Tin Tin	106
Rings, Miscellaneous	107
Rocky Jones, Space Ranger	109
Rocky Lane	109
Rootie Kazootie	109
Roy Rogers	109
"Scoop" Ward	110
Seckatary Hawkins	110
Secret Three, The	110
Sgt. Preston (The Challenge of the Yukon)	111
Shadow, The	114
Sherlock Holmes	115
Singing Lady, The	115
Skippy	115
Sky King	116
Smilin' Ed's Gang — See Buster Brown Gang	
Space Patrol	117
Speed Gibson of the International Secret Police	119
Spider, The	119
Spirit, The	119
Spy Smasher	119
Straight Arrow	119
Super Circus	120
Superman, The Adventures of	121
Tarzan	123
Tennessee Jed	123
Terry and Ted (Uncle Don)	124
Terry and the Pirates	124
Thurston, The Magician	125
Tom Corbett, Space Cadet	125
Tom Mix	126
Vic and Sade	132
Wild Bill Hickok, The Adventures of	132
Wizard of Oz	132
World War II	133
Early Shows and Premiums 1928-34	134
Chronological List of Premiums, When Offered, and Number Distributed	140
Where to Buy and Sell	148
Bibliography	158

COLOR PLATES

Collection of old radio premiums	49
Popular maps	50
Rare maps	51
Paper premiums	52
Prototypes and rare premiums	53
Rings	54 & 55
Comics and other paper premiums	56
Badges	97
Decoder manuals	98
Decoders	99
Paper premiums	100
Space Patrol	101
Signs	102
Cereal boxes	103
Pinback buttons	104

ABOUT THE AUTHOR

Tom Tumbusch has had a life-long interest in popular culture subjects. He is a graduate of the University of Dayton where he studied fine art, communications, and business. He became involved in dramatics in high school which lead to a long association with amateur and professional musical theatre. A series of articles published in *Dramatics Magazine* was collected into his first book, a small paper back of production tips entitled *A New Look at Musical Theatre*.

He became a correspondent for *Variety* while working for a leading regional advertising agency. The paper back was expanded into the *Complete Production Guide to Modern Musical Theatre* published by Richard Rosen Press as part of their Theatre Student series in 1969. *Guide to Broadway Musicals* followed in 1972, was revised in 1978, and completely rewritten and expanded in 1983.

Concurrently in the mid-seventies an advertising campaign lead Tumbusch to old radio broadcasts. Included in some programs were commercials offering premium giveaways. The search for information on these items came up blank and the idea for the *Illustrated Radio Premium Catalog and Price Guide* was hatched. At first small collector's booklets were published by Tomart Publications. Interest and acceptance continued to grow resulting in this volume.

Tumbusch contributed to other publications including *The Nostalgia Bible* and the Time-Life *Encyclopedia of Collectibles*.

"Reconstructing history from bits of information scattered all over the nation was a welcome relief from the hectic pace of the advertising world," he said. "And I felt the system used to develop the premium information could be used for other collecting areas." His next choice was the field of Disney collectibles.

Tomart's *Illustrated DISNEYANA Catalog and Price Guide* was the resulting four volume work. This definitive series covers the entire spectrum of Disney merchandise manufactured or licensed for sale in the U.S. The books also include collector's information plus a history of Walt Disney, his characters, and The Walt Disney Company.

He has been a guest at conventions featuring musical theatre or nostalgia collecting of Disneyana and other popular culture subjects. He has appeared on TV and radio talk shows and been consulted on nostalgia subjects by such publications as the *Chicago Tribune*, *Los Angeles Times*, *Orlando Sentinel*, *USA Today*, *The Wall Street Journal*, and *Money Magazine*.

FOREWORD

This book has been a work in progress for over 15 years. There have been previous presentations, but this volume is significantly different . . . nearly twice the size, representing years of additional research . . . including valuable information provided by some of the cereal companies and other sponsors which originally offered the premiums.

The pre-network programs of the late 20's and early 30's are covered in greater detail. Thanks to a 1935 study on children's listening habits, we even know what premiums these early local or regional shows offered in the greater New York City market. Other shows from around the country were picked up based on data gathered from publicity material, old radio magazines, and the actual premiums.

Many collectors have been diligent in sending in photo copies of premiums not listed in previously published materials. Contributors are noted in the acknowledgements. Everyone interested in premiums owes them a debt of gratitude for helping reconstruct obscure events from the past.

MARKET REPORT

The interest in premium giveaways and the value buyers placed on them is a curious trend to follow. If this book were published three years ago, the report would have been of a mature market with sales and values fairly stagnate. A revitalization was prompted by several events.

The only two premium events ever promoted since the hobby began were taking shape in two different parts of the country. The first announced was a convention of collectors, long talked about, but finally promoted by "Little Jimmy" Dempsey at Evansville, Indiana, July 28-29, 1984. Ironically, an auction of General Mills premiums benefiting the Como Zoo of St. Paul, Minnesota was planned for the same days.

Hundreds of premiums changed hands at these two events and interest broadened beyond the 200 or so hard-core collectors. Then in 1986 it was announced an annual convention of premium collectors would be held in conjunction in what is now known as the Big D Show (formally Childhood Treasures) held each July in Dallas. The availability of premiums at this show is incredible as collectors and dealers convene from all over the nation.

Another trend began to take form in 1987. Collectors who hadn't sent away for items as a kid began to take an interest. A new generation of collectors is finding these amazing gadgets, decoders, and rings as fascinating as the folks who once sent a box top and a dime to get them.

The demand for character related rings is the most acute with values topping $1,000 for the extremely choice items. Other premiums values are rising to a less degree and paper premiums, with the possible exception of the Buck Rogers Cut-Out Adventure Book and a few others, are in less demand.

Overall there is definitely a growing interest in character premiums, cereal boxes, and related items.

WHAT IS THE "RAREST" PREMIUM?

The Jack Armstrong glo-in-the-dark crocodile whistle was only offered in two cities as a test premium. Only 809 were mailed. How many crocodile whistles were scraped, jobbed to a premium liquidator or sold in stores is unknown. In the case of the Lone Ranger meteorite rings only 85 were given out during premium testing. However, Kellogg offered the same item as a Gold Ore Ring on their packages. So, many thousands more of an identical ring were given away under another name. Kellogg's refused to provide the exact number. They cited a company policy not to reveal competitive marketing statistics. It's difficult to understand how information over 30 years old could impact on Kellogg's marketing, but big companies do have policies.

Tracking premiums since 1970 has proven rarity seldom relates to interest or value. The rarest premiums are undoubtedly the items from local and regional radio programs from the late 20's and early 30's; and perhaps some of the plastic TV premiums of the 50's. The "rarest" premiums are often rare because they were duds when they were issued. Lack of interest seems to carry over on some extremely rare premiums. Many are unmarked and communicate little identification with the character.

More important to value is the desire to own a particular item.

In choosing the "rarest" premiums careful consideration was given to nationally available premiums most often requested and the ones seen the least. Perhaps your rarest is among them.

Ten most sought after premiums available nationally
Superman Secret Compartment Ring (2 versions)
Radio Orphan Annie Altascope Ring
Captain Marvel Statuette
Captain Midnight Mystic Sun God Ring
1955-56 Captain Midnight Decoder and Manual
Space Patrol Cosmic Smoke Gun (2 versions)
Green Hornet Secret Compartment Seal Ring
Buck Rogers Cut-Out Adventure Book
Comic Book Club Pinback Buttons for Wonder Woman, The Flash, and the Fawcett set of 10 buttons
Complete Captain Video Flying Saucer Ring

Ten rarest premiums available nationally
Tom Mix Live Turtle (or remaining shell w/decal)
Sgt. Preston Camp Stove and Tent
Doc Savage Medal of Honor
Spider Ring
Lone Ranger National Defenders Warning Siren
Betty's Luminous Gardenia Bracelet (Jack Armstrong)
Cisco Kid Secret Compartment Ring
Don Winslow Lt. Commander Pin
Dick Tracy Inspector General Badge
Radio Orphan Annie Secret Guard Initial Ring

There are many rarer premiums used in isolated tests to determine which premiums consumers wanted more than others; and ones only offered on a local or regional basis. There are also existing one-of-a-kind prototypes and short run premiums which were never manufactured.

Many of the General Mills test premiums surfaced in the Como Zoo auction. Eight different production variances of the Tom Mix wrangler badges and never produced premiums surfaced in the large find of Robbins Company material back in the fall of 1974. Large quantities of premiums manufactured by the Brownie Manufacturing Company were found in December 1974 when the firm was liquidated. Orin Armstrong's son sold many of his dad's handmade prototypes to a Chicago comic book dealer. Examples of these items are with premiums seen on color page 53. The Sky King secret compartment decoder belt buckle pictured is the only one ever made. The Jack Armstrong Listening Squad whistle badges were test premiums. The eight variations of the Tom Mix wrangler badge, the Tom Mix secret compartment signal mirror 45 caliber bullet, Valric the Viking magnifying ring, D.A.S.C. siren ring and the so called "Phantom" voodoo pendant came from the Robbins Company warehouse find and most were never released for use as premiums.

There is also one more large accumulation of premiums being stored. More on that subject later.

If you attended the Dallas show in 1987 or 88 you know you could have purchased just about any premium ever made.

In a sense, every premium is rare, yet most still are available for sale on a fairly regular basis.

There are many ways to define "rarest". There are the rarest national release premiums . . . the rarest local and regional premiums . . . and the one-of-a-kind premiums. In the end, the rarest are the ones you want, but don't have . . . or in the case of some dealers, the ones they happen to have for sale.

"HOW IT ALL BEGAN"

The idea of a premium - a tangible incentive given "free" - goes back to ancient times. This book deals with a particular type premium which developed along with the invention of the radio and the marketing advantages it offered. The ball got rolling back in 1915. The idea of a "Radio Music Box" was outlined in a brief memo from David Sarnoff (later to head NBC and its parent company - Radio Corporation of America) to his superiors at the American Marconi Company. It reads as follows:

"I have in mind a plan of development which would make radio a "house-hold Utility" in the same sense as the piano or phonograph. The idea is to bring music into the home by wireless.

While this has been tried in the past by wires, it has been a failure because wires do not lend themselves to this scheme. With radio, however, it would be entirely feasible . . .

The "Radio Music Box" can be supplied with amplifying tubes and a loud-speaking telephone, all of which can be neatly mounted in one box. The box can be placed on a table in the parlor or living room, the switch set accordingly and the music received. There should be not difficulty in receiving music perfectly when transmitted within a radius of 25 to 50 miles . . .

The same principle can be extended to numerous other fields as, for example, receiving lectures at home which can be made perfectly audible; also, events of national importance can be simultaneously announced and received. Baseball scores can be transmitted in the air by the use of one set installed at the Polo Grounds. The same would be true of other cities. This proposition would be especially interesting to farmers and others in outlying districts removed from cities. By the purchase of a "Radio Music Box" they could enjoy concerts, lectures, music, recitals, etc. which may be going on in the nearest city within their radius.

While I have indicated a few of the most probable fields of usefulness for such a device, there are numerous other fields to which the principle can be extended."

The success of radio transmission was based on a number of earlier patents - principally on the wireless and the "Audion" vacuum tube, so the development field was wide open. American Marconi, General Electric, Westinghouse and other companies scrambled to produce practical receivers.

The breakthrough came in 1919, when Dr. Frank Conrad, an engineer at Westinghouse, started an experimental radio station in his East Pittsburgh garage. He tested this equipment with phonograph records and by occasionally reading from the newspaper. Wireless operators were able to receive his "broadcasts" and the first radio station - KDKA - was born.

Thirty radio stations were on the air in late 1920, when the first presidential election returns between two Ohioans - Warren G. Harding and James M. Cox - were broadcast. If you wanted to listen, you did so on a "crystal set".

In 1922, slightly over 100,000 receivers were sold; in 1923, over a half million were purchased; with three times that number being bought in 1924. Sales were so brisk the giant Sears Roebuck

[1] David Sarnoff by Eugene Lyons, Harper and Row, 1966.

Company put out a special catalog for radio sets and the parts to build your won. And to insure buyers had a source of programming, the company started station WLS, the call letters standing for World's Largest Store.

Radio was here to stay and attention turned to the best method to pay for the programming. Various methods of public support were tried, the most acceptable was a primitive form of what we now call the commercial.

The exact date of the first true "commercial" is a subject for debate. WAAT, Newark, NJ, January 1, 1922; WGAZ (now WSBT), South Bend, IN, July 3, 1922; and WEAF, New York, NY on August 28, 1922 all claim the fame.

Of greater importance to premium collectors, however, is a 1922 broadcast by a beautiful movie queen named Marion Davies. She took to the radio airwaves to deliver a talk entitled, "How I Make Up for the Movies". The sponsor was "Mineralava" - a manufacturer of facial mudpacks - who offered an autographed picture of the star. This was radio's first recorded premium offer. Reportedly some 15,000 requests were received.

Radio developed a mass audience about the time movies were starting to take over from vaudeville. The squeeze wasn't felt at first as many vaude comic and singing performers switched to the radio medium. At the time, every local station had to generate its own programming so there was plenty of work.

That began to change on November 15, 1926, the date the National Broadcasting Company (NBC) went on the air with 26 interconnected stations. Nearly a year later on September 18, 1927, the Columbia Phonograph Broadcasting System of 16 interconnected stations took to the airwaves. NBC added stations so rapidly a second network was created in 1927. The Red Network continued to operate out of WEAF, New York while the new Blue Network was anchored from WJZ, New York. The government broke up the act in 1943 when it forced NBC to sell the Blue Network. It was renamed the American Broadcasting Company (ABC).

The immediate effect of the networks was better programming. Big vaudeville and movie stars had been waiting and watching radio from the wings. The networks gave them the opportunity to reach millions of listeners and that was the key.

This turn of events left non-network stations with no alternative. They had to improve the quality of their own programs. Thus program syndication was an early off-shoot in the fledgling broadcast industry. Syndication is the term given to programs produced by one station or an independent company and sold to whatever station will buy them. The quality of writing and performance of early syndicated programs was usually better than what could be produced on a local station basis. The main attraction of syndication, however, was stations could buy the program for less than the cost to produce a studio show locally . . . and be more competitive with network quality programming.

Syndication played another major role in the early days of radio. The networks were preoccupied with "prime time" evening and daytime adult programming . . . the market segments of greatest interest to sponsors.

Thus, the task of programming to kids was left primarily to the local stations and the independent syndication producers.

In 1936, a study entitled "Children and Radio Programs" was published. Over 3,000 children were interviewed to determine which shows they liked best, the influence the shows had on them, the influence of advertising, the power of premium offers, and similar data. Today this volume provides a detailed insight into the programs of the 1928-1934 era and the premiums they offered. There are brief descriptions of 67 early programs. A table of 107 children's radio programs broadcast on the four New York radio stations WEAF, WJZ, WABC, and WOR lists the name of the show, sponsoring product, station, years on the air, type of program and typical offers.

The children interviewed reported they received 1,726 different

[2]Children and Radio Programs by Azriel L. Eisenberg, Columbia University Press, 1936.

items by sending in a box top, label, aluminum inner seal, green triangle or other proof-of-purchase. Many, however, were product samples, magazines, recipes for children, theater or sports tickets, poems, or store items given away. (See page 134.)

Nearly all early shows offered membership cards and some sort of pin or badge. There were also maps, adventure booklets, song sheets and assorted other items that tied in with the sponsor. Without network access, early children's programs had a choice of local production or syndication via electrical transcription.

One of the most ambitious of these sponsor/syndicators was Ovaltine with their "Radio Orphan Annie" program. The Chicago produced show began in 1930, before a coast-to-coast network link was possible. A second West Coast cast was formed in Los Angeles to air the same scripts for the western U.S. Both casts continued until 1933, when the Chicago cast became the first kid's show to use the national network hookup.

The networks began responding to the demand for other top-flight kid's adventure serials. The result was Wheaties' "Jack Armstrong, the All American Boy" and Ralston's "Tom Mix" in 1933. Together with Ovaltine's "Radio Orphan Annie" and "Captain Midnight", who replaced her in 1940, "Jack Armstrong", "Tom Mix", and one other were to become the main-stay of juvenile adventure serials (and hundreds of radio premiums) over the next 17 years.

"The Air Adventures of Jimmie Allen" was an important syndicated show that began in 1933 in Kansas City. In 1939, the character matured into Stuart "Red" Albright, later known to friend and foe alike as Captain Midnight. As indicated earlier, Ovaltine secured the rights to the program in 1940, and took it coast to coast.

Selecting the programs that were turning points for radio could trigger a great debate. However, one other became a legend . . . and gave rise to a whole new network in the process.

In 1932, George W. Trendle, owner of radio station WXYZ in Detroit, decided to go forward with a new western story idea. He envisioned his western program as a keystone in the development of a statewide Michigan network. The idea was so good, however, the payoff was much larger. "The Lone Ranger" went on the "Michigan Network" in January, 1933, but additional markets were needed to make the project financially feasible. An advertising salesman friend of Trendle's named H. Allen Campbell sold the idea to stations WOR in Newark, WGN in Chicago and WLW in Cincinnati. The Mutual Radio Network with WXYZ and these three stations as the base, was operating by mid-1934 and at one time became the largest radio network. WXYZ later gave birth to "The Green Hornet" and "The Challenge of the Yukon", the story of Sgt. Preston and his dog King.

The latter two WXYZ-based shows achieved a degree of popularity and eventually both crossed the bridge into TV along with The Lone Ranger. Bret Reid, the Green Hornet, was related to the Lone Ranger's nephew, Dan Reid (Bret was his grandson). However, the overpowering stature of the Lone Ranger was too formidable for WXYZ - and for all of radio - to top. The only consolation is that many Green Hornet and Sgt. Preston premiums are rarer today. The rights to all three programs were eventually sold to the Wrather Corporation.

WHITE HATS, BLACK HATS AND THE THEATER OF THE MIND

Early radio heroes may have been bigger than life, but they were united in the basic principle of communicating right from wrong. Violence, if ever, was usually brief. Rarely was anyone killed in juvenile programming. The bad guys were blood-thirsty and cunning, but the heroes outsmarted them with superior logic, cleverness, and many intriguing devices we now call radio premiums.

It was easy to feel close to the principles of radio adventure heroes because all the activity took place in the listener's mind's eye. As a listener you were really part of what was happening. Perhaps, adventure radio was a superior form of entertainment because the listener could "view" the action with as much as or as little violence as he wanted to get out of the "scene". But that's a subject for the psychologists to ponder.

The twinge of nostalgia which makes us want to step momentarily out of today's hectic pace and back to those thrilling, less pressured, days of yesteryear has created a big demand for the old radio programs on tape. Over 50,000 transcriptions have been found to date. Those in the hands of disc collectors have been reproduced on reel-to-reel and cassette tapes for the thousands of old radio show fans and collectors nationwide.

Since many of the programs still contained commercials offering premiums it is common for people to hunt for them. Less than a thousand radio premium collectors have been identified. However many other people discover items in family trunks and pick up new items when they find them. So the number of collectors continues to grow. Some look at premium collecting as an investment. Most seek to acquire items they owned in their childhood. Still others would like to collect, but shy from prices in today's market. However, prices are continuing to rise. In view of that fact, some people have found collecting a single character to be the answer to financial limitations.

AND NOW AN IMPORTANT WORD FROM OUR SPONSOR

Today the words, "and now an important word from our sponsor" often signal an irritating delay in the program. We tolerate these commercials only because we understand that there would be no programs without them. There was a time, however, when a message from Captain Midnight, Jack Armstrong, Sgt. Preston or the Lone Ranger was welcome . . . even awaited with great anticipation.

All that stuff about the cereal - that was for Mom. But oh how we waited to hear Franklin McCormack, Mike Wallace or Fred Foy lead off the program with an announcement something like this:

"Say boys and girls get your pencil and paper ready because today we have some exciting news for you. At the conclusion of today's episode (insert hero's name) will personally tell how you can get in on an exciting new offer. We're sure you won't want to miss out. So get that pencil and paper ready now . . . or ask Mom to take it down for you. It's the best offer we've ever made; so be sure to stand by your radio at the conclusion of today's exciting adventure."

Where did you put that scratch pad? The search was on. To heck with the gripping drama currently unfolding. You found your pencil and paper, but, drat, there is still seven minutes to go. Finally the closely guarded secret was out . . . and we were seldom disappointed. All too well we knew it meant eating or drinking something absolutely awful, but it was worth it to be the first kid on our block to get one.

Return with us now to those thrilling days of yesteryear when a box top and a dime were the key to untold hours of fun and fantasy. Remember when we hung on the announcer's every word as he revealed:

"Now, this is your last chance! Yes, this is your last chance to join the new 1949 Secret Squadron. This is the last day I can tell you about it. Supplies are almost gone. So many fellas and girls are sending in that we must close this offer at midnight Sunday. So send in tonight . . . or tomorrow for sure. Now remember, you send no money. Not one cent. You get all the wonderful new Secret Squadron equipment free of charge . . . if you are one of Captain Midnight's Ovaltine drinking friends. Now isn't that swell? You don't send any money. Not a single penny. And think of what you get! Well, first you get that amazing Key-O-Matic Code-O-Graph; the most amazing code-o-graph the Secret Squadron has ever issued. It's really a honey. Big, full two inches long and made of strong, durable metal so it can last a lifetime. It's bright . . . shiny as gold. Has a rich gold-colored finish with bright red gears for automatic decoding. Here on the top are the words, "Captain Midnight" . . . and the letters "S.S." . . . which you know stand for Secret Squadron . . . and the famous winged insignia of the Secret Squadron in raised design and in big numbers, the date of this wonder new Secret Squadron . . . 1949. Say-y-y, w-h-e-n you see your Key-O-Matic Code-O-Graph you'll say it's the best looking piece of secret equipment you ever saw. And think how many ways you'll use this wonderful code-o-graph. With this amazing Key-O-Matic Code-O-Graph you can decode the secret messages sent to you by Captain Midnight . . . automatically. And, of course, if you don't have it you can't decode the secret messages. You can't be on the inside of all the exciting events coming. It's twice as secret. Twice as mysterious. Twice as much fun as any code-o-graph the squadron's had before.

Now! Here's the secret! The Key-O-Matic Code-O-Graph has two parts to it. Besides the code-o-graph, there's a special secret little key . . . you must have it to operate the code-o-graph. Only with this special key can you operate the master code setting. Actually set your code-o-graph for any one of six hundred and seventy-six master code designations and then decode automatically. But someone who hasn't got a separate key can't operate the master code! Why, if even some enemy of the Squadron should get your code-o-graph he couldn't use it at all without the key. You can actually hand your code-o-graph to a friend and ask him to decode a message and he can't set and work it without that all important key. Now think of the fun you'll have while you mystify your parents and friends when you can change master codes and decode automatically . . . and they can't tell how you do it! And besides all this, you also get the new official handbook of the 1949 Secret Squadron. Eight pages in full color with pictures of Captain Midnight, Chuck, and Joyce . . . and new secret passwords and signs and signals. And remember! It doesn't cost you a single penny. Not even one cent . . . if you're one of Captain Midnight's Ovaltine drinking friends.

Now here's all you do to get your official 1949 Key-O-Matic Code-O-Graph and your new official Secret Squadron handbook without charge! Just tear the label (the entire label) from your jar of chocolate flavored Ovaltine. Print your name, address, city and state on the back of the label. Put it in an envelope and mail to Captain Midnight, Chicago, Illinois, but do it now . . . it's your last chance. This offer closes midnight Sunday. Tear the whole label from your jar of Ovaltine. Print your name and address on the back of the label and mail to Captain Midnight, Chicago, Illinois, TONIGHT or by Sunday for sure." (Running time: three minutes, 20 seconds.)

Well, gang, if you didn't send in then it was truly your last chance. There were more premiums, but most were plastic items. But as the above "official" Captain Midnight radio commercial transcript related (probably with a much greater degree of finality than the advertising writer ever intended) this was truly your last chance to obtain a bright and shiny, sturdy metal with rich gold-colored finish, rugged piece of secret equipment that would last a lifetime.

The majority of fellas and girls found the novelty of decoding, along with the rich gold finish, wore off in a few weeks. Most were broken, lost or discarded.

Yet, if you suffer a long-suppressed desire to own a 1949 Key-O-Matic Code-O-Graph, the chances of finding one at your neighborhood antique show or flea market are pretty good. Finding the official secret handbook and the special little key will be a lot tougher, but I'm sure the old Captain won't mind your knowing that a girl's hairpin will work the master code gears just as well as the little

8

key most kids lost the day they opened their envelope from Captain Midnight - Chicago, Illinois.

You remember the cost of "not one cent to Captain Midnight's Ovaltine drinking friends". Wel-l-l-l . . . things certainly have changed. Three decades later the same "big, full two inch" mechanism of brass and red plastic gears that used a key to change master codes and then decode automatically in a condition you would be proud to show your family or friends would command between $20 and $35.

They would be amazed to learn what you paid for it, but your safety deposit box would be the envy of your neighborhood. The terrific badges, decoders, other secret equipment offered on radio commercials, comic books, cereal packages, and in the Sunday funnies section seem even more fascinating today than when you waited the eternal "couple of weeks" it took to complete the cycle from box top to your mailbox.

There were hundreds, perhaps thousands, of such items offered during the golden age of radio . . . between 1930 and 1950. There were a few premiums offered earlier. And, of course, similar premium offers continue to the present day. But the items offered during this period were in a class by themselves.

There are several reasons.

The Depression era 30's made it possible to produce intricate objects of apparent value at low cost. Times were difficult, even for the family with a working breadwinner. Tales of the less fortunate had everyone watching their money. The public was ripe for offers of free gadgets coupled with an inexpensive food product which promised improved nutrition.

Radio itself was new. Its marvels were still not completely understood. Programs and commercials were aired to the undivided attention of an audience of people who bought the products they heard advertised.

Mom was reinforced in her decision to buy products the kids needed to send for premiums because she overheard the commercials. Sponsors wisely supported their claims with even more detailed health and energy information in women's magazines.

The best part was the sponsors didn't let you down. When the package arrived and your nervous fingers somehow managed to get it opened you weren't disappointed. The secret compartment wasn't quite as big as you pictured it. The magnet ring you got from Tom Mix wasn't as powerful as the one Tom used to magnetize the ring of keys from across the room . . . and you soon found coding and decoding was more trouble than it was worth. But you were still glad you sent away for it. Many happy hours were spent playing and fantasizing with your treasure. But most of all, there was the fun of being the first kid on your block to own one and to show it off to your friends. Oh, the superiority you felt as they turned green with envy. It mattered little the amazing gold-colored ring was producing an identical effect on your finger.

The offers were truly amazing because in those days the premium items offered could easily cost the advertiser more than the box top and the dime we sent in. Back then the number of premium requests were used to gauge how many kids were listening and to get them to try the product.

Today it would cost over $10 each to produce a rather simple ring in the original brass material (if it were still available). Even though many of the original dies still remain, the special high-speed, injection-forming equipment on which they were used faded from the scene in the early 60's. Cheap plastic forced in a new era of premiums. The lacquered gold flashed, brass rings and decoders "as shiny as gold" became the thing of the past.

According to the recollection of a man who represented the Robbins Company at the time, the most successful premium offer ever was the Lone Ranger Kix Atomic Bomb ring. Three separate manufacturing runs were required to meet the first avalanche of orders. Over 6 million rings were produced . . . from 1948 to 1957. General Mills confirmed this information.

Part of the success of premiums during the golden age was the close association of the character and the products they represented. Ralston owned the rights to Tom Mix. General Mills owned Jack Armstrong and presented the Lone Ranger in all but seven states. Ovaltine controlled Radio Orphan Annie and Captain Midnight while Nabisco owned all rights to Straight Arrow.

By the mid-50's companies could no longer sponsor an entire show. The tremendous cost of producing and airing children's programming became prohibitive. But every now and then a super premium is created. Some of the best I've seen in recent years are the Cheerios' Super Hero dart game, the General Mills' Battlestar Galactica cockpit and the Superman ring from Nestles'.

Every now and then manufacturers once again realize the value of adventure heroes kids recognize rather than the characters the brand creates and tries to get the kids to accept. Ovaltine has issued some modern Orphan Annie premiums tied to the 50th anniversary of the radio show and some additional movie tie-ins. There was a Lone Ranger movie membership kit offered by Cheerios and Ralston made an aborted attempt to revive the old Tom Mix Straight Shooters Club - complete with a photo, membership card, cereal bowl, patch, radio show record, and a spectacular wristwatch. Captain Midnight resurfaced in 1987 to offer a T-shirt and a watch.

THE PREMIUM CREATORS

A surprisingly few people were responsible for creating the vast majority of all premiums produced during the golden age.

The major focal point of premium creators was a middle man named Sam Gold. From his base in Chicago he made the rounds of cereal companies, advertising agencies, and radio show producers. He had a knack of selling premium ideas and the ability to round up free lance premium creators and manufacturers. Sam Gold was a visualizer. The box top boys would hire him to conjure up just the premiums they needed to accomplish their sales and promotion objectives.

Sam Gold

People who worked with Sam Gold reflect him as a bit of an actor who could dramatize an infant idea in great detail, get the order, and then figure out how to do what he said he could.

The Gold Company produced hundreds of premiums. The March 14, 1949 issue of LIFE Magazine chronicled a bit of Sam Gold and the box top premium business at its zenith. The article depicts many popular premium rings and some obscure soap opera jewelry. The Life issue is available at some back issue magazine stores and can be found at most public libraries for reading.

Gold counted on Orin Armstrong for the design of many of the metal objects. Armstrong was both an artist and sculptor who produced ideas and finished mock-ups for Gold's presentations to ad agencies and sponsors.

Often several different designs were made for the same premium. In the mid 70's a large find of radio premium items produced examples of different designs of the Tom Mix Wrangler badge with variations in the metal and other materials used. A Tom Mix bullet with secret signal mirror, a bullet ring with concealed ballpoint pin, a Valric of the Vikings ring with magnifying lens similar to the Radio Orphan Annie ring and other items were also found. Perhaps these were test premiums, but the author knows of none found in the original mailer . . . or any others found outside this one "warehouse" batch.

Armstrong's son, Russell, sold some of his dad's prototypes to a Chicago dealer. Among them were the Sky King secret compartment decoder belt buckle, a Sky King kaleidoscope ring, and several Green Hornet type rings with a plain silver metal disc covering the secret compartment. An enterprising dealer put a picture of the Red Goose inside one in order to pass it off as a production piece.

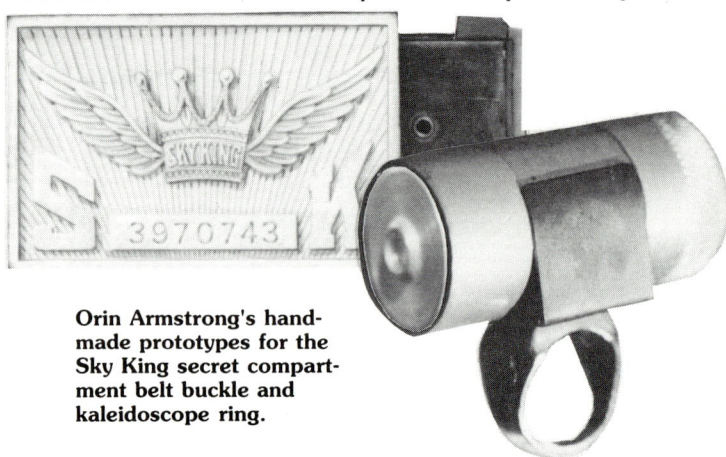

Orin Armstrong's handmade prototypes for the Sky King secret compartment belt buckle and kaleidoscope ring.

Another Gold employee, John Walworth, designed many plastic items. The Straight Arrow Mystic Wrist Kit, arrow ring and bandana were among the many items he designed for the character. John also created over 600 plastic toys for Cracker Jack; plastic premiums for Kool Aid; football and Flintstone figures for Post cereals; and miscellaneous figures for Nabisco and Kellogg's. When two of Gold's key employees split off to formed their own company Walworth stepped in to fill their shoes. Paper items designed by him include Howdy Doody puppets for Poll Parrot; Straight Arrow puzzles, drums, and headbands; the Tom Corbett membership kit; and the second Howdy Doody end seal poster. He also designed the Space Cadet and Straight Arrow shoulder patches.

There were probably other designers Sam Gold turned to for the gold flashed, brass rings, badges, decoders and other objects. Unfortunately, research to date has not produced information about any others. However, inquiries have unearthed some interesting facts on how the items themselves were produced.

Metal premiums started like any other form of advertising: with a handmade conceptual layout or mock-up. Paper items were drawn or painted while metal items were fashioned, however crudely, from the materials planned for production. Dies were then made and proofed in lead. After any required corrections a small run of 20 to 100 pieces were produced for final approval. Sometimes alternate designs were tested to determine the most cost effective production method or the most appealing design.

Anywhere along the line the premium could be abandoned in favor of a better premium or the failure to sell the idea.

Lead proofs for Jack Armstrong Whistling Squad Lieutenant and Captain badges, watch fob decoder, and All–American Boy ring.

10

Paper premium engineers Fred Voges (l.) and Wally Wiest (r.) in a photo they staged for use in promotional material. (circa 1952)

Premiums were usually approved for manufacture after the first several ads and commercials had run. The initial response was used to gauge the size of the production run. The majority of metal premiums were manufactured in Massachusetts and shipped to Battle Creek or the greater Minneapolis, Chicago or St. Louis areas for fulfillment. Yea, gang, that's what was going on while we were checking our mailboxes each day . . . and why we must still "allow 6-8 weeks for delivery".

The Einson-Freeman Company of Long Island City produced paper premiums of all types throughout the 30's and 40's. Sam Gold turned to them often for production of masks, games, punch-out kits and other paper premiums. Most were designed by Fred Voges and Wally Weist. When World War II came along the materials shortage virtually killed metal premiums and the use of paper premiums increased. In 1942 Sam Gold joined Einson-Freeman as a vice-president.

All indications suggest Gold maintained his offices in Chicago. Material from the Voges estate relates Fred worked for Gold in Chicago during this period . . . and until 1946 when he and Weist formed their own company.

Some of the rarest of all premiums are punch-out and other paper premiums. A lion's share of these were created by Voges and Weist. Voges was the paper engineer - one of the most creative to come along since the oriental origami masters. Wally Weist was a versatile artist in his own right, but was an accomplished "swipe" artist as well. He was equally at home copying a Rembrandt in oils as he was at reproducing the styles of Disney or Milt Caniff on premiums.

Presently more is know of Fred Voges. The saga began at his father's Chicago paperboard printing and die cutting shop in the early 30's. The major product at the plant was gambling punch boards. Somehow Blue Ribbon Books of New York came to the elder Voges with a new idea for children's books they had just patented - the "Pop-Up" book. Young Fred, fresh out of Emmington High School, was intrigued with the concept. In short order he produced mock ups of the earlier titles. His father's shop got the work and Fred did the paper engineering on all the "pop-up" titles, as well as the Mickey Mouse and Wizard of Oz "Waddle Books".

His work came to the attention of the Einson-Freeman Company. Fred did a lot of design work for them from about 1934 until he went to work full-time for Sam Gold. During this time Fred's designs included Disney board games, maps and movie viewers; the Tarzan map game for Kolynos toothpaste and other sponsors, rubber band guns for Buck Rogers, Dick Tracy (and many other characters), paper ventriloquist puppets, and the Captain Sparks/Orphan Annie pilot cockpit trainer.

Not too much is know about Wally Weist before the time he joined the Gold Company the same week Fred Voges did in the early 40's. At Gold's shop they did the Terry and the Pirates, Disney, and PEP airplane premiums, as well as designs for hundreds of game oriented cereal box backs. The most notable work done after they formed their own company was a series of premiums for the Howdy Doody TV programs including puppets, masks, a magic kit, several bread end seal and punch-out promotions. A large number of miscellaneous paper premiums were done for the Mars candy company including many items for the Super Circus TV show.

Fred and Wally continued to do a number of Disney premiums including numerous bread end seal promotions which grew out of the famous Donald Duck bread series. A favorite is the Peter Pan Pan-o-rama. It combined bread end seals with a cardboard punch-out scene received in store or by mail to create a composite scene from the movie.

Their other work included cereal box backs, punch-outs for Captain Kangaroo, plus Hopalong Cassidy and the Cisco Kid bread end seals albums.

Wally Weist died in 1957 and the company was dissolved. The firm's records, along with original art and thousands of sample paper premiums, were stored in the Voges home in Chicago. Over

Unsold premium ideas for the Tom Mix Rodeo (envelope pictured). Terry and the Pirates glo-in-the-dark photos, and the Capt. Sparks Airport.

the years many premiums were dispensed to neighborhood children as Halloween favors.

Fred Voges went to work for a packaging design and manufacturing company and did no further premium work. Later, in retirement, he learned of the nostalgia boom and began to make the rounds to comic and memorabilia shops in the Chicago area gradually selling off his work.

In 1978 Joe Sarno and later George Hagenauer began to help. Our hobby, and this author in particular, is indebted to George for preserving the work of these two men. When Fred Voges' health was failing George made many trips to his home to sift through hundreds of boxes to sort out the most marketable material.

George related a couple of interesting stories Fred Voges once told him. The first dealt with the PEP paper airplanes. Fred and Wally were working for Sam Gold at the time. Their office was in the upper floors of a building located in the Loop near State on Wacker Drive. The design for each of the 40 different planes was finalized by "test flights" of various prototypes launched high above the "El" trains much to the surprised pedestrians below. The in-pack premiums were so successful the two underpaid artists ($25 per week) found they could trade large stacks of the planes at local grocery stores for rationed meat. Storekeepers then sold the planes to build traffic and to profit from their investment . . . and the kids could pick the planes they needed to complete their sets.

Another great story concerned Mary Hartline, the voluptuous blond star of TV's "Super Circus." Fred and Wally worked up the art for a paperboard puppet of Mary leading the Super Circus band. There was an initial print run of 100 to proof the printing and check the die-cut. It looked exactly like Mary and several were routinely sent to the producer for final approval. To everyone's surprise, Mary Hartline's manager, her husband, rejected the proof and required that the job be done over because he objected to her bust being too large. (Do you suppose he knew different?) A less profound Mary Hartline puppet was the result.

Sam Gold's son entered the business somewhere along the line. Now retired to a warmer climate, he has written to say the Gold family has retained quantity samples of the premiums the Gold Company produced. So there is still hope out there for everyone looking for a Superman secret compartment ring or other spectacular premium.

HOW TO FIND RADIO PREMIUMS

"How do I find premiums?" is an often asked question by numerous new and old collectors. The answer really depends on how aggressive they want to be. One collector acquired nearly everything in less than three years. Some people prefer to take their time and buy the items they want at the best possible price.

The more aggressive collectors will get in touch with everyone they can find who collects premiums (by mail and phone) and subscribe to the major premium mail auctions. Some of these are found in the "Where to Buy and Sell" section.

The next step is to attend all antique toy and antique advertising shows within reasonable driving distance. These specialized shows attract dealers who specialize in premiums. They learn to know these nostalgia dealers. If they are looking for a special list of items, they let their dealer friends know. Some dealers will even hold a needed item until they see them.

Of course, the best way to find radio premiums is at the source . . . the original owner, auction, garage or estate sale where they just surface. Often items can be acquired at a fraction of their normal values. It's also a way to get first chance at extremely rare items as well. Unfortunately, this is by far the most time consuming and most often frustrating method.

A handful of collector/dealers advertise for premiums in the various antique publications. This is probably the most expensive way to locate premiums, but you get first choice on much of what is uncovered nationwide. Advertisers in Box Top Bonanza, the hobby's newsletter, usually have items at more realistic prices and will perhaps suggest a favorable trade for an item you have.

There is one method of finding premiums which appears to be exhausted. Most of major warehouse type premium finds are history - the Dille Chicago warehouse of Buck Rogers material, the Fawcett Publication files, the Voges estate, the excess General Mills samples auctioned for the benefit of the Como Zoo, the excess stock of the Brownie Manufacturing Company and the warehouses where the Robbins Company stored their samples. While it can't be said all large concentrations of premiums have been uncovered, it can be said many, many people have searched without much success.

It seems sometime in the life of each collector there's a spark of inspiration to trace down the original sponsor or premium manufacturer. While many discoveries were made in the 70's, not much has been found in quantity in the last 10 years.

Mention of the Robbins Company in a previous publication prompted the following letter:

Dear Mr. Tumbusch,

Richard King of Providence was recently kind enough to show me a copy of your book which I enjoyed reading. I'm at the right age to relate closely to the olden, golden days of radio. Your book is very well done and I'm sure of great interest to collectors of radio memorabilia.

We were, however, disturbed by the reference to the Robbins Company on page 8. We have checked out the possibility that "thousands of items were uncovered" in our warehouse and believe there is no way this could be true. All overruns, cancelled orders, etc., are quickly scrapped. This coupled with our excellent plant housekeeping makes it impossible that a quantity of old premiums could have been found here.

The possibility does exist that some of our older or retired employees may have some of the old medallions, decoders, etc., that we made years ago, but we would doubt that there would be significant quantities involved.

We would very much appreciate your correcting what has to be erroneous information about the Robbins Company when your next catalog is published.

Thanks again for an otherwise excellent publication.

Sincerely,
F. W. Munro, Jr.
The Robbins Company

The following letter was sent in response:

Dear Mr. Munro:

The help you have provided through Rich King is greatly appreciated. When he told me of all you did I sent along a personal copy of the book for you.

Then it was a surprise to hear from you directly. You can be assured that in the future I will make clear all the material that has turned up is not from your company warehouse . . and that you no longer have any samples on hand.

We get more letters on the big premium finds than all other subjects combined. That's why I'm trying to clear the air and save us all a lot of correspondence.

Here is the story as I've been able to piece it together.

In November and December of 1974 two large stocks of old radio premiums were uncovered. The first was that of the Brownie Manufacturing Company. The firm was liquidating and one of the lawyers involved knew an antique dealer who in turn contacted me. I have a complete inventory of the material found . . . mostly plastic pieces with optics. Since that is not an issue to you, I'll stick to the story as it concerns Robbins.

Apparently, acting quite independently but perhaps as a result of the Brownie material being sold for $2,000+, someone else went to work tracking down the Robbins leftovers . . . and from wherever he got it, he turned up a bunch of it.

First, the finder tried to sell the stuff to the dealers who found the Brownie material. It was a truck-load deal just too big for them to handle so the finder started to retail it in the New York City area. Collectors bought everything he had with him. That was his first tip off to the value of his find. A steady flow of material has been placed throughout the country - and still keeps turning up periodically.

Over the years I've been running down every lead I can find. My file folder on this subject is full of lists, photos, interviews and correspondence documenting the following facts:

- There were many thousands of "like new" premiums, parts and a few dies of Robbins Company manufacturer offered for sale since 1974.
- Many prototypes, alternate designs of known premiums and finished premiums that were never actually offered have also turned up during this period.
- Everything found is metal. No premiums are found with the instructions or in the mailer. (However, Lone Ranger Six Gun rings have been shipped by the dozens in chipboard boxes.)
- All trails trace back to the state of Rhode Island.

Your information has convinced me the material was not harbored at the Robbins plant warehouse. Yet such a large quantity of material had to be stored somewhere other than by a private collector or employee. The very nature of material indicates it was put into storage by the Robbins Company . . . because only they would have had possession of the dies, parts, prototypes and unissued premiums . . . or any interest in storing them.

The theory that seems most likely is a public warehouse . . . one your company would have used in the years 1936 or 37 to around 1950. (All the premiums found in quantity were offered during those years . . . most from 1936 to 1941.) Perhaps your company even paid storage charges until the 60's or early 70's and then decided to abandon it. It could have stayed there until the warehouse needed the space or until the finder located the material.

That is probably more than you wanted to know, but I'm stuck with a moral dilemma of publishing the most accurate prices possible based on the buying, selling and trading experience of hundreds of collectors.

Should you wish to help further, you might try looking into the possibility of public warehouse usage during the period mentioned. (Such use would seem highly likely since your company was turning out so many high-volume orders within a short period back then.)

In any event, I wish to personally thank you for your interest and cooperation. And as mentioned at the outset, you can rest assured the subject of your letter will be cleared in future publications.

Sincerely,
Tom Tumbusch

Nothing further was received and it seems highly unlikely files on warehouse contents 30-40 years old would still be available. The Robbins Company is in business to manufacture metals and awards and not to provide historical data on premiums. They are more polite than most of the old sponsors in answering letters on a subject which no current employees have much interest or knowledge. Even the specialized equipment on which most premiums were made was scrapped in 1962.

The premiums are out there to be found in all price ranges. Aggressive collectors will get first choice through established channels, but experience proves good things also come to those collectors with perhaps less money and more patience. A big part of the fun is the thrill of the hunt. It's a vast field of collecting and often full of surprises.

THE VALUES IN THIS PRICE GUIDE

This book is a collector's guide to average prices, according to condition. Prices listed are for collector transactions at the time research was completed. The real value of any collectible is what a buyer is willing to pay. No more. No less. Those prices are constantly changing . . . up and down.

Many factors have a bearing on each transaction. Not the least of these are imagined value, emotional desire, or competitive drive for ownership.

Most dealers want the highest price they can get and continually test collectors with prices higher than guide.

Prices listed are based on the author's experience and are presented as a guide only. No offer to buy or sell at the prices listed is intended or made. If there is any question as to the prices listed, please direct them in writing to the author c/o Tomart Publications, P.O. Box 292102, Dayton, OH 45429. Buying and selling is conducted at the reader's risk. Neither the author or publisher assumes any liability for any losses suffered for use of or any typographic errors contained in this book.

Supply and demand - always factors in measuring value - are a bit more predictable for those knowledgeable in a given area of collectibles. They have a feel for how often they see a given item come available for sale. However, since everyone has different experience there are a lot of different ideas on which items are rarer and more valuable.

The availability of the items listed in this book is definably limited. No more originals will be manufactured.

The quantities of vintage radio premium production ranged anywhere from hundreds up into the millions. Generally, the items which generated the greatest interest originally were the items produced in the largest quantities. These were the rings, decoders, and badges which continue to be the most popular premiums today. And since there were more of them produced back then, they still turn up on a regular basis in attics, old chests of drawers, and even warehouses.

Premiums from the last 50-60 years just aren't old enough to consider the known universe as a valid basis for establishing values. Hopalong Cassidy hat/compass rings were thought to be very rare until a quantity was uncovered in 1987 . . . over 25 years since it was used as a premium. They sold for $20 each. The supply of newly discovered items helps meet the demand of new collectors coming into the hobby and influences the value of many premiums. Of course, this isn't always the case. There are rare and even some rather common items in high demand . . . and the value of these items outperform the radio premium market as a whole . . . at least until supply catches up with demand.

Memory recalls the sale of three Lone Ranger Frontier Towns in the same mail auction. For years a complete punched town had sold in the $150-$300 range. The first of the three in our example sold for $360, the second of $2,000 and the third for $400. There were a few buildings missing the last case, but the real point is the final bidders in the second sale were a major oil company executive and a Texas cattleman. The Texan vowed to get it for a party and did. Several Lone Ranger towns ranging in price from $300 to $700 went ownerless at the 1988 Big D show in Dallas.

Was a Lone Ranger Frontier Town ever worth $2,000? It was for a brief time, but that market force has been satisfied and "current" values are more in the line with the historic progression for this item. Ironically, a complete town was purchased at a local flea market within a few months of the $2,000 sale for just $20.

The idea the value of collectibles rise automatically with inflation or to the highest price one person is willing to pay at an auction has slightly less creditability than the fellow in the alley who is offering to sell you a solid gold 17-jewel watch for $10. Values rise and fall at the whim of the people who are ready buyers.

There is no ready market for an entire radio premium collection at retail value. There have been numerous examples in recent years where collections of nostalgia collectibles were sold at estate and sheriff sales at a fraction of the estimated value. Except for a very limited number of high demand items the process of turning a good size collection of radio premiums back into cash can be a long and expensive one.

This book reports market prices based on items sold at leading antique shows and flea markets, as well as toy and antique advertising shows. No attempt has been made to report auction prices.

Collectors who buy at shows can generally purchase for less. Often they have first choice of items offered for sale; sometimes at exceptional bargain prices. But they also incur substantial time and travel expenses.

Mail and gallery auctions are preferred by collectors who don't have the time or the ability to visit major shows. Money spent and current resale value also tend to be of less concern to the auction buyer. The winning bidder must outlast the others who have an emotional fix on ownership or perhaps need the specific price to "complete" a collection.

It's difficult to say who actually spends more money in pursuit of their collecting interest . . . the show goer or the auction buyer. This much is sure. There are substantial costs involved beyond the money spent on collectibles by the show goer not normally considered in the "price". In mail or gallery auction sales, however, the "price" includes all the costs.

Collecting should be pursued for the interest and satisfaction involved. There are much better investments at most financial institutions. Both Fortune and Business Week magazines have done extensive articles on the pitfalls of speculating in what these magazines categorize as "exotics".

Every attempt has been made to have this price guide reflect the market in its broadest sense. The research effort covers over 40,000 miles of travel each year to attend leading antique, toy, and advertising shows from Boston to Glendale, California. Mail auctions are monitored and many sales lists are received. Collectors and dealers from across the country call to report sales of collections or premium finds in their area. Major criteria used are prices at which items do not sell even though they are seen show after show and cooperating dealers who report sales and trends. The up-to-date values in this book are a compilation of information received through October 1988.

There are two more factors affecting value which can be measured more precisely - rarity and condition.

RARITY

Some premiums were available for years after they were first offered. Examples of this type of continuous distribution include almost all early Tom Mix premiums, the Dick Tracy Quaker badges from 1938 to 1940, the non-decoder Captain Midnight premiums from 1945 to 1949 and Lone Ranger Safety Club badges. Most premiums, however, were offered for only a couple of months or so before the offer was terminated. Betty's luminous gardenia bracelet was offered only on two Jack Armstrong programs in 1941 and surely holds the record for brevity of an offer. However, it was also offered as a soap opera premium by General Mills.

Almost every premium sent out had a "bounce back" offer of yet another premium. Such premiums are rarer because only the people sending for the original premium knew about them. Many of these were so difficult to get few could qualify. You had to eat 39 boxes of cereal to get the Dick Tracy Inspector General badge.

Paper and plastic items had less kid tolerance than sturdy brass ones - and thus are rarer - especially cut-out paper premiums which self-destructed when used. Other premiums had parts that were easily lost. Some premiums were offered only regionally or before too many kids had radios. And some items were bummers and are today extremely rare.

Rarity doesn't always equate to value. Fibber McGee and Molly spinners come from one of the top shows of all time. Less than five sets are known to the author. Yet the Lone Ranger Atomic Bomb ring - the most prolific premium - often brings more. The strongest demand is generated by people wishing to recover items they had as a child. Thus rarity plays only a part of value. Character popularity, cross-overs to other collecting fields (such as collectors of pocket knives, Buck Rogers, western items, etc.) and the type of item (ring, button, badge, paper, punch-out) are all factors as collectors often specialize in certain items.

Price also has some regional influences. In Los Angeles and New York, prices are substantially higher. Selling prices are lowest in the Midwest - especially around Chicago and in Indiana, Ohio, Minnesota and Pennsylvania. Here premiums are found on a regular basis and thereby fulfill demand. Realizing these regional price situations exist - and that isolated individuals will always pay more in auction bidding, the values represented in this guide are an average of what the majority of a given item has sold for in the last two years.

Another factor enhancing value is the completeness of the original mailing package. Premiums were usually mailed with instructions. Many had booklets, manuals, catalogs and extra parts which made having the premium more fun. The actual mailing box or envelope may be worth a little more to some collectors, but mainly it's the additional items included within the package which increase value and demand by perhaps 20 to 50 percent.

All values shown in this book are U.S. dollar values with the dollar signs removed to avoid repetition.

CONDITION

Condition, like beauty, is in the eye of the beholder. When money becomes involved, the eye seems to take on an added dimension of x-ray vision or rosy colored glasses. Which one depends on whether you are buying or selling.

However, let there be no mistake about the price categories set down on the following pages. The "Mint" column refers to items in like-new condition - no scratches, never polished, free of any defects whatsoever. If paper, a mint item must be free of marks, creases (other than original folds), ragged edges or corners and any other defect or blemish. Mint items were probably never in circulation . . . and if mailed, were put away and not used.

"Good" condition means first and foremost the item is complete with absolutely no parts or pages missing. Creases, dirt, marks, tears, bends, scratches, missing paint, excessive polishing, rust or corrosion damage, repairs with non-original materials, and similar shortcomings are factors which depreciate value and relegate such items to the complete, but good classification. Of course, some complete items with excessive wear, rust, deep cuts or other mistreatment are less than good. Buying items in poor condition or incomplete ones is a decision usually regretted.

"Fine" condition is harder to pin down in writing. It is obviously the mid-ground between good and mint. In general a fine item would still be in a condition you would be proud to show your family or friends. There is minor wear, scratches, blemishes, etc. The item has been in circulation - used, but was given great care.

There are some items that don't fit within these standard grading breakdowns. Between fine and mint the term normally used is "near mint". "Very good" is the designation used for less than fine, but better than good condition. To determine prices on such items simply figure an appropriate mid-point between listed values.

BE SURE TO LISTEN NEXT TIME FOR MORE EXCITING OFFERS

Every radio and related premium verified by the publication deadline has been included. It is the most complete illustrated list ever published. Yet by no means is it all inclusive. There are over 3,000 items listed. Yet, there are premiums to be found, photographed and listed in future editions. If you'd like to help by supplying information on premiums not listed or spot a date that is wrong, please send a xerox copy or other data to the author c/o Tomart Publications, P.O. Box 292102, Dayton, OH 45429.

PREMIUM NEWSLETTER

Box Top Bonanza is the established newsletter for premium collectors. For subscription details see the ad in the "Where to Buy and Sell" section or write Joel Smilgis, Editor of Box-Top Bonanza, 153-1/2 - 15 Avenue, East Moline, IL 612244.

Free Inside is a publication for those interested in keeping up with cereal boxes new and old. For subscription information write Mike Vollmer, P.O. Box 1071, Spokane, WA 99210.

NUMBER CODE SYSTEM

The purpose of the number coding system developed for the illustrated Radio Premium catalog and price guide is two-fold - 1) to match illustrations to the column listings and 2) to provide collectors and dealers with a positive identification number to use in advertisements and in personal communications.

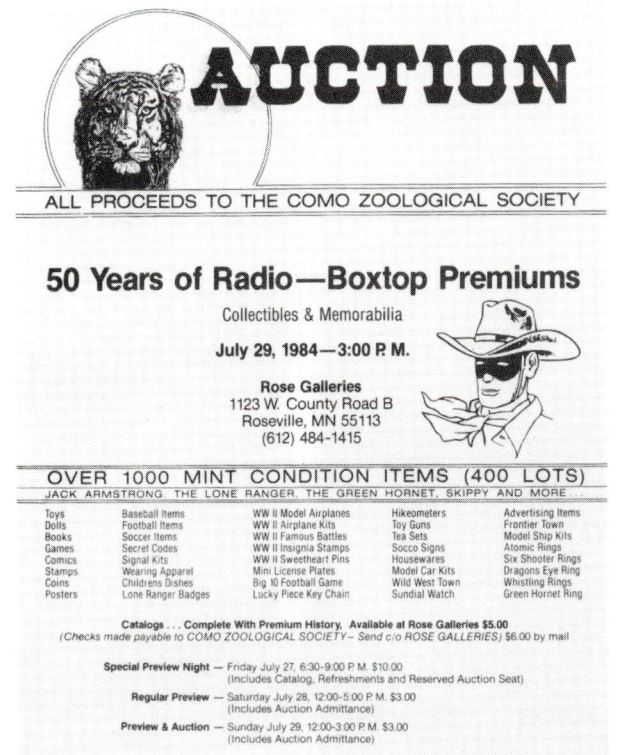

Here's how the alpha-numeric system works. The letter is based on the first letter of the program as listed. The individual numbers for each alphabetical program series begins with 001. Every attempt has been made to list items in the sequence they were issued. The numbers used in this book supersede all previous publications.

Dealers and collectors are encouraged to use Tomart's numbers in sales material or correspondence. Use in whole or part in any other price guides, however, would be an infringement of the author's copyright. Violators have and will be prosecuted.

DATING RADIO PREMIUMS

The first goal of this guide was to determine accurate name and date information. A close secondary goal was to research and present a current guide to selling prices.

An attempt has been made to list premiums chronologically. Where a specific date is shown it was taken from a primary source, i.e., a copyright date on the item, instruction sheet, premium catalog, newspaper or magazine ad or other source where an actual date appeared in print. A large percentage of the items were tracked down, but there are still a number of premiums which eluded diligent efforts to date them. Where this has happened the items are not date grouped.

Undated items are inserted in the chronological order where best available information indicates they should appear. Anyone having precise information on an undated item please send a xerox copy of the source information to the illustrated Radio Premium catalog and price guide c/o Tomart Publications, P.O. Box 292102, Dayton, Ohio 45429.

Many radio premiums, particularly early Tom Mix items, were offered several times. Where this is the case, the year of first issuance is the year shown. Also, the normal radio season spanned two years . . . the same as a new car model year or the modern-day television season. The 1940 Captain Midnight Skelly Spinning Medal of Membership, for example, was first offered around October of 1939. However, since the date of 1940 appears on the item it appears in the 1940 date group rather than 1939 to avoid confusion.

16

A505

A507

A508

A550

ADMIRAL BYRD

The second Admiral Richard E. Byrd expedition to the South Pole (1933 to 1934) provided a major first in radio broadcasting. Long before the network of satellites made worldwide live coverage possible, broadcasts from the Byrd expedition pioneered the communication of history in the making. The shortwave hook-up originated from the ship Ruppert (and from Byrd's outpost at Little America once the expedition landed) to Buenos Aires, Argentina. The signal was relayed to CBS in New York where the live two-way communication between the expedition and newscasters in the studio was broadcasted over the network.

The broadcasts spanned approximately 1-1/2 years. They were sponsored by General Foods, maker of Grape-Nuts, selected by Admiral Byrd as "the breakfast food his men should eat to fortify themselves against the punishing cold and hardships of the Antarctic." Premiums included issues of the *South Pole Radio News* and a colorful map listeners used to follow the expedition.

		Good	Fine	Mint
A505	South Pole Radio News #1	5	10	15
A506	South Pole Radio News #2	5	10	15
A507	Byrd Map of Antartica	10	25	55
A508	Note from Adm. Byrd sent w/Map	3	7	12

ADVERTISING DISPLAYS AND SIGNS

Point of purchase signs and store displays were a very prevalent form of advertising in the 30's, 40's and early 50's. It was not unusual to have several different window signs and displays for each premium offer. There were signs for the grocer's window; large and small stand-up counter displays; product displays for aisle ends featuring a character or program tie-in; and banners which hung over wires strung above supermarket aisles. Dangle signs were suspended from a ceiling or light cord. Signs and banners were usually paper and displays were die-cut cardboard. Even some metal signs were produced.

A wealth of material has survived to provide a representation of how consumers of all ages visualized their radio heroes at the point of purchase. Displays and signs from the children adventure serials command the greatest values ranging from 50 to 500 and up. Point of purchase material from adult comedy programs start at about 10 up to 75 depending upon the desirability of the piece. Spectacular metal signs can command up to a 1,000 or more.

18

ALLEN'S ALLEY — See Fred Allen

AMERICAN EAGLE DEFENDERS
The American Eagle Defenders was a comic book club with a pinback button and membership card the only premiums known.

		Good	Fine	Mint
A550	Pinback Button	30	60	90
A551	Membership Card	10	20	30

AMOS AND ANDY
Freeman Gosden and Charles Correll were two small-time vaudeville performers when they met in Durham, North Carolina. Their interest in radio resulted in a 1926 Chicago radio show called "Sam and Henry." The show was highly successful and the boys wanted to take it to the soon-to-be-formed NBC network. But station WGN owned the show title and wouldn't go along. So they quit to go it on their own. They kept the black humor idea, but new characters had to be developed. They were, of course, Amos and Andy. The program aired for the first time on Aug 19, 1929. By 1931, "Amos and Andy" had become a national legend. Few Americans missed a single broadcast. Theaters even timed film showings to allow a 15-minute break to pipe in the program. Relatively few premiums were offered during the 27 years the show was on the air. Most came during the early Pepsodent years when the program enjoyed its greatest popularity.

1929		Good	Fine	Mint
A600	Photo	8	14	20
A601	Story of Amos & Andy Folder	4	10	15

1930				
A610	Cardboard Stand-up Figures (2) & Folder	15	23	30

1931				
A619	Check 'N Double Check Sheet Music	5	10	15
A620	Smaller Cardboard Figures, 6	20	35	45
A651	Puzzle	10	20	30

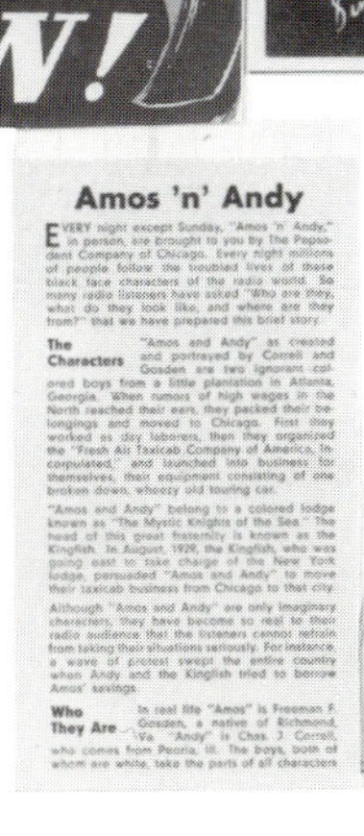

1935

A652	Map of Weber City - complete with letter and envelope	12	20	30
A655	Amos Wedding Script Reprint, Dec 25, 1935	5	10	15
A660	Perfect Song Sheet Music	4	8	14

1936

| A680 | Contest Winner Check | 50 | 100 | 175 |

AUNT JENNY'S TRUE-LIFE STORIES

Each week Aunt Jenny set the stage for soap opera type dramatizations designed to solve one of her neighbor's problems. Unlike most "soap operas" the story was normally completed in five daily episodes. The casts changed as the stories required and there were two Aunt Jenny's (Edith Spencer and Agnes Young) over its run of nearly 20 years (Jan 1937 to late 1956). The program was "brought into your kitchen" by Spry.

In addition to her common sense solutions to the family problems for the housewives of Littleton, where the show supposedly originated, Aunt Jenny always had cooking tips on how to use Spry. Premiums included recipes, cookbooks and cooking utensils.

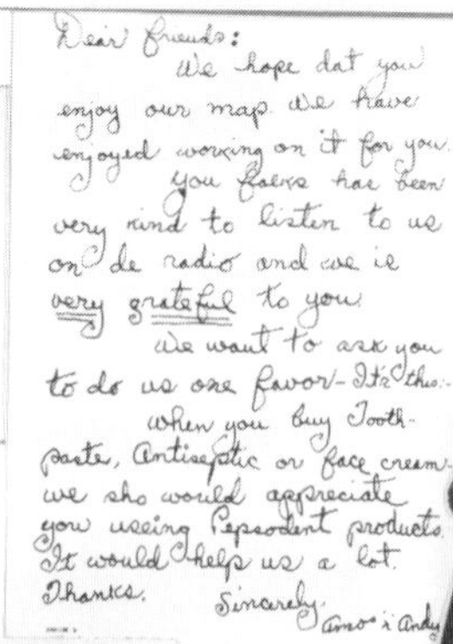

		Good	Fine	Mint
A800	Cookbooks, each	2	4	7
A804	Recipes from Spry Lids	1	2	3
A806	Cake Knife or Other Cooking Utensil	3	8	20

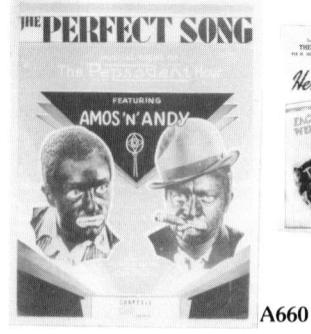

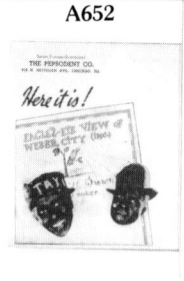

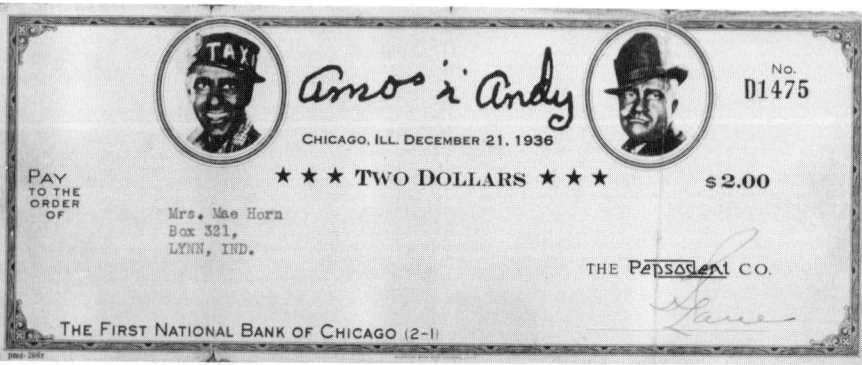

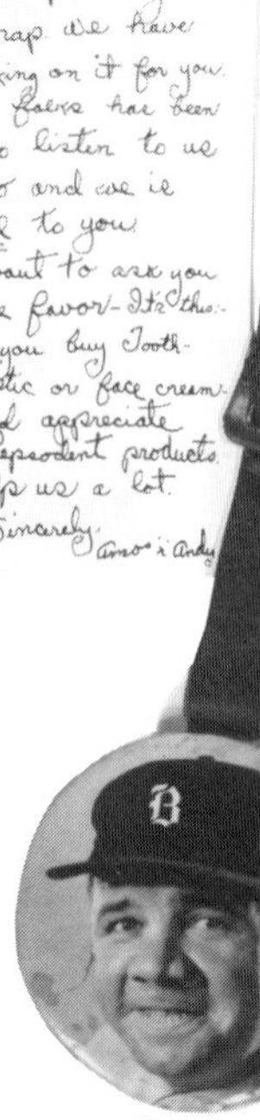

20

BABE RUTH BOYS' CLUB

Babe Ruth introduced his Boys' Club as a local program under the sponsorship of a gasoline company in 1934. He told stories about baseball and gave advice on how listeners could become better players. Balls, bats, and game tickets were somehow awarded. Quaker Puffed Wheat, Rice and Muffets took the program national the same year with more traditional premiums awarded for box tops. Evidence indicates the program only lasted one season. The Wheaties flip book on how to hit a home run is a Jack Armstrong premium.

		Good	Fine	Mint
B100	Ring	10	22	35
B101	Charm Bracelet	10	22	35
B102	Umpire Scorekeeper w/Photo	20	35	50
B103	"Ask Me" Game	15	30	45
B104	Membership Button	8	15	25
B105	Pinback Button	10	17	28
B106	Big Book of Baseball	8	15	25

BABY SNOOKS

Fanny Brice was a star singer and comedienne in the Ziegfeld Follies from 1911 through the early 20's. She developed the Baby Snooks character over the same period to amuse her friends. The movies *Funny Girl* and *Funny Lady* are based on this portion of her life. Radio audiences heard the "Baby" character for the first time in 1936. By 1938 the successful formula fell into place and Baby Snooks became a permanent fixture on the airwaves until her death in 1951. Tums offered the one premium known.

		Good	Fine	Mint
B115	Dancing Puppet	15	25	35

21

B175

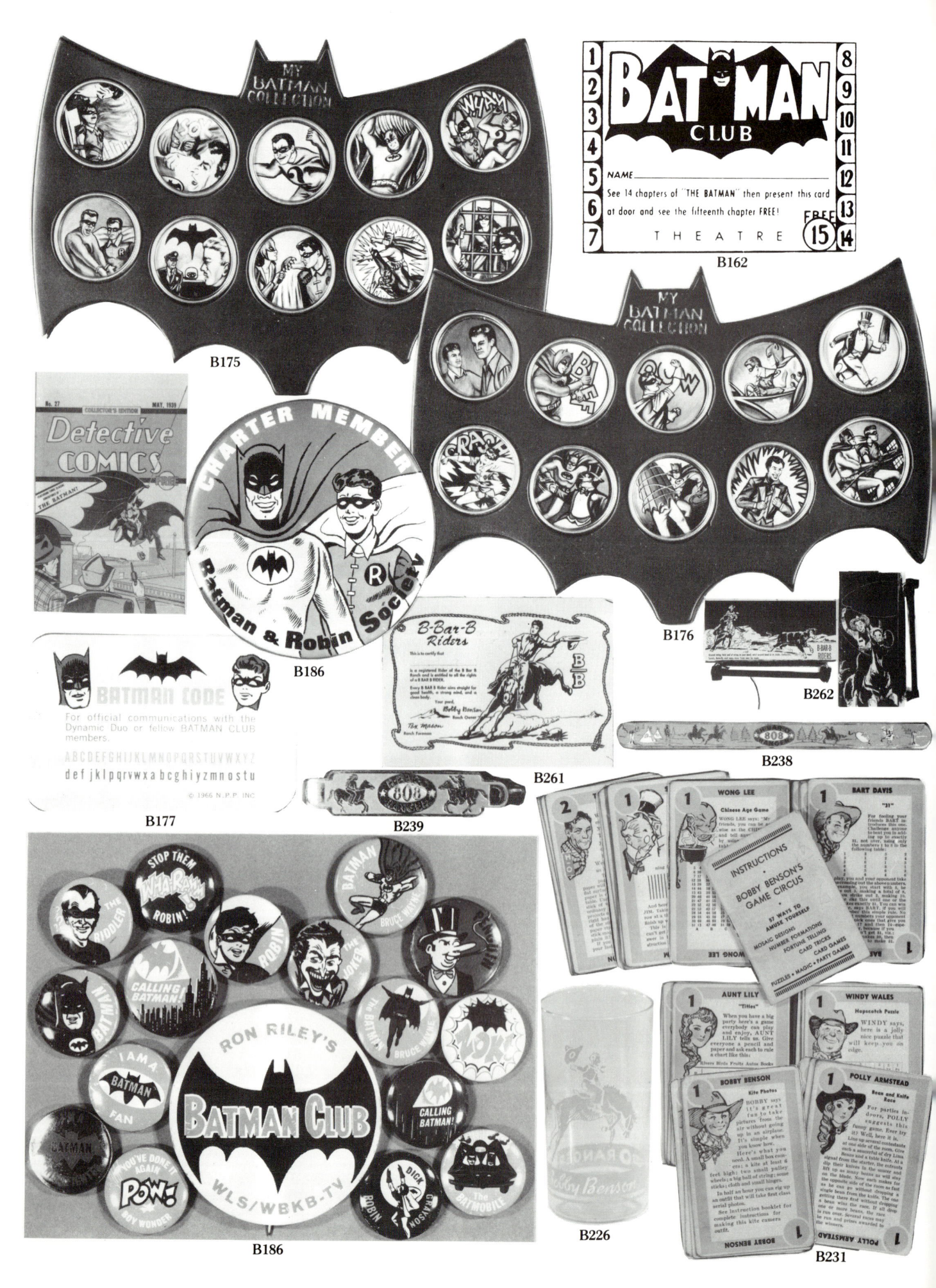

B162

B176

B186

B262

B177

B261

B238

B239

B186

B226

B231

22

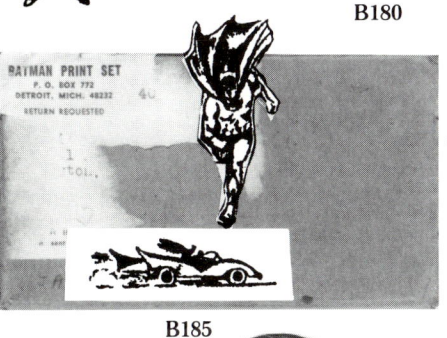

BATMAN

Batman and Robin made many guest appearances on the Superman radio show sponsored by Kellogg's. The dynamic duo of Batman and Robin, created by Bob Kane, was unquestionably the second most popular hero in the National (now DC) Comic Book line. Curiously, however, there was no Batman Club as there was for Superman, The Jr. Justice Society and many other comic book heroes. Nor were Batman and Robin included in any of the other clubs. The characters first appeared in *Detective Comics* #27 in 1939 and the first comic under the *Batman* title in 1940. However, there was one premium photo and several items connected with the movie serial which appeared in 1943.

The real popularity of Batman surged in 1966 as a "camp" TV production starring Adam West and Burt Ward. The outrageous production style caught viewers' fancy and revitalized interest in the character. Hundreds of toys and premiums resulted.

		Good	Fine	Mint
B150	Infantile Paralysis Postcard	30	50	75
B160	Batplane Punch-out, movie serial	80	150	275
B161	Batmask, movie serial	30	60	100
B162	Batman Club Card, movie serial	10	25	65
B175	Coins, each	1	2	4
B176	Coin Holders for 10 coins	2	5	12
B177	Membership Card	1	3	6
B180	Batman and Robin Posters, set	20	50	80
B185	Printing Set	15	30	45
B186	Pinback Buttons, 1966-67, each	1	2	3

BLACK FLAME OF THE AMAZON, THE

"The Black Flame of the Amazon" was a syndicated show. Known sponsors were Hi Speed Gasoline in the areas where the brand was sold and Mayrose Ham in the greater St. Louis area. The program was based in part on the travels of 30's explorer Harold Noice who led an expedition along the Rio Vaupes to the mountains of Columbia where gold was discovered. Materials from the program modestly proclaimed it was based on the "adventures of Harold Noice, adventurer, explorer, and scientist, in the darkest jungles of South America."

Other characters in this children's adventure serial were Jim and Jean Brady who were friends of Noice; his right hand man, Pedro; and Keyto, a friendly native. They battled jungle renegades and Amazon pirates. In addition to being "thrilling", the broadcasts contributed to the listener's knowledge of "strange savage customs, fierce animals, and weird tropical plants" found in South America. The program aired Monday through Friday each evening. The Hi Speed membership pinback is particularly colorful. Other premiums found are some of the most interesting and creative identified for a regional program.

		Good	Fine	Mint
B200	Membership Litho Tin Pinback	5	12	20
B201	Educational Map of South America	15	45	70
B202	Cardboard Ruler	10	20	30
B203	Compass Ring	50	125	200

BOBBY BENSON OF THE H-BAR-O

"Bobby Benson" first aired Monday through Friday over CBS in 1932, sponsored by the H-O Oats Company. Young Bobby and friend, Polly, were the hero and heroine of many colorful adventures set on the H-Bar-O ranch located in the Big Bend country of Texas. Each day's action was intermixed with Western songs. The kids' two guardians were Aunt Lil and Black Bart (a good guy in this case). There was a Chinese cook and the villain, Little Snake, leader of a band of Mexican desperados. When the H-O Company dropped sponsorship the name of the ranch was changed to B-Bar-B. Three notable actors to play on early episodes were Don Knotts, Al Hodge and Tex Ritter. The show was revived on Mutual in 1949 and ran until 1955.

		Good	Fine	Mint
1932-35				
B220	H-Bar-O Ranger Club Button	4	7	12
B223	Cardboard Code Rule	12	15	20
B224	Code Book	12	16	20
B225	Cereal Bowl, 3 different colors, each	5	9	15
B226	Drinking Glass, 3 different colors, each	4	7	12
B228	Map	20	40	60
B230	Photos of Bobby, Polly, Windy Wales, Tex Mason, Aunt Lilly, and Friend Jack, each	5	10	15
B231	Circus of Games, set of cards & booklet	15	22	30
B232	Africa Scene Production Photo	8	12	20
B237	Card Game	15	22	30
B238	Bracelet, enameled	15	25	35
B239	Tie Clasp, enameled	15	25	35
1936 Combination Story/Comic Books:				
B250	Tunnel of Gold	10	15	20
B251	The Lost Herd	10	15	20
1937				
B255	2-1/2 Cent Money	5	10	15
1948-49				
B260	Photo of Bobby	2	4	8
B261	Membership Certificate	2	4	8
B262	Humming Trick Lariat	5	10	15

BREAKFAST CLUB — See Don McNeill

BUCK JONES (HOOFBEATS)

Based on the popular movie cowboy hero, "Hoofbeats", starring Buck Jones, aired briefly during 1937 on a syndicated basis.

		Good	Fine	Mint
1937				
B300	Horseshoe Pin	10	20	30
B302	Horseshoe Ring	15	25	35
B305	Manual and Premium Catalog	10	16	24
B310	Jr. Sheriff Badge	6	8	10

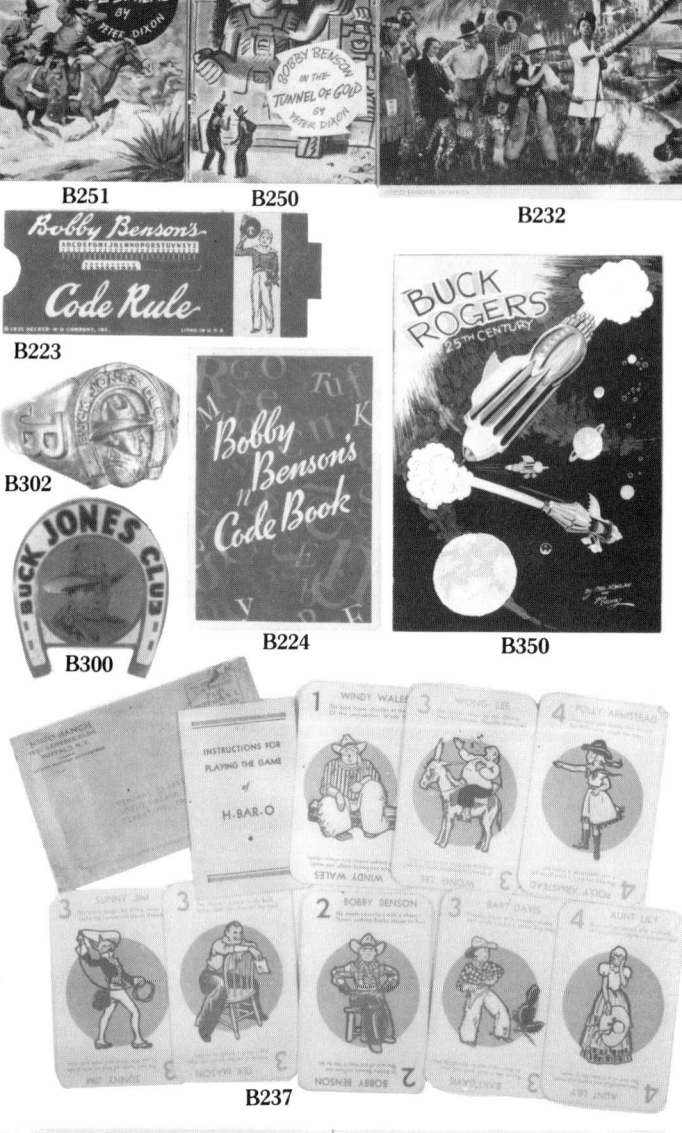

24

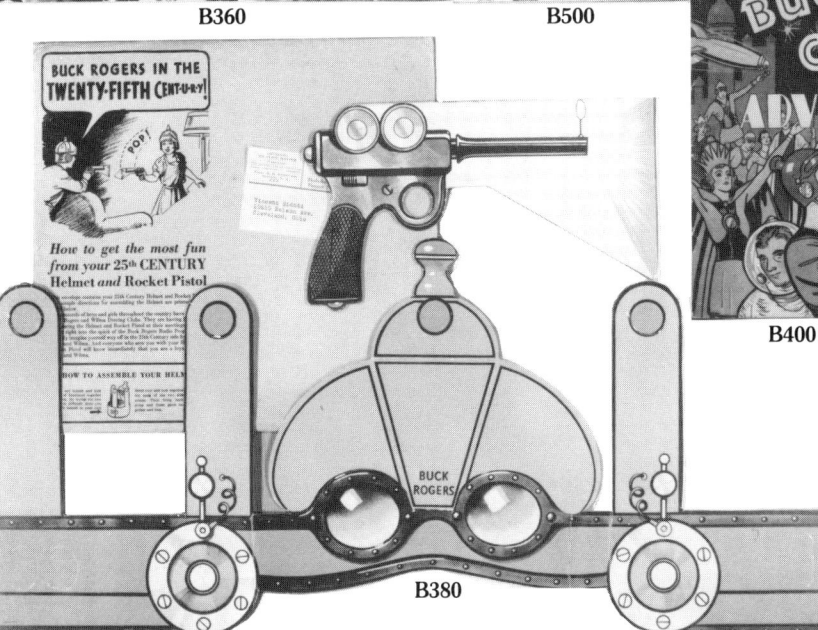

BUCK ROGERS IN THE 25TH CENTURY

Buck Rogers was the sensation of the early 30's. He was epitomized in pulps, newspaper comic sections, movie serials, plus countless children's toys, games, costumes, ray guns, etc. He seemed a natural for radio (and premiums). But the program was never a great success. Perhaps because too much time was spent describing Dr. Huer's inventions. A long series of advertisers tried the show. Kellogg's began it in 1932. Cocomalt took over as sponsor until 1935, Cream of Wheat picked it up for a season or two in 1936, and Popsicle returned the show to the air from 1939-42. Newspapers and comic books promoted clubs in the early to mid-40's and radio adventures continued to air until 1947 on a local syndication basis. Buck Rogers items are sought by a wide variety of collectors beyond the radio premium collecting hobby.

		Good	Fine	Mint
1932 Newspaper Comic Strip Premiums:				
B345	Drawing of Buck	50	100	150
B346	Drawing of Wilma	50	100	150
1932-33 — Kellogg's				
B350	Kellogg's Buck Rogers Origin Story Book	40	65	110
B351	Letter	5	12	20
B355	Kite Folder (PEP)	4	8	12
1933-35 — Cocomalt				
B360	Picture of Buck and Wilma	30	50	85
B375	Solar Map	175	275	400
B380	Paper Gun and Helmet, comes in both Buck and Wilma versions	120	180	400
B399	Cocomalt Adventure Book Offer Sheet, four-color	35	60	80
B400	Cut-out Adventure Book, uncut	300	600	1000
B425	Cocomalt Big Little Book — Buck Rogers in the 25th Century, 1933	15	22	35
B426	Cocomalt Big Little Book Buck Rogers City of Floating Globes, 1935	30	50	70
B450	Painted Lead Figures w/ Cocomalt folders — Buck, Wilma and Killer Kane, set	18	35	60

25

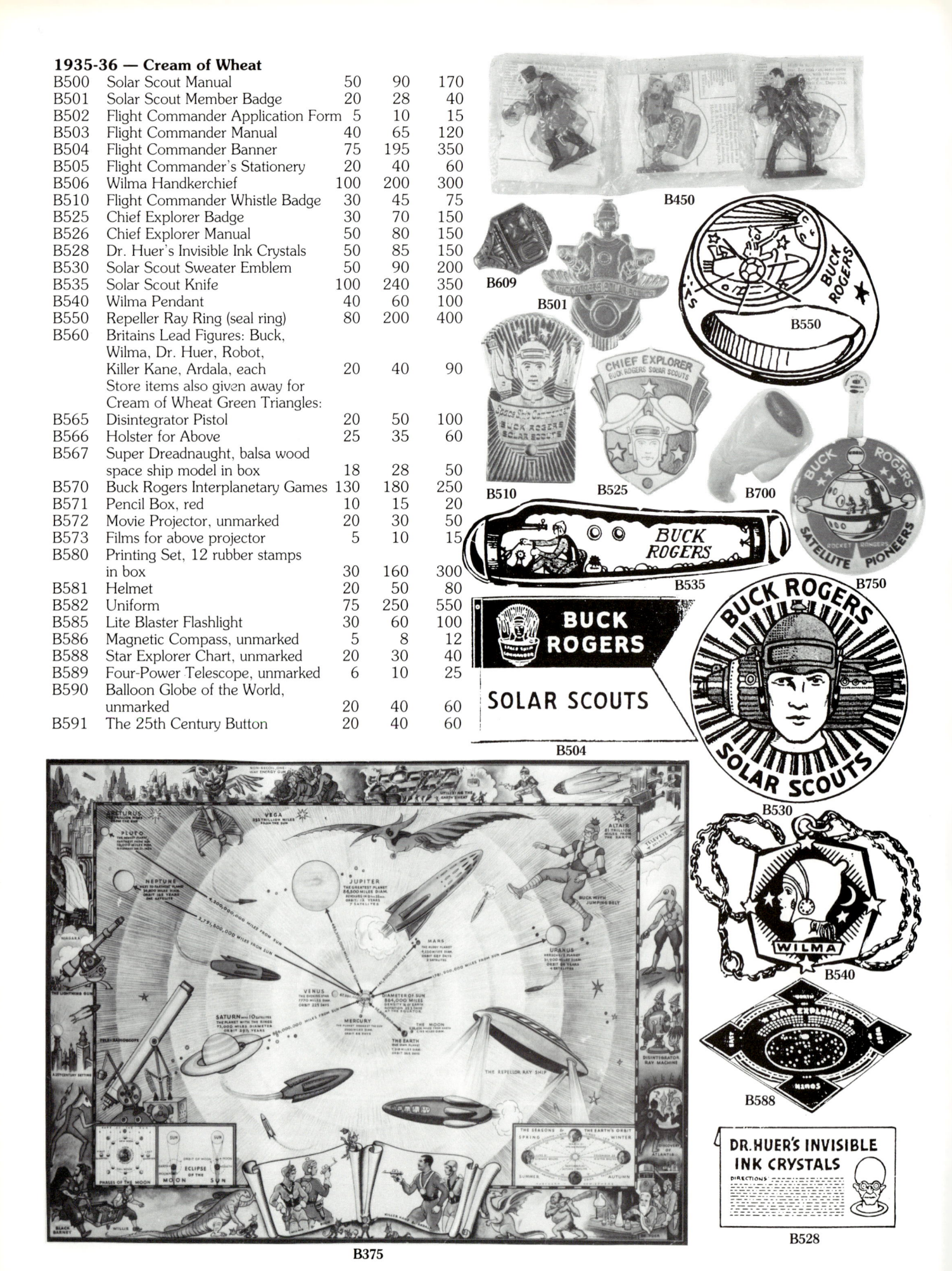

1935-36 — Cream of Wheat

B500	Solar Scout Manual	50	90	170
B501	Solar Scout Member Badge	20	28	40
B502	Flight Commander Application Form	5	10	15
B503	Flight Commander Manual	40	65	120
B504	Flight Commander Banner	75	195	350
B505	Flight Commander's Stationery	20	40	60
B506	Wilma Handkerchief	100	200	300
B510	Flight Commander Whistle Badge	30	45	75
B525	Chief Explorer Badge	30	70	150
B526	Chief Explorer Manual	50	80	150
B528	Dr. Huer's Invisible Ink Crystals	50	85	150
B530	Solar Scout Sweater Emblem	50	90	200
B535	Solar Scout Knife	100	240	350
B540	Wilma Pendant	40	60	100
B550	Repeller Ray Ring (seal ring)	80	200	400
B560	Britains Lead Figures: Buck, Wilma, Dr. Huer, Robot, Killer Kane, Ardala, each	20	40	90

Store items also given away for Cream of Wheat Green Triangles:

B565	Disintegrator Pistol	20	50	100
B566	Holster for Above	25	35	60
B567	Super Dreadnaught, balsa wood space ship model in box	18	28	50
B570	Buck Rogers Interplanetary Games	130	180	250
B571	Pencil Box, red	10	15	20
B572	Movie Projector, unmarked	20	30	50
B573	Films for above projector	5	10	15
B580	Printing Set, 12 rubber stamps in box	30	160	300
B581	Helmet	20	50	80
B582	Uniform	75	250	550
B585	Lite Blaster Flashlight	30	60	100
B586	Magnetic Compass, unmarked	5	8	12
B588	Star Explorer Chart, unmarked	20	30	40
B589	Four-Power Telescope, unmarked	6	10	25
B590	Balloon Globe of the World, unmarked	20	40	60
B591	The 25th Century Button	20	40	60

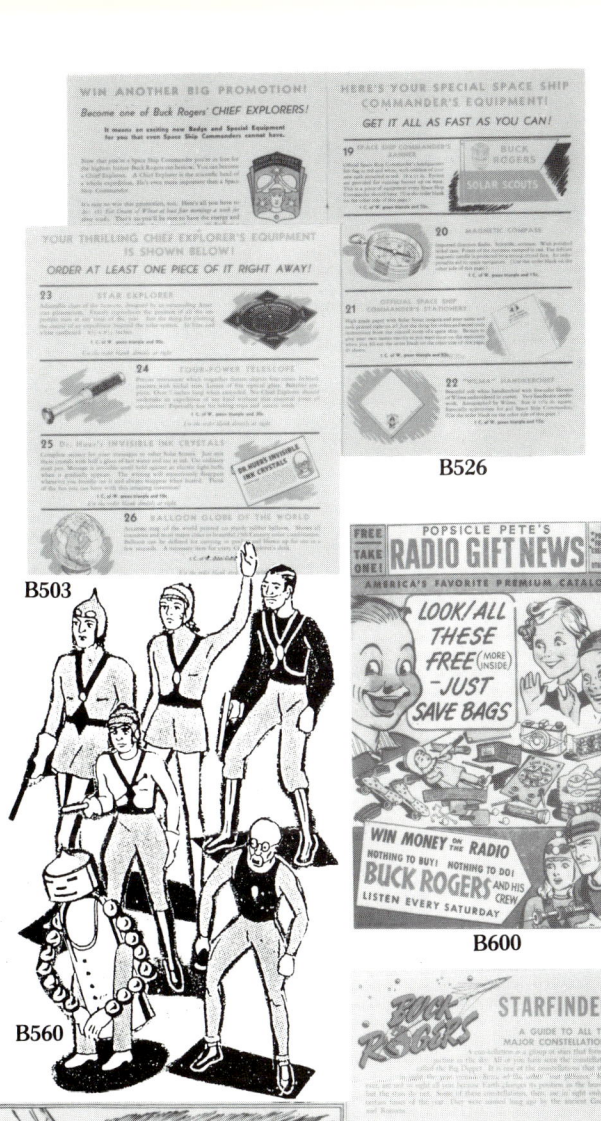

1939-41

B600	Popsicle Pete Radio News Premium Catalog (shows birthstone ring)	10	20	35
B609	Birthstone Initial Ring (generic premium offered by others)	35	85	135
B610	Match Book	2	5	12
B615	Whistling Rocket Ship (Muffets)	70	120	175

1942

B650	Space Ship (Morton Salt)	15	25	35

1944-50

B700	Ring of Saturn Ring, red stone, glow-in-the-dark crocodile base	75	185	350
B725	Rocket Rangers Tab	25	30	40
B750	Satellite Pioneers Tab	20	25	35
B751	Satellite Pioneers Bulletin	18	25	35
B760	Satellite Pioneers Starfinder	18	25	35
B765	Drawing of Pluton, 1947	4	7	10
B775	Sylvania Space Ranger's Kit, punch-out equipment, TV off	25	50	100

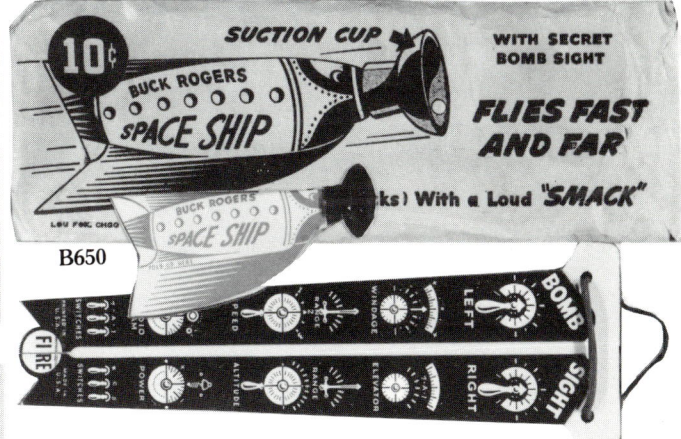

The ring, three badges, and Wilma pendant from the 1936 Cream of Wheat Solar Scout promotion were reused in the early 40's. Readers of *Famous Funnies* and *Buck Rogers Comics* were invited to join the "Buck Rogers Rocket Rangers." Apparently an excess supply of the Solar Scout items were used up before the Rocket Rangers tab was issued.

BUSTER BROWN GANG (SMILIN' ED'S GANG)

A Buster Brown program was heard over CBS for a brief time in 1929. The show was revived on NBC in 1943 as a Saturday morning show with Smilin' Ed McConnell as host. The show continued on radio until the early 50's when it was also seen on TV. Andy Devine succeeded McConnell. The show originated from Hollywood under the sponsorship of the Brown Shoe Company of St. Louis. Premiums were picked up at the department stores and "leading" shoe stores which sold Buster Brown shoes. The high spot in each program was the arrival of Froggy, the Gremlin, who burst upon the scene amidst the screams of the delighted young audience. Ed: "Plunk your magic twanger, Froggy." Froggy: "Hiya kids, hiya, hiya." (Then Froggy would stick out his tongue in adult defiance and give a Bronx cheer.) We all went wild.

		Good	Fine	Mint

1945

B900	Froggy 5" Rubber Doll (larger size was a store item)	5	10	22

1945-56

B850	Buster Brown Gang Comics #1	10	15	25
B851-60	#2-#10	3	5	10

27

B861-93 #11-#43	2	3	5

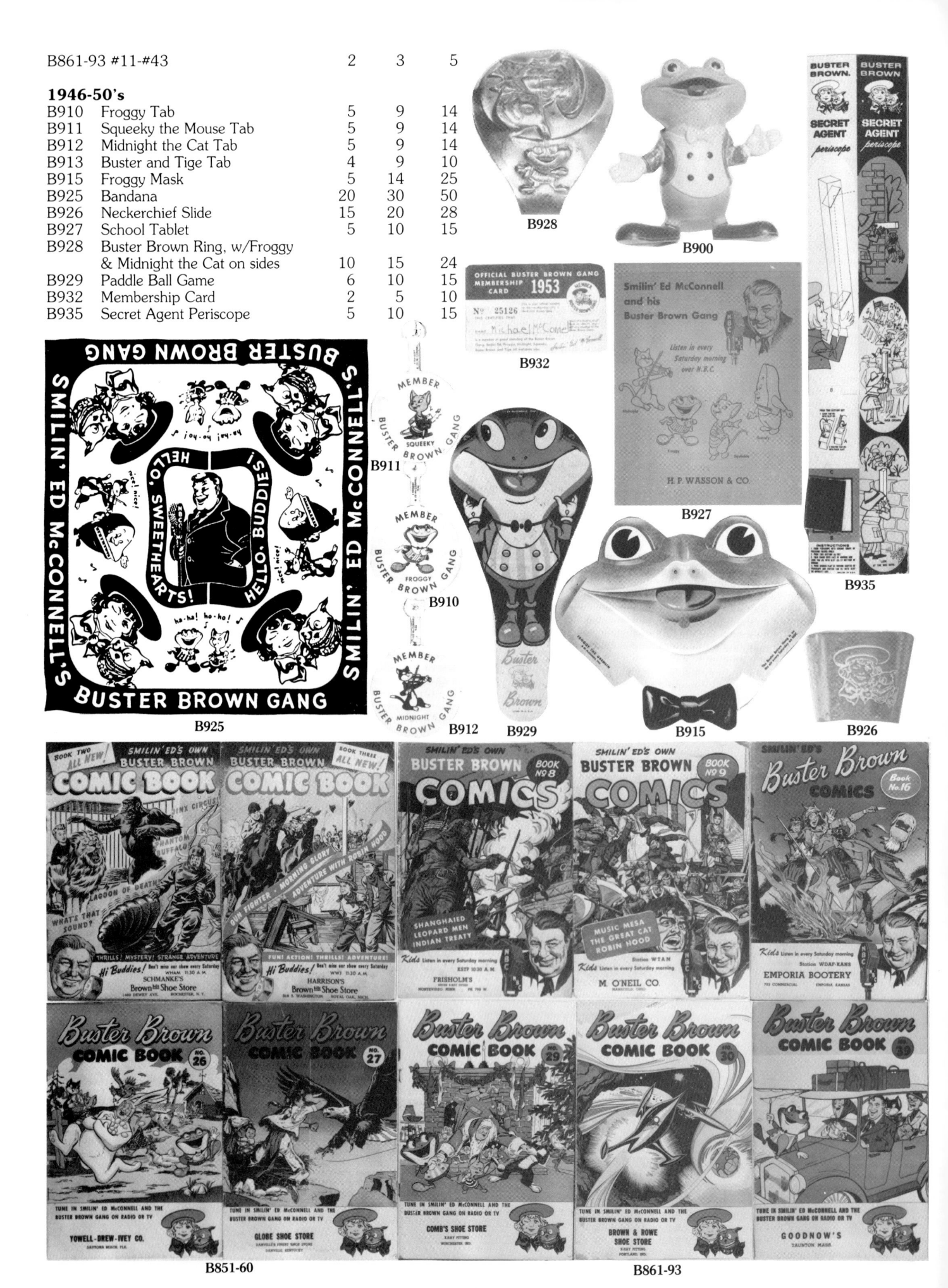

1946-50's

B910	Froggy Tab	5	9	14
B911	Squeeky the Mouse Tab	5	9	14
B912	Midnight the Cat Tab	5	9	14
B913	Buster and Tige Tab	4	9	10
B915	Froggy Mask	5	14	25
B925	Bandana	20	30	50
B926	Neckerchief Slide	15	20	28
B927	School Tablet	5	10	15
B928	Buster Brown Ring, w/Froggy & Midnight the Cat on sides	10	15	24
B929	Paddle Ball Game	6	10	15
B932	Membership Card	2	5	10
B935	Secret Agent Periscope	5	10	15

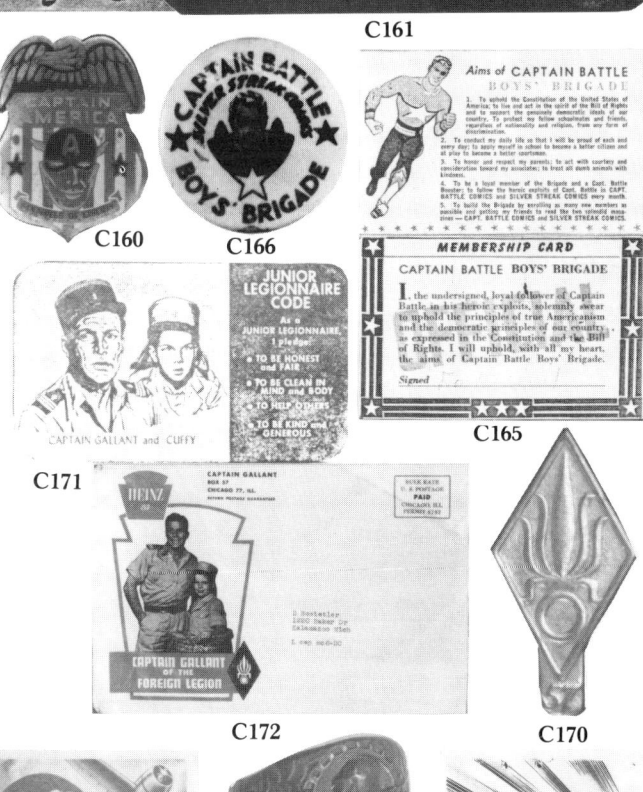

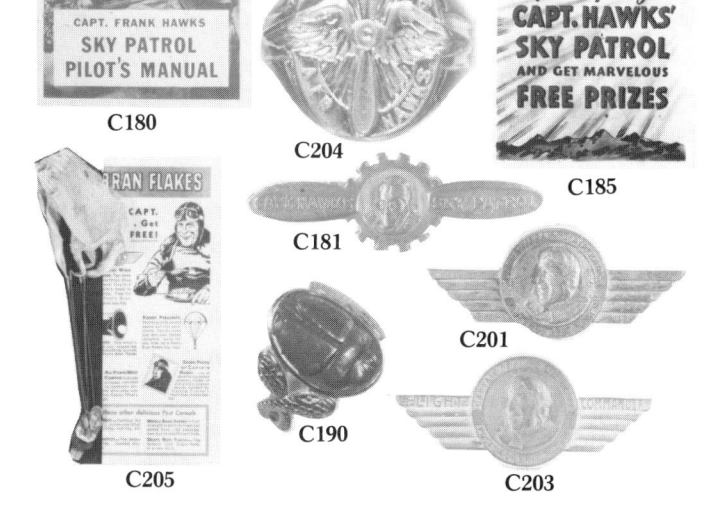

CAPTAIN AMERICA

Captain America premiums were comic book connected. An ad for his "Sentinels of Liberty" club appeared in the very first issue of *Captain America Comics* (Mar 1941). You got both the badge and a membership card for only 10 cents. Issue #33 (Dec 1943) asked kids to stop sending dimes for the badge because Uncle Sam needed the metal to make "guns, tanks, bullets, ships, planes!" In the same ad Captain's young assistant, Bucky, added "How about using that dime for a war savings stamp?" The character was a product of the war. His short-lived premiums were a victim of the shortages it caused.

1941-43

		Good	Fine	Mint
C160	Sentinel of Liberty Badge	75	200	300
C161	Membership Card	10	25	50

CAPTAIN BATTLE BOY'S BRIGADE

Captain Battle appeared in *Captain Battle Comics* and *Silver Streak Comics* in 1941-42. He was around long enough to get a small club going.

		Good	Fine	Mint
C165	Membership Card	20	40	60
C166	Pinback Button	50	175	350

CAPTAIN GALLANT OF THE FOREIGN LEGION

Captain Gallant of the Foreign Legion was played by Buster Crabbe on TV. The show was sponsored by Heinz. It was short-lived and the premiums are scarce.

		Good	Fine	Mint
C170	Membership Badge	15	30	45
C171	Membership Card	10	20	30
C172	Letter and Envelope	5	12	20

CAPTAIN FRANK HAWKS

Captain Hawks was a personable aviator when aviators were the darlings of a country in need of heroes. He was not a radio program personality, but rather a real-life aviator contracted to endorse Post cereals on-pack and in newspaper advertising. Hawks often did press interviews and he appeared as a guest on many radio programs. His exposure made him an ideal personality to compete with the radio serials which were capturing the imagination and buying power of young product users. The promotion ended before Hawks was killed in an airplane crash in 1938.

1935-36

		Good	Fine	Mint
C180	Manual	12	18	25
	Propeller Pins:			
C181	Member	5	7	10
C182	Flight Lieutenant	5	8	12
C183	Flight Captain	6	9	15
C184	Sky Patrol Ring	12	22	30
C185	Sky Patrol Prize Folder	5	8	15
C190	Scarab Ring (also offered by other Post personalities)	40	70	120

1936-37

		Good	Fine	Mint
C200	Air Hawks Manual	10	15	22
	Air Hawk Flight Wings:			
C201	Silver - Member	3	5	10
C202	Brass - Squadron Leader	3	6	10
C203	Bronze - Flight Commander	4	8	15
C204	Air Hawks Ring	12	22	30

29

C240 C259 C271 C255 C290 C241 C243

C242 C247

C248 C246 C244

C249 C296 C250

C245 C267 C256 C260

C261 C268 C263

C262 C257 C266

C280

30

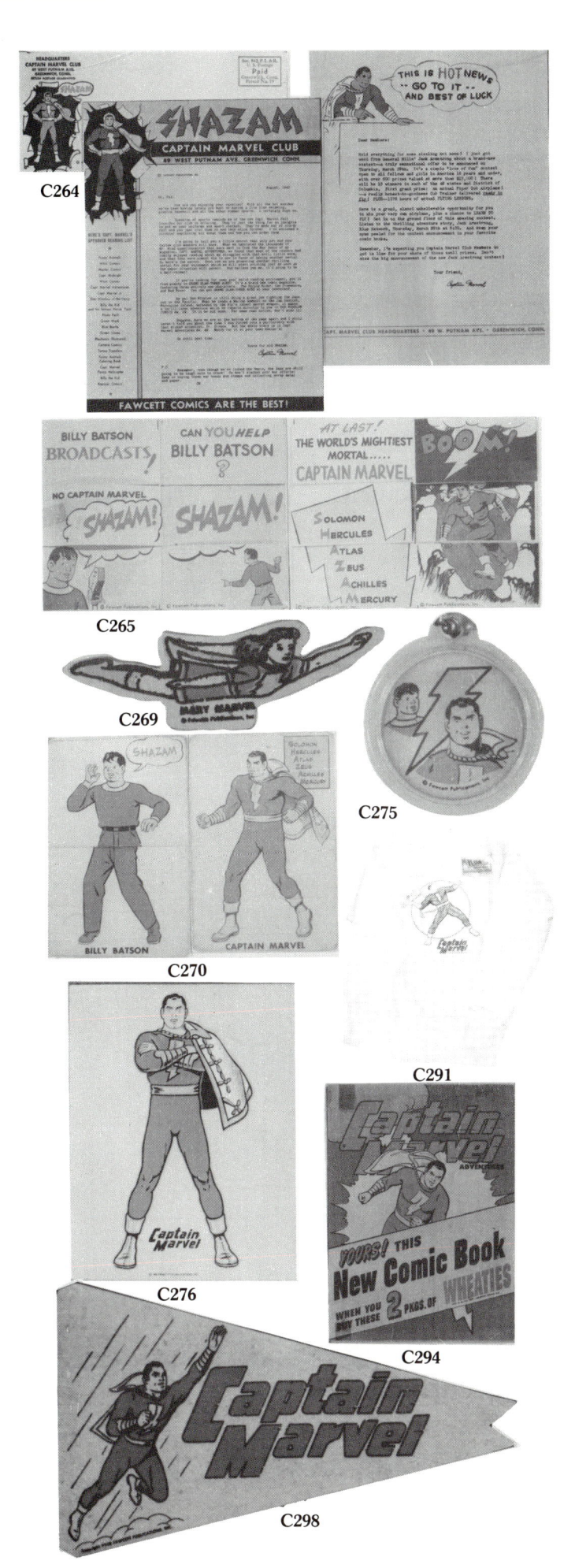

C205	Rocket Parachute, unmarked	8	15	25
C210	Sepia Autographed Photo	5	12	25
C220	See-Back-O-Scope, unmarked	10	12	15
C221	Newsletter (Bike Contest Winner)	3	4	5

CAPTAIN MARVEL

Captain Marvel was the top superhero of the 40's. He first appeared in *WHIZ Comics* in Feb 1940. Captain Marvel, with art by C.C. Beck, far outsold *Superman Comics* and over a million kids joined the Captain Marvel fan club. In 1948 Superman's publisher, National Periodicals, sued Fawcett, the publisher of Captain Marvel, because they felt the character was a copyright infringement. In a gross miscarriage of justice, the long, drawn-out suit was settled in 1953. Fawcett was forced to give up all rights to the Captain Marvel character to National's DC Comics. In the interim, however, the "big red cheese" gave away some of the "swellest" premiums ever.

The first button and card were issued in Nov 1941, but the best items appeared in the club's heyday of 1944-46. The Captain Marvel Club continued until the very end, but the promotion was interrupted in 1946 as noted in the following P.S. from a Fan Club letter:

"P.S. - Now I'm afraid I have to tell you some bad news. Until we are able to get larger quarters, we are going to be forced to discontinue the regular monthly letters. This makes me very unhappy, but you can be sure that I'll remember you and will begin to write them again in a few months."

Fawcett resumed the club in 1947 with a new logo, but the rarity of items with Captain Marvel preparing to throw an airplane indicates the premium promotion had run out of steam. The momentum had been lost.

In addition to the comic book premiums listed below, there were variations in membership cards... and throughout the club's years there were numerous letters from Captain Marvel. The contents of these ranged from club news to pitches for other Fawcett publications... even one for Jack Armstrong. The letters are fairly common, but items included with them, such as offer forms, war bond stamp book envelope, and other small paper giveaways, are sought after by collectors.

		Good	Fine	Mint
1941				
C240	Membership Button, tin litho	10	15	25
C241	Membership Code Card	5	12	25
C242	Color Photo	20	50	75
C243	Letters on b&w stationary, each	10	20	30
C244	Offer Forms, each	15	25	40
C245	Felt Emblem	20	45	75
C246	Letters on four-color stationery, each	15	25	35
C247	Christmas Card	15	30	50
C248	War Bond Stamp Book Envelope	20	40	60
C249	Necktie	20	40	60
1943				
C250	Paper Decoder	65	125	250
C255	Membership Button (Cello)	15	20	25
C256	Secret Message Postcard	15	30	50
C257	Toss Bags - Capt. Marvel flying, standing at attention, Mary Marvel flying, standing alert, or Hoppy, each	10	25	45
1944-47				
C259	Membership Button	10	15	20
C260	Statuette (supplies ran out)	400	800	1200
C261	Felt Pennant, blue	25	50	85
C262	Cloth Emblems: Captain Marvel, Mary Marvel, CM Jr., each	20	30	40
C263	Overseas Cap	25	50	80
C264	Letters, w/blue and red letterhead, each	6	12	20

31

C265	Magic Folder	40	55	65
C266	Felt Hat (beanie)	25	85	135
C267	Pencil Clip	15	22	30
C268	Skull Cap	25	50	80
C269	Mary Marvel Pin, fiber board	20	45	70
C270	Shazam Membership/Code Card	18	25	32
C271	Membership Button	15	20	25
C275	Key Chain	20	35	50
C276	Marvel Glow Pictures, set of four: Captain Marvel, Mary Marvel, Captain Marvel Jr. and Hoppy the Marvel Bunny, each	30	50	100
C280	Comic Buttons, set of 10: CM, MM, Billy B, CMJ, Hoppy Bunny, Ibis, Radar, Golden Arrow, Bulletman and Nyoka	100	250	450

1947-48

C290	Membership Button	15	30	50
C291	Sweatshirt	20	40	80
C292	Magic Flute	12	15	20
C293	Balloon Flute	12	15	20
C294	Captain Marvel Giveaway Comic (Wheaties)	15	25	60
C295	WHIZ Giveaway Comic (Wheaties)	15	25	60
C296	Magic Whistle in envelope	20	40	60
C298	Felt Pennant, yellow w/ flying Capt. Marvel	35	60	100

Fawcett published a couple dozen or so paper punch-out items designed to sell in stores for 10¢ each. The Marvel Family, the Marvel Bunny, and a variety of Fawcett publication's funny animal characters were the subject of these paper toys. They were also offered through the mail to members of the Captain Marvel Club. A vast quantity of these were found in a warehouse back in the 60's. They have been routinely sold for $5 to $10 each over the years and the quantity available has been reduced, but most titles are seen regularly. The most difficult to find are the Captain Marvel Magic Lightning Box and Magic Eyes. Other Captain Marvel items include The Buzz Bomb, his Rocket Raider, Magic Picture, Shazam game and a puzzle entitled "One Against Many." There was also a Flying Captain Marvel, The 3 Famous Flying Marvels and a Capt. Marvel, Jr. Ski Jump. These paper toys were copyrighted in 1944 and 1945 by Reed and Associates.

Similar to the paper toys were series of Fawcett character iron-ons and tattoo transfers. These, too, were distributed in nice illustrated envelopes. Three different Marvel Family character sets have been seen. Other characters included Don Winslow, the Blue Beatle, Spy Smasher, Prince Ivis, Captain Midnight, and envelopes of assorted Fawcett characters.

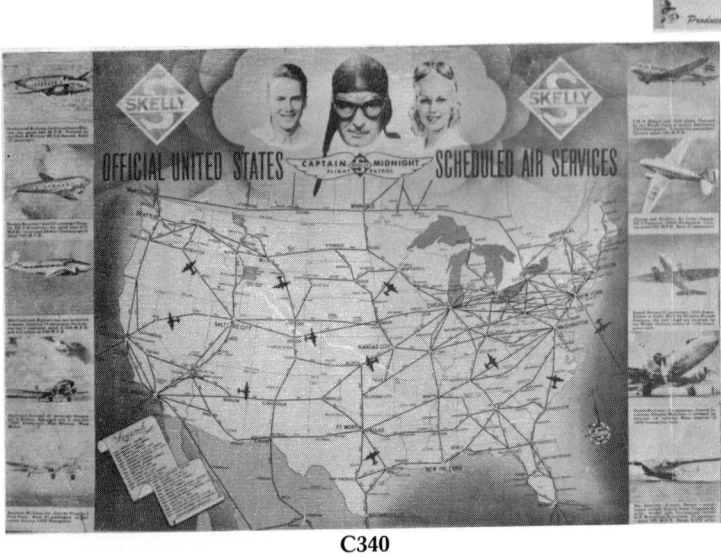

C292

C293

C340

C300

32

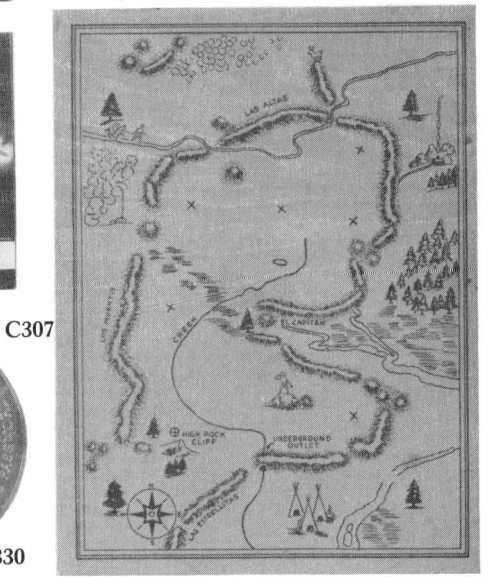

CAPTAIN MIDNIGHT

"Captain Midnight" started as a regional program produced in Kansas City sponsored by Skelly gasoline and oil products. He was the successor to Jimmie Allen as the trend in hero worship shifted from boy aviators to more mature fighter pilots. World War II was brewing and everyone knew it. The same writing team — Robert Burtt and Willfred Moore — who wrote Jimmie Allen, penned Captain Midnight (and later Hop Harrigan and Sky King). Ovaltine also realized times were changing and sought the rights to the "Captain Midnight" show to replace "Radio Orphan Annie." So in the fall of 1940 — September 30 to be exact — "Captain Midnight" went network from Chicago. The origin was retold how a daring captain of World War I penetrated deep into enemy ranks to complete a highly secret mission against 100 to 1 odds. The real identity of the pilot was to forever remain top secret, but he returned exactly at the stroke of midnight.(Since readers of this book are privileged to know old radio's top secrets the true identity of Captain Midnight can be revealed. His name was Stuart "Red" Albright.) Together with his ward, Chuck Ramsey, the good Captain tamed the sinister Ivan Shark and his daughter, Fury. Chuck's father, Robert, a test pilot of experimental aircraft, was a long time friend of "Red" Albright. His work was top secret and even Capt. Midnight wasn't totally sure of his fate. The female interest was at first Patsy Donovan, but was changed to Joyce Ryan in the Ovaltine years. Due to war shortages premiums were largely suspended from late 1942 until the fall of 1945. Captain Midnight served courageously during the balance of the 40's on radio and had a resurgence on television in the 50's. In the video version he was also known as Jet Jackson in certain non-Ovaltine sponsored cities and in re-runs. There is a strange phenomenon connected with Captain Midnight. Nearly everyone who has ever heard of the program can conjure up a "decoder ring."Yet, exhaustive research has failed to prove there ever was such a premium.

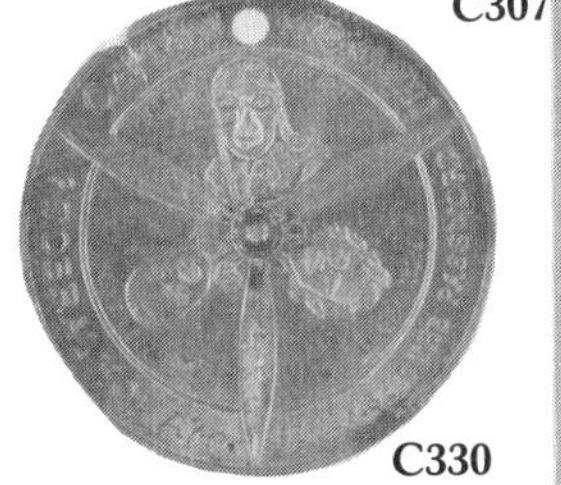

1939 — Skelly Premiums

		Good	Fine	Mint
C299	Membership Card	10	30	50
C300	Mysto-Magic Weather Forecasting Flight Wings	5	7	10
C301	Photo of Captain Midnight wearing Secret Ring	15	18	24
C302	Photo of Chuck Ramsey	8	10	12
C304	Photo of Captain, Chuck and Patsy together	12	16	20
C305	Flight Commander's Pin	100	250	400
C306	Letter from Chuck's Dad	10	25	45
C307	Chuck's Treasure Map	20	50	75
C308	Photo of Capt. Midnight (same as C301) w/Treasure Hunt rules on the reverse	20	25	30
C310	Trick and Riddle Book	12	20	25
C315	Stamp Album of Air Heroes, w/16 stamps	10	15	25
C319	Spartan Bomber Model Kit	20	50	100
	Flight Patrol Reporter Newspapers:			
C320	Vol. 1, No. 1, Spring 1939	20	30	40
C321	Vol. 1, No. 2, June 15, 1939	17	25	35
C322	Vol. 1, No. 3, Aug 1,1939	17	25	35
C323	Vol. 1, No. 4, Dec 1939	17	25	35
C325	Vol. 1, No. 6, Mar 1940	15	20	30

1940-41 — Skelly Premiums

C329	Membership Card	10	30	50
C330	Brass Spinner Membership Token, original	6	8	10
C331	Reproduction (small "r" under S in Skelly logo)	1	1	2
C332	Pewter Spinner Membership Token, repro of C330	1	2	3
C335	Ringo Jumpo Jumping Bean Game	15	25	50

33

| C340 | Airline Map of America | 50 | 125 | 250 |

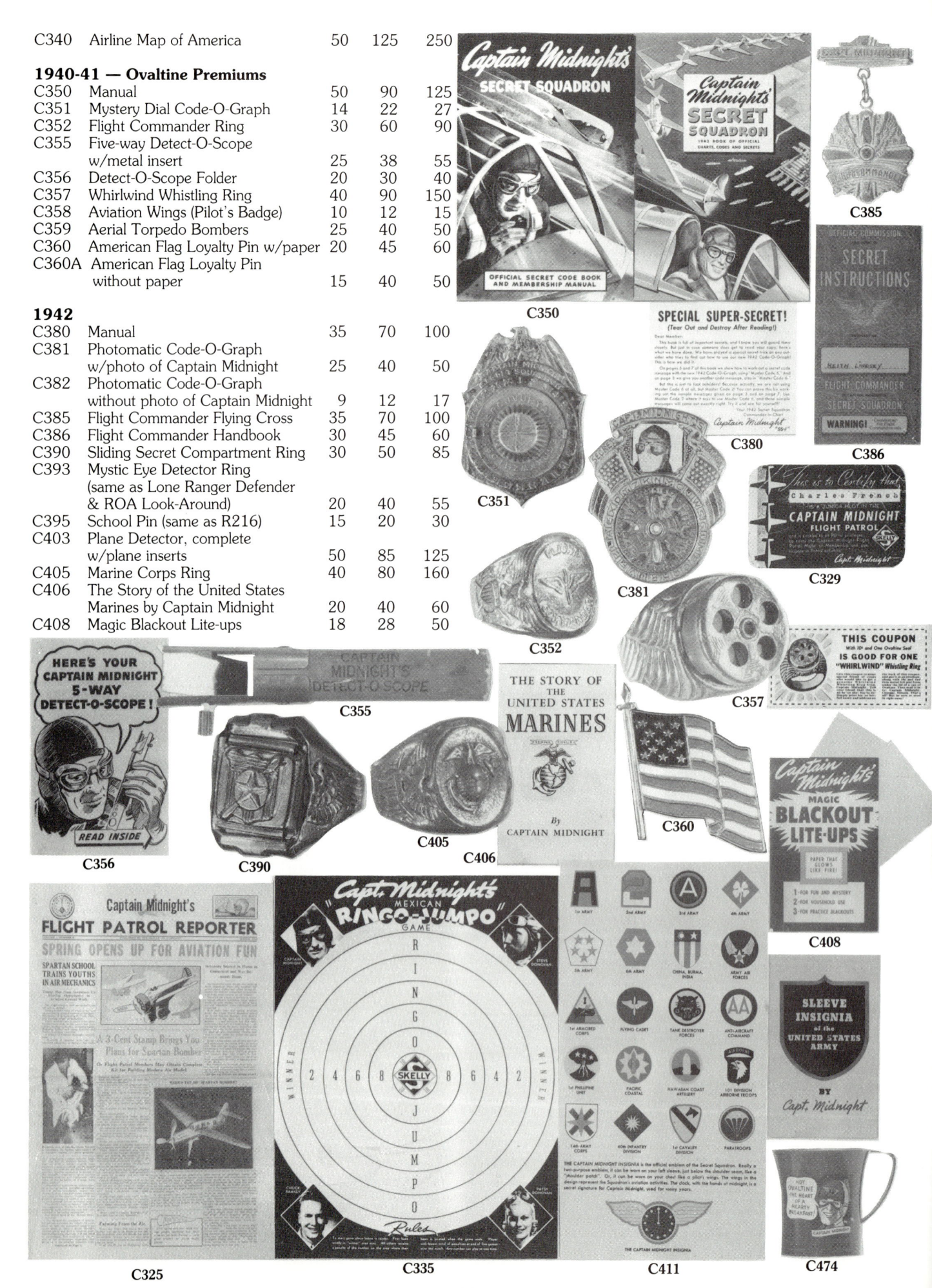

1940-41 — Ovaltine Premiums
C350	Manual	50	90	125
C351	Mystery Dial Code-O-Graph	14	22	27
C352	Flight Commander Ring	30	60	90
C355	Five-way Detect-O-Scope w/metal insert	25	38	55
C356	Detect-O-Scope Folder	20	30	40
C357	Whirlwind Whistling Ring	40	90	150
C358	Aviation Wings (Pilot's Badge)	10	12	15
C359	Aerial Torpedo Bombers	25	40	50
C360	American Flag Loyalty Pin w/paper	20	45	60
C360A	American Flag Loyalty Pin without paper	15	40	50

1942
C380	Manual	35	70	100
C381	Photomatic Code-O-Graph w/photo of Captain Midnight	25	40	50
C382	Photomatic Code-O-Graph without photo of Captain Midnight	9	12	17
C385	Flight Commander Flying Cross	35	70	100
C386	Flight Commander Handbook	30	45	60
C390	Sliding Secret Compartment Ring	30	50	85
C393	Mystic Eye Detector Ring (same as Lone Ranger Defender & ROA Look-Around)	20	40	55
C395	School Pin (same as R216)	15	20	30
C403	Plane Detector, complete w/plane inserts	50	85	125
C405	Marine Corps Ring	40	80	160
C406	The Story of the United States Marines by Captain Midnight	20	40	60
C408	Magic Blackout Lite-ups	18	28	50

C350

C385

C386

C329

C380

C351

C381

C357

C352

C355

C356

C390

C405

C406

C360

C408

C325

C335

C411

C474

34

1943

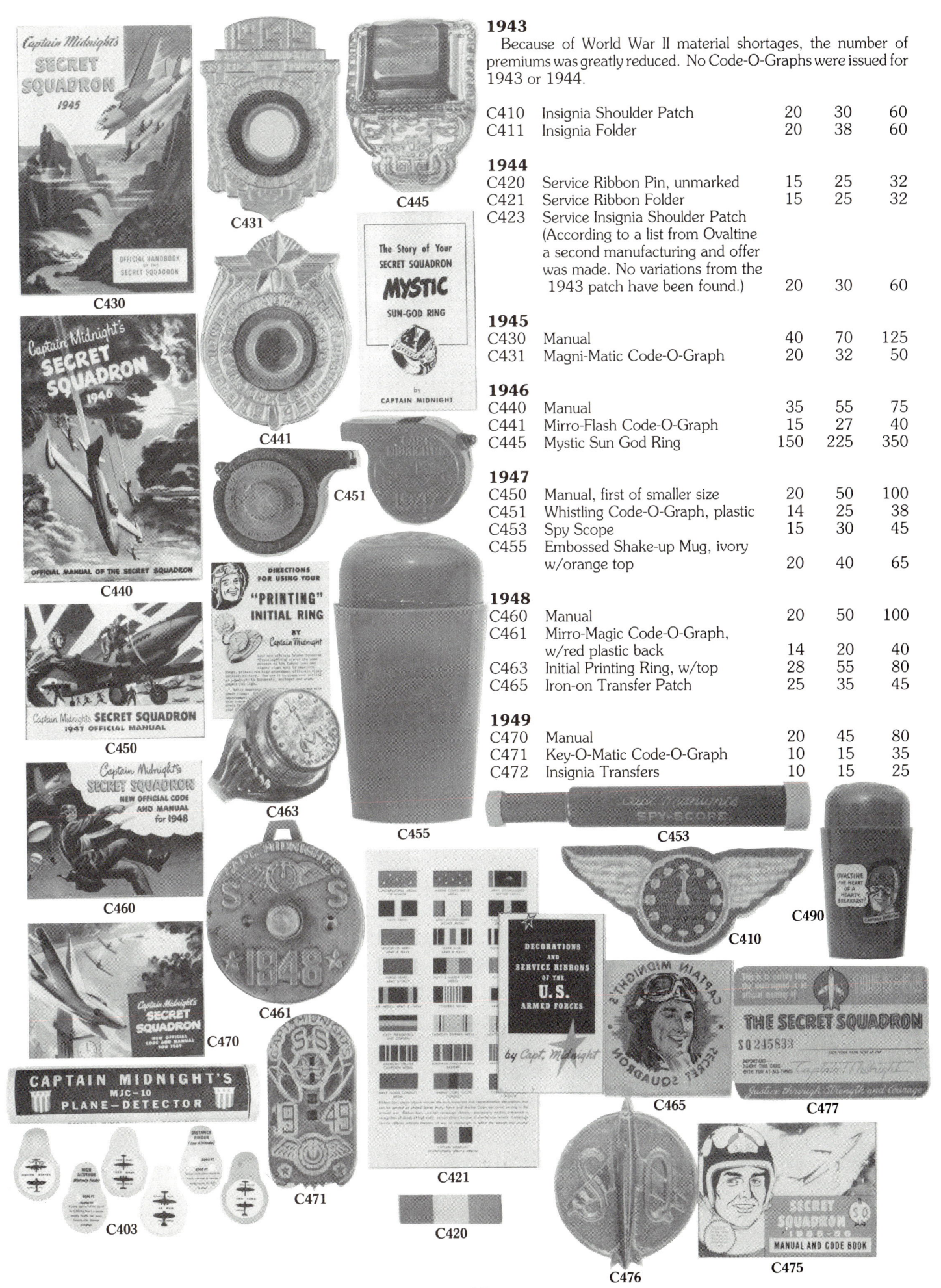

Because of World War II material shortages, the number of premiums was greatly reduced. No Code-O-Graphs were issued for 1943 or 1944.

C410	Insignia Shoulder Patch	20	30	60
C411	Insignia Folder	20	38	60

1944

C420	Service Ribbon Pin, unmarked	15	25	32
C421	Service Ribbon Folder	15	25	32
C423	Service Insignia Shoulder Patch (According to a list from Ovaltine a second manufacturing and offer was made. No variations from the 1943 patch have been found.)	20	30	60

1945

C430	Manual	40	70	125
C431	Magni-Matic Code-O-Graph	20	32	50

1946

C440	Manual	35	55	75
C441	Mirro-Flash Code-O-Graph	15	27	40
C445	Mystic Sun God Ring	150	225	350

1947

C450	Manual, first of smaller size	20	50	100
C451	Whistling Code-O-Graph, plastic	14	25	38
C453	Spy Scope	15	30	45
C455	Embossed Shake-up Mug, ivory w/orange top	20	40	65

1948

C460	Manual	20	50	100
C461	Mirro-Magic Code-O-Graph, w/red plastic back	14	20	40
C463	Initial Printing Ring, w/top	28	55	80
C465	Iron-on Transfer Patch	25	35	45

1949

C470	Manual	20	45	80
C471	Key-O-Matic Code-O-Graph	10	15	35
C472	Insignia Transfers	10	15	25

35

Captain Midnight switched to TV in the 50's. His image was changed to a jet pilot and The Secret Squadron designation was changed at this time from "SS" to "SQ."

1953
C474	Hot Ovaltine Mug		5	10	15

		Good	Fine	Mint

1955-56
C475	Manual		50	90	200
C476	SQ "Plane Puzzle" Decoder, plastic		35	75	150
C477	Membership Card		14	18	28
C479	Flight Commander Certificate		4	5	5
C480	Flight Commander Secret Handbook		15	25	45
C481	SQ Cloth Patch		8	15	26
C484	Photo (General Mills)		10	20	30

1957
C485	Manual		35	60	110
C486	Silver Dart SQ Decoder, plastic		35	60	110
C487	Membership Card		14	18	28
C488	Flight Commander Signet Ring, plastic		40	80	160
C489	Flight Commander Handbook		35	70	150
C490	Shake-up Mug, 15th Anniversary Offer, red w/blue top		8	12	18
C493	SQ 15th Anniversary Cloth Patch		9	13	20

There is no evidence of any premiums marked Jet Jackson. However, there has been several paper Captain Midnight items produced recalling the "old radio" days. There have been at least two different paper 1942 Code-O-Graphs produced. There was a set of thin vinyl sound sheet records produced by the Longines Symphonette Society in the late 60's or early 70's using the comic book style artwork never associated with the distinctive radio Captain Midnight as visualized in manuals and other printed material. Ovaltine offered a record of old radio broadcasts in the late 70's.

C494	Longines Symphonette Society package		15	30	45
C495	Ovaltine Record (also available in stores		5	10	15

In 1987 Ovaltine revived the 50's version of the character and once again offered premiums free for proof of purchase from a new "classic" Ovaltine jar and special coupons from newspaper ads.

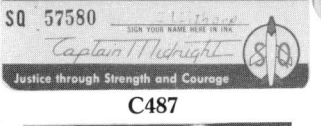

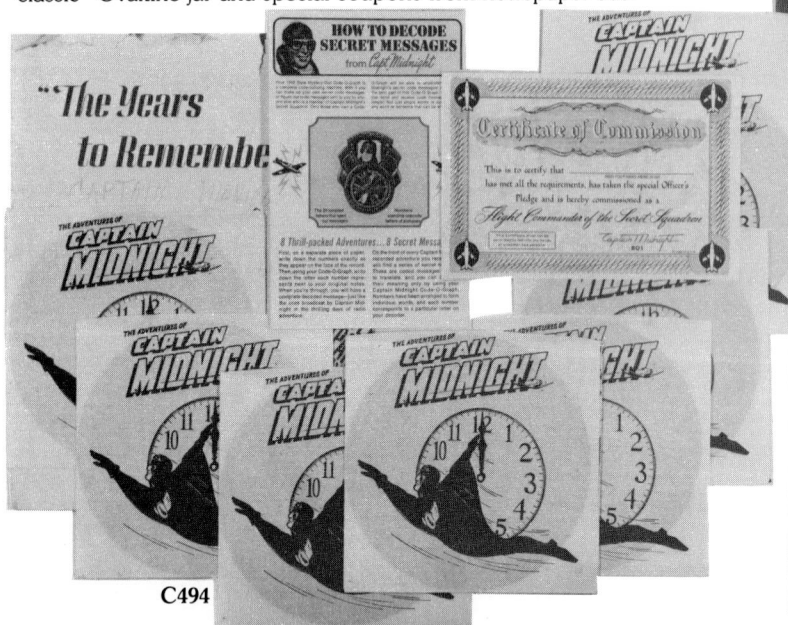

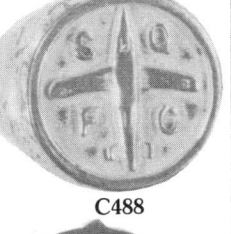

36

C496	T-Shirt		5	10	15
C497	Watch		10	25	35

CAPTAIN TIM HEALY'S IVORY STAMP CLUB

Stamp collecting was the hobby craze during the early 30's. Jack Armstrong, Radio Orphan Annie, Jimmie Allen, and several others had give-away promotions offering stamps or stamp-related prizes. Captain Tim Healy's Ivory Stamp Club was on the air Tuesday, Thursday and Saturday from 6:30-6:45 PM starting in 1934. The show featured stories about stamps and collecting tips . . . and encouraged the formation of stamp clubs in school.

		Good	Fine	Mint
C500	Membership Pins, red or black	3	5	8
C501	Stamp Album, 1934	8	9	10
C503	Stamp Album, 1935	9	10	12
C504	Kellogg's "Know Your Stamps", package backs, each	2	4	6

CAPTAIN VIDEO

In the age of Star Wars, the space exploits of Captain Video are remembered as being rather pedestrian. The budget for props was only $25 a week (5 programs). The cameras stayed focused on the Captain and the Video Ranger as they described and reacted to the action. The scripts were written like radio scripts. Models and sets were few. The exception was the command station of the Captain's spaceship - The Galaxy. It became indelibly burned in the viewer's mind. But while Captain Video scrimped on production budgets, the premiums offered were some of the best of the TV era. The program aired on the Dumont network from 1949 to 1956 when the network folded and refused to sell the show to NBC.

		Good	Fine	Mint
C510	Membership Card	8	12	16
C511	Photo of Captain Video	5	10	15
C512	Photo Ring	25	32	40
C513	Secret Seal Ring	35	45	190
C515	Flying Saucer Ring, w/both saucers	40	75	325
C516	Rite-O-Lite Gun Kit	15	20	25
C517	Space Gun Ring (has since been identified as a Space Patrol premium)			
C518	Plastic Space Men, 12 different - came in Post Raisin Brand, each	3	4	9
C520	Purity Bread Tab	10	25	50
C521	Glo-Photo Pendant, plastic	40	70	140
C522	Mysto-Coder	35	70	110

CASEY, CRIME PHOTOGRAPHER

Casey was a photographer for the *Morning Express*, but he spent most of his time solving murder mysteries with reporter Annie Williams at his side. He enjoyed great rapport with long-suffering Inspector Logan of Homicide and the entire group commiserated with Ethelbert, the bartender at the Blue Note Cafe. The program was first heard under the title of "Flashgun Casey" in 1943 and remained on the air until 1955.

C530   Cast Photo   15   25   30

CEREAL BOXES

Cereal boxes are miniature point-of-purchase displays - often colorful - used to promote premiums as well as the product.

Interest in cereal boxes has grown even more rapidly than the desire to own the premiums themselves. In the case of the Lone Ranger Frontier Town Cherrios boxes and the Sergeant Preston Yukon Trail packages, the premium and cereal box are one and the same. Premium collectors are mainly interested in packages depicting a character or premium offer. However, samples of the sponsor's product package have long accompanied the collection of the premiums themselves. There is also competition from antique advertising collectors for available material.

Manufacturers have recognized the collectibility of their packages and have even started issuing limited edition collector's boxes with sports heroes, teams or merchandizing devices such as holograms to encourage retention of modern day cereal boxes.

Then too, many brands are offered for only a brief time - often based on a popular TV, comic or toy "hero."

The accelerated interest has been reflected in rapidly increasing prices. Boxes form the last 5 to 10 years command $5 each if a character or popular premium offer is shown on the front of the box. Boxes from the 50's and 60's are commanding $10 to $50 or so depending on the character and the demand. Prices on choice boxes from the 30's, 40's and 50's have achieved the stature of popular culture art and can command prices ranging into the hundreds of dollars for exceptional specimens of complete boxes. Completeness is the key. A complete box has a full top and bottom, separated where the box would normally be joined. Condition, design, premiums, and what's on the front then add to the value of the complete box.

Top cereal boxes are: any of the Ralston Tom Mix or Space Patrol premium boxes, Cheerios Lone Ranger Frontier Town boxes, Quaker Sergeant Preston Yukon Trail boxes, and Superman PEP boxes. There were over 75 different Mickey Mouse and Disney character Post Toasties boxes. These are sought after by Disney as well as premium and antique advertising collectors and range from $25 to $100 or more per complete box. Disney package backs only with uncut cut-outs range from $10 to $45 each.

40

41

NEW! Send for This Complete, Authentic
TOTEM POLE COLLECTION
Get a Hand-Painted Miniature Model of any ONE of
5 NORTHWEST INDIAN TOTEM POLES
EACH ONLY 25¢
ALL 5 TOTEM POLES ARE THIS LARGE!
THUNDERBIRD
THE FIGHT WITH THE OTTERS
BURIAL POLE
KILLER WHALE
SUN AND RAVEN
Money-Saving Offer!
SUPPLY LIMITED! ORDER TODAY! USE HANDY ORDER BLANK ON TOP OF PACKAGE!
Quaker Puffed Rice
Roy Rogers MICROSCOPE RING!
MOTHER'S OATS
BOYS! GIRLS! Get ROY ROGERS "BRANDING IRON" RING
WHOLE GRAIN OATS - The Richest Thrifty Natural Source of VITAMIN B
The Quaker Oats Company
5 GABBY HAYES COMIC BOOKS
QUAKER PUFFED WHEAT
SPECIAL OFFER!
GET 2 "Challenge of the Yukon" DOG PICTURE CARDS
inside this package
YOURS..at no extra cost!
QUAKER Puffed Wheat
INSIDE THIS PACKAGE ARE 2 DOG PICTURE CARDS IN FULL COLORS!
WIN ONE OF 6000 GILBERT TOYS IN THE
Post TOY SWEEPSTAKES
1000 FIRST PRIZES
2000 SECOND PRIZES
3000 THIRD PRIZES
SPECIAL BONUS OFFER! SEE SIDE PANEL
GRAPE-NUTS FLAKES
TOY SWEEPSTAKES OVER 6,000 PRIZES!
Post
GRAPE-NUTS FLAKES
LIGHT-CRISP WHEAT FLAKES
CAUTION!
Get these keen scaled RAILROAD models on KIX boxes!
KIX
CORN CEREAL
KIX STREAMLINER
Cheerios
FREE INSIDE!
Cocoa Puffs
Chocolate Flavor Frosted Corn Puffs
STAR WARS
Cheerios
SPECIAL OFFER!
Kellogg's PEP
THE SOLAR CEREAL
Kellogg's PEP
WHOLE WHEAT FLAKES
"TOM CORBETT SPACE CADET"
CUT OUT THIS AMOOZIN' LI'L ABNER POP-OUT PICTURE!
NABISCO
the Original SHREDDED WHEAT
FREE INSIDE
LOCOMOTIVE
INSIDE THIS BOX ONE PINK PANTHER 5-IN-1 SPY KIT
Cheerios
THE OAT CEREAL READY TO EAT
FREE!
Mickey Mouse Circus
WIGGLE PICTURE BADGE
Cheerios
Get your MICKEY MOUSE CIRCUS WIGGLE PICTURE BADGE
FREE Mickey Mouse Circus Wiggle Picture Badge
HOW TO GET IT:
OR... for 25¢ and one Cheerios boxtop... get all 6 Wiggle Pictures and Badge!
HOW TO GET THEM:
Cheerios
Cheerios
MOTHER'S
CRUSHED OATS WITH CHINA
The Quaker Oats Company

43

CHANDU THE MAGICIAN

"Chandu the Magician" aired originally as 15-minute daily episodes beginning in 1932. It aired in 30 eastern cities sponsored by Beech-Nut products . . . and on the West Coast by White King soap. It dealt with the adventures of the Regent family in various parts of the world. It combined magic, occult, mystery, romance, travel and foreign lure. A survey of 3,000 New York area school children rated it the top juvenile show in 1934, but it bowed to the network shows in 1936. In 1948, it reappeared briefly with White King as the sponsor. White King's name appeared on a boxed set of Chandu magic tricks which is not a premium.

		Good	Fine	Mint
C540	Photo of Gayne Whitman, Chandu	4	6	8
C541	Photo of Chandu in costume	8	12	16
C542	Photo of Dorothy Regent	4	6	8
C543	Photo of Bob Regent	4	6	8
C544	Photo of Betty Regent	4	6	8
C550	Chinese Coin Trick	15	20	25
C551	Buddha Money Mystery	20	25	30
C552	Holiday Trick	20	25	30
C553	Svengali Mind Reading Trick	15	20	25
C554	Galloping Coin Trick	15	20	25
C555	Choco-mint Mystery	15	20	25
C556	Mysterious Bottle Trick #5	10	15	20
C560	Chandu White King of Magic Card Miracles	15	25	40

CHARLIE McCARTHY

"The Edgar Bergen and Charlie McCarthy Show" first aired on May 9, 1937 and continued throughout the 40's as a weekly half hour prime-time comedy show. They shared his half hour with Mortimer Snurd and Effie Klinker. There were classic running rivalries between Charlie and such notables as W.C. Fields. The little wooden dummy was as hopelessly in love with movie queens like Dorothy Lamour as we listeners were. During the sponsorship of Chase and Sanborn Coffee a few premiums were offered.

		Good	Fine	Mint
C570	Photo of Edgar and Charlie	4	6	8
C572	Spoon	3	5	8
C573	Personalized Fan Card	10	18	25
C575	Charlie McCarthy Radio Game, 1938	8	12	22
C580	Cardboard Dummy of Charlie	8	12	22
C581	Cardboard Dummy of Mortimer (may not be a premium)	10	15	30
C582	Ring	40	80	130

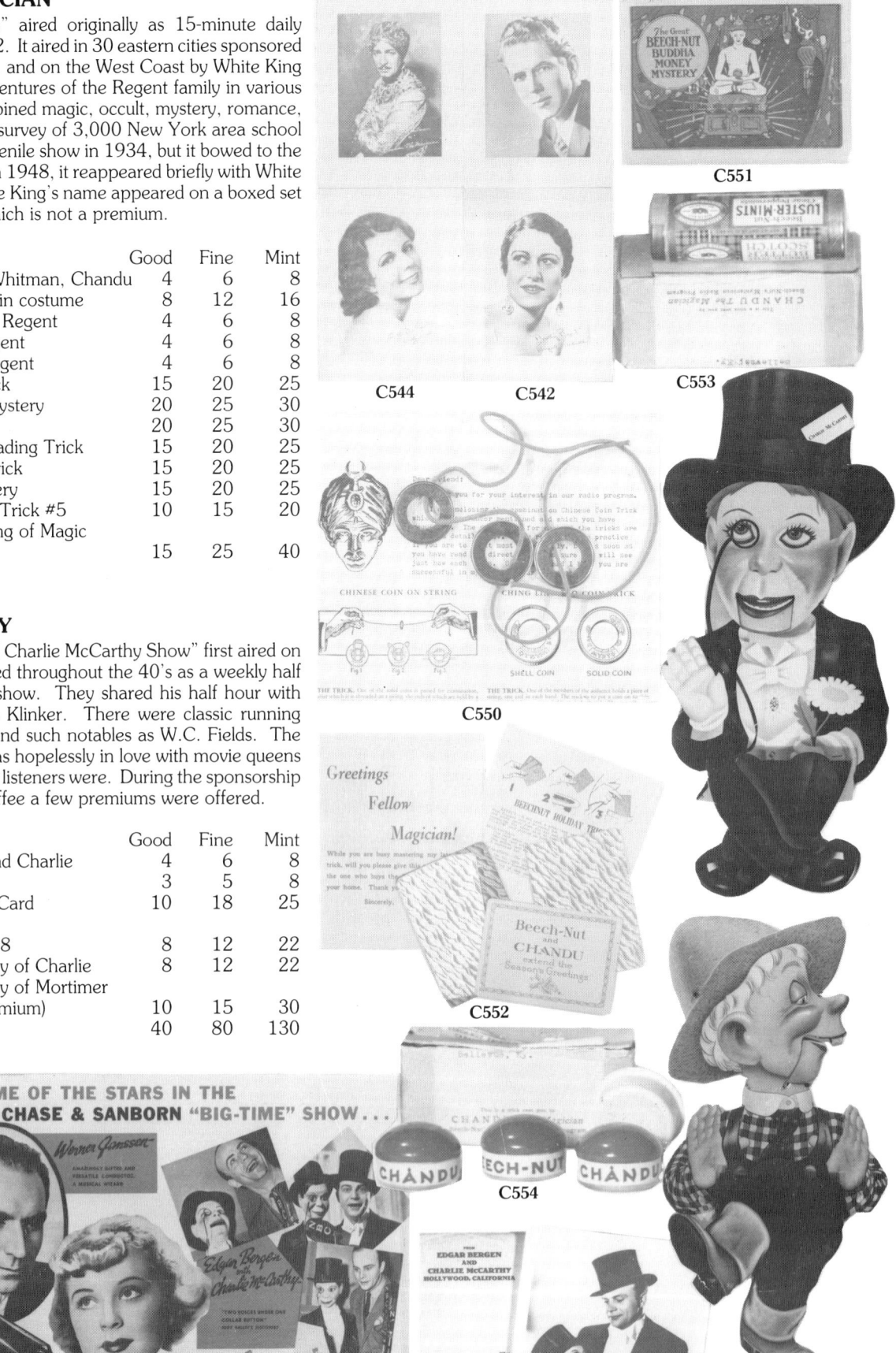

CINNAMON BEAR, THE

"The Cinnamon Bear" was an imaginative, extremely well written and produced children's radio serial. It aired each weekday between Thanksgiving and Christmas. Designed for department store sponsorship, it first appeared in 1937, and yearly thereafter for over a quarter of a century. The serial is available on tape and still provides vivid entertainment for today's TV generation youngsters. Metro Golden Memories, 5425 W. Addison, Chicago, IL 60641 has reproduced the coloring book children colored to obtain their silver star. They sell for $1 plus postage and applicable sales tax.

		Good	Fine	Mint
C640	Coloring Book, printed on newsprint paper	15	25	50
C640A	Coloring Book, reproduction printed on white bond paper	1	1	1
C641	Foil Silver Star w/Paddy Picture	20	40	60
C642	Stuffed Bear	35	60	100
C655	Wieboldt's TV Badge, complete w/paper bear	20	40	80

CISCO KID, THE

The Cisco Kid and his sidekick, Pancho, rode the radio range on Mutual starting in 1942. The program lasted into the early 50's and on TV sponsored by a variety of local bread brands. Cisco was an obvious ladies' man quite contrary to the leading horse-loving, six gun heroes of the time. Pancho provided the comic relief between the kissing and shooting. The show would usually end with a bad pun from Pancho that would trigger the line every kid waited to hear, "Oh, Pancho!" and his reply "O-O-O-O-h-h-h, Sissss-co!"

		Good	Fine	Mint
C675	Secret Compartment Picture Ring	150	250	500
	Butternut Bread Tabs - each available in five different color hats:			
C680	Cisco	5	10	16
C681	Pancho	2	3	5
C682	Cisco & Pancho Weber Bread Tabs, pair	10	15	20
C683	Cisco & Pancho Blue Seal Bread Tabs, pair	10	15	20
C685-89	Tip-Top Bread Giveaway Photo Postcards	4	6	10
C693	Tip-Top Puzzle, in illustrated envelope	10	15	20
C695	Triple S Club Letters, 1951	25	45	65
C696	Triple S Club Button	15	30	45
C700	Cisco Radio Face Mask	4	8	10
C701	Pancho Radio Face Mask	4	8	10
C705	Paper Cricket Gun	8	12	16

45

1953 - Conclusion

C710	Cisco TV Face Mask	4	6	8
C711	Pancho TV Face Mask	4	6	8
C720	Rancher Club Button	10	18	25
C721	Rancher Club Card	5	6	7
C722	Rancher Club Certificate	5	10	15
C723	Rancher Club Photo	10	18	25

46

		Good	Fine	Mint
C725	Cisco Texas Citizenship Certificate	6	9	10
C727	Cattle Brands Manual	15	20	25
C729	Range War Game	25	35	50
C730	Name-the-Pony Newsletter	8	12	16
C731	Cisco 8-1/2" x 11" Photos	2	4	8
C732	Pancho 8-1/2" x 11" Photos	2	4	8
C735	Humming Paper Lariat	10	17	30

CLARA, LU & EM

Clara, Lu, and Em made their pretend apartment house gossip into a comic soap opera. It all started as a skit three college students did at Northwestern University in the mid-20's. A friend got them on a local Chicago station in 1930. An ad agency executive liked what he heard and was instrumental in placing the show on the NBC Blue Network in 1931. The show lasted to 1936. A puzzle is the only premium found to date.

C755	Clara, Lu & Em Puzzle	5	10	15

COUNTERSPY

As a rule, the countless adult/juvenile-styled mystery shows didn't offer premiums. David Harding, Counterspy, tried one badge offer before deciding his time would be better spent fighting crime. Pepsi Cola made the offer. The show began on ABC in 1942 and ran until 1957 for a parade of sponsors.

1949

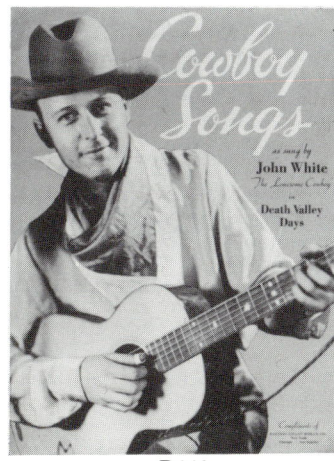

		Good	Fine	Mint
C775	Junior Counterspy Agent Photo Badge	15	22	40
C776	Membership Certificate	8	15	20
C780	Match Book	2	3	6

CRANKY CROCODILE

A short lived show apparently targeted for younger children aired in 1933. The only description of the show found appears in *Children and Radio Programs* as the "Adventures of the Cranky Crocodile with a musical background." A paper Cranky Crocodile was sent free to listeners who wrote asking for one. The value wouldn't be much.

C790	Paper Cranky Crocodile	10	15	25

DAVEY ADAMS SHIPMATES CLUB (D.A.S.C.)

The Davey Adams Shipmates Club identified premiums with a simple D.A.S.C. The sponsoring product was Lava soap. The commercial jingle for the product also pounded home the name letter by letter . . . L-A-V-A; L-A-V-A . . . in time with a kettle drum beat. Premiums make mention of Captain Davey Adams, Steve Wood and a Wah Ling "battling the gangsters in Bayport" . . . suggesting a radio show connection, but any other references to any broadcast connection were elusive. Coded dates on the printed pieces indicate the materials were printed in 1939 and 40. The manual reprints pages on sailor knots, semaphore signaling code, and international Morse code from the *Sea Scout Manual* published by the Boy Scouts of America. What appears to be a decoder is actually a secret compartment membership badge. Four secret passwords appear in the upper windows when the numbers 1 thru 4 are positioned in the lower opening. The letters on the center hub, SLC, stand for "Strength - Loyalty - Courage".

		Good	Fine	Mint
D110	Charter Member Certificate	10	17	25

47

		Good	Fine	Mint
D111	Letter offering Secret Compartment Badge	5	12	20
D112	DASC Manual	10	20	30
D115	Secret Compartment Membership Badge	15	45	60
D117	Siren Ring	100	200	300

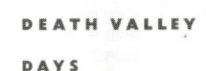

DEATH VALLEY DAYS

One of radio's earliest programs, it aired on the NBC Blue Network from Sept 1930 to well into the TV years of the 60's. The same basic "stories of the Old West" format never changed over the years even though the program title did. It was called "Death Valley Sheriff" in 1944, and simply "The Sheriff" in 1945. The yarns were spun by the Old Ranger who sometimes doubled as the pitchman for Borax and Boraxo. He was replaced in the TV version by spokesman Ronald Reagan.

		Good	Fine	Mint
D125	1931 Story of Death Valley	3	4	5
D130	1932 Story of Death Valley	3	4	5
D135	1933 Old Ranger's Yarns of Death Valley	3	4	5
D136	20 Mule Team Jigsaw Puzzle, 1933	10	15	20
D140	1934 Death Valley Tales as told by the Old Ranger	3	4	5
D141	Cowboy Songs in Death Valley, 1934	2	3	5
D145	World's Biggest Job Script in Folder, 1935	4	5	8
D150	High Spots of Death Valley Days Vol. 1, No. 1, 1939	3	4	5
D155	1950's Model of 20 Mule Team and Wagon	10	15	22
D156	Old Ranger's Seed Packets	5	12	18

DETECTIVES BLACK AND BLUE

"Detectives Black and Blue" was an early syndicated program, one of the first to incorporate music to build suspense and production quality. It aired from 1932 to 1934 featuring two amateur detectives (graduates of a detective correspondence course) who had more of a knack of slapstick radio comedy than solving mysteries. Dialogue was rhymed throughout the broadcast including their catch phrase: "We're detec-a-tives Black and Blue... good men tried and true."

		Good	Fine	Mint
D170	Badge	15	23	30
D171	Cap	30	40	50

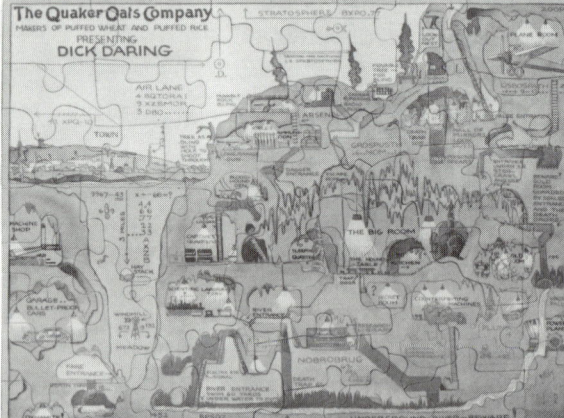

DICK DARING, A BOY OF TODAY

Quaker Oats presented "Dick Daring" on NBC in 1933-34. The main character was a thinly veiled copy of Jack Armstrong, but the premiums weren't nearly as good. The two jigsaw puzzles depicting elaborate underground secret chambers and passageways are the most interesting. The two books are both on magic. Pocket magic tricks (all store items) were also redeemed for Quaker trademarks. Secret chambers and magic tricks are a curious combination of premiums which make one wonder how it all fit together. However, other than the premiums themselves there is a void of information.

		Good	Fine	Mint
D221	City Underground Jigsaw Puzzle & Picture	8	18	30
D222	Mountain Underground Jigsaw Puzzle & Picture	8	20	35
D225	Bag of Tricks Book	4	8	15
D226	New Bag of Tricks Book	3	7	12

48

WRANGLER
TOM MIX RALSTON STRAIGHT SHOOTER
STRAIGHT SHOOTER
SHERIFF
GOOD LUCK TOM MIX RALSTON
SECRET OPERATOR MELVIN PURVIS LAW AND ORDER PATROL
LIEUTENANT SECRET OPERATOR MELVIN PURVIS LAW AND ORDER PATROL
SECRET OPERATOR MELVIN PURVIS LAW AND ORDER PATROL GIRLS DIVISION
GIRLS JUNIOR G-MAN DIVISION
MELVIN PURVIS JUNIOR G-MAN CORPS
ROVING OPERATIVE MELVIN PURVIS JUNIOR G-MAN CORPS
CHIEF OPERATIVE MELVIN PURVIS JUNIOR G-MAN CORPS
DREIKORN'S BREAD Speed Gibson's FLYING POLICE
RED RYDER Victory Patrol
BOBBY BENSON RANGER H-O
OFFICIAL PHILLIPS H. LORD'S GANG BUSTERS
TARZAN RADIO CLUB BURSLEY COFFEES
TARZAN RADIO CLUB DRINK MORE MILK
Langendorf PHANTOM PILOT PATROL
HOWIE WING CADET
MARY MARVEL
BUCK JONES CLUB
CHIEF EDITOR
SPECIAL COUNTER-SPY JUNIOR AGENT
CAPTAIN AMERICA
SUPERMAN JUNIOR
SUPERMAN AMERICA
REPORTER DICK STEEL NEWS SERVICE
LI'L ABNER
SG CAPTAIN
SG CAPTAIN '42
THE SHADOW CLUB
THE SECRET 3 DETECTIVE SERVICE
Bond Bread LONE RANGER SAFETY CLUB
QBC LONE RANGER SAFETY CLUB
LONE RANGER SAFETY SCOUT SILVER CUP
LONE RANGER SAFETY SENTINEL
CHIEF SCOUT
LONE RANGER SILVER'S LUCKY HORSESHOE
1942
BUCK ROGERS SOLAR SCOUTS
CHIEF EXPLORER BUCK ROGERS SOLAR SCOUTS
ROY ROGERS RIDERS LUCKY PIECE
MEMBER DICK TRACY SECRET SERVICE PATROL
DICK TRACY SECRET SERVICE PATROL MEMBER
DICK TRACY SECRET SERVICE PATROL SECOND YEAR MEMBER
DICK TRACY SECRET SERVICE PATROL SERGEANT
DICK TRACY SECRET SERVICE PATROL LIEUTENANT
DICK TRACY SECRET SERVICE PATROL CAPTAIN
INSPECTOR GENERAL DICK TRACY SECRET SERVICE PATROL

Radio Orphan Annie's Secret Society
WARNING!
HERE'S OUR BRAND NEW SECRET CODE AND SIGNS AND SIGNALS FOR 1935!
Radio Orphan Annie's Secret Society 1935
RADIO ORPHAN ANNIE'S SECRET SOCIETY 1936
BIGGER AND BETTER THAN EVER
NEW
SIGNS
SIGNALS
CODES & SECRETS
PASTE
Radio Orphan Annie's Secret Society
1937
BIGGER AND BETTER THAN EVER
Radio Orphan Annie's Secret Society
1938
5TH ANNIVERSARY YEAR
BIGGER AND BETTER THAN EVER!
Secret Society News
EXTRA
FOR MEMBERS ONLY
RADIO ORPHAN ANNIE'S 1939 SECRET SOCIETY!
New Mysterious Secret Language Amazes Millions!
MOST SECRET CODE EVER INVENTED!
Outsiders Mystified by New Secret Symbol!
RADIO ORPHAN ANNIE'S 1940 Secret Society
BIGGER N' BETTER THAN EVER!
7TH ANNIVERSARY STREAMLINER
NEW
Codes....Signals
Signs...Secrets
Captain Midnight's SECRET SQUADRON
OFFICIAL SECRET CODE BOOK AND MEMBERSHIP MANUAL
Captain Midnight's SECRET SQUADRON
1942 BOOK OF OFFICIAL CHARTS, CODES AND SECRETS
Captain Midnight's SECRET SQUADRON 1945
OFFICIAL HANDBOOK OF THE SECRET SQUADRON
Captain Midnight's SECRET SQUADRON 1946
OFFICIAL MANUAL OF THE SECRET SQUADRON
Captain Midnight's SECRET SQUADRON
1947 OFFICIAL MANUAL
Captain Midnight's SECRET SQUADRON
NEW OFFICIAL CODE AND MANUAL for 1948
Official Handbook for members of FRANK BUCK'S ADVENTURERS CLUB
(BRING 'EM BACK ALIVE)
Frank Buck's
MOST THRILLING ADVENTURE
BUCK ROGERS SOLAR SCOUTS
SECRET CLUB OF THE RADIO FRIENDS OF BUCK AND WILMA
BUCK ROGERS IN THE 25TH CENTURY
Captain Midnight's SECRET SQUADRON
NEW OFFICIAL CODE AND MANUAL FOR 1949

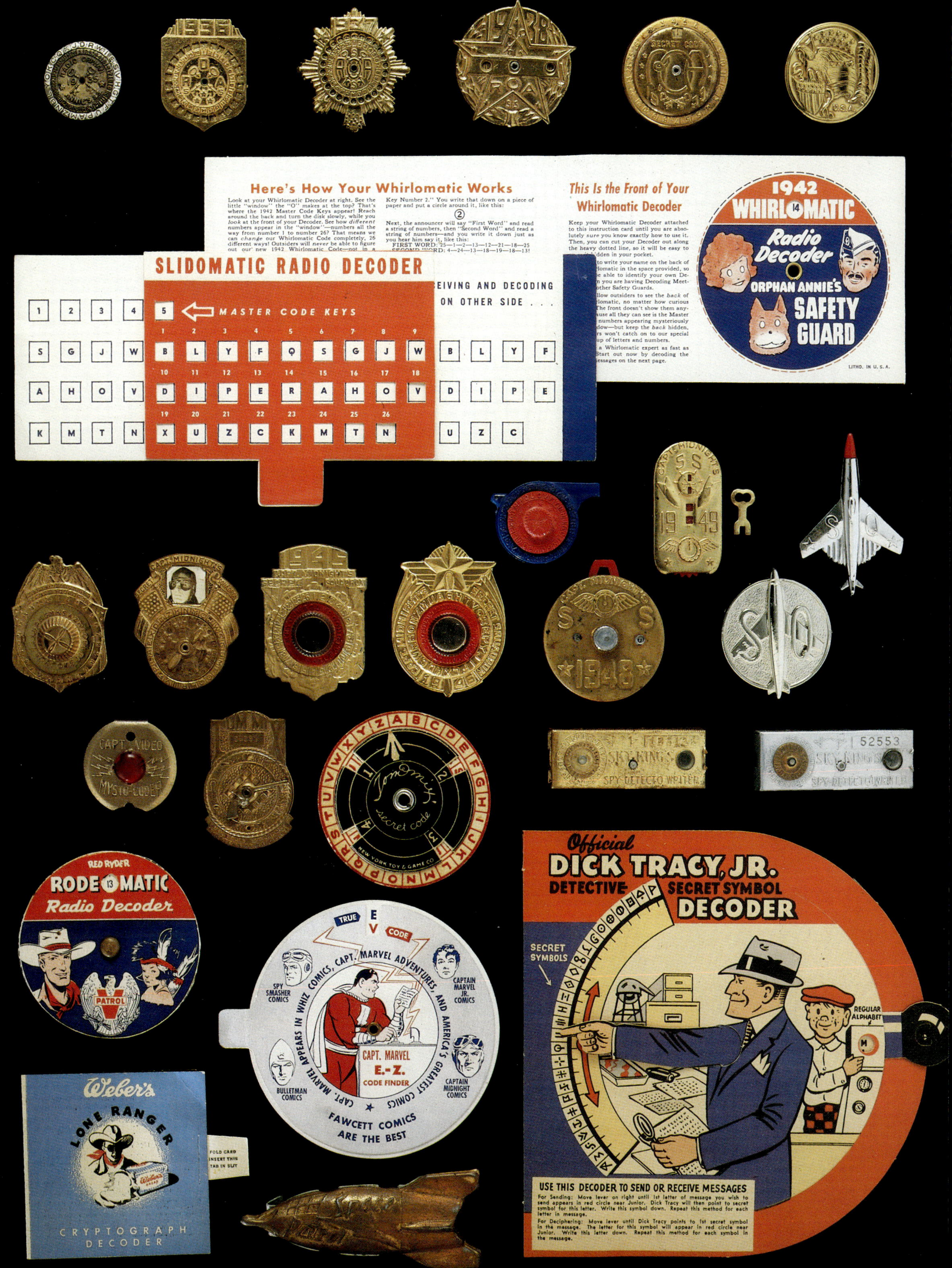

Here's How Your Whirlomatic Works
Look at your Whirlomatic Decoder at right. See the little "window" the "O" makes at the top? That's where the 1942 Master Code Keys appear! Reach around the back and turn the disk slowly, while you *look* at the front of your Decoder. See how *different* numbers appear in the "window"—numbers all the way from number 1 to number 26? That means we can *change* our Whirlomatic Code completely, 26 different ways! Outsiders will *never* be able to figure out our new 1942 Whirlomatic Code—not in a
Key Number 2." You write that down on a piece of paper and put a circle around it, like this:
②
Next, the announcer will say "First Word" and read a string of numbers, then "Second Word" and read a string of numbers—and you write it down just as you hear him say it, like this:
FIRST WORD: 25—1—2—13—12—21—18—25
This Is the Front of Your Whirlomatic Decoder
Keep your Whirlomatic Decoder attached to this instruction card until you are absolutely *sure* you know exactly how to use it. Then, you can cut your Decoder out along the heavy dotted line, so it will be easy to
1942
WHIRLOMATIC
14
Radio Decoder
ORPHAN ANNIE'S
SAFETY GUARD
LITHO. IN U. S. A.
SLIDOMATIC RADIO DECODER
MASTER CODE KEYS
ON OTHER SIDE . . .
CAPT. MIDNIGHT'S
1949
1948
CAPT. VIDEO
MYSTO-CODER
SKY KING'S
SPY-DETECTO WRITER
52553
Tom Mix
secret code
NEW YORK TOY & GAME CO.
RED RYDER
RODE-O-MATIC
13
Radio Decoder
PATROL
TRUE
CODE
CAPT. MARVEL APPEARS IN WHIZ COMICS, CAPT. MARVEL ADVENTURES, AND AMERICA'S GREATEST COMICS
SPY SMASHER COMICS
CAPTAIN MARVEL JR. COMICS
BULLETMAN COMICS
CAPTAIN MIDNIGHT COMICS
CAPT. MARVEL
E.-Z.
CODE FINDER
FAWCETT COMICS ARE THE BEST
Weber's
LONE RANGER
FOLD CARD INSERT THIS TAB IN SLIT
CRYPTOGRAPH DECODER
Official
DICK TRACY, JR.
DETECTIVE
SECRET SYMBOL
DECODER
SECRET SYMBOLS
REGULAR ALPHABET
USE THIS DECODER TO SEND OR RECEIVE MESSAGES
For Sending: Move lever on right until 1st letter of message you wish to send appears in red circle near Junior. Dick Tracy will then point to secret symbol for this letter. Write this symbol down. Repeat this method for each letter in message.
For Deciphering: Move lever until Dick Tracy points to 1st secret symbol in the message. The letter for this symbol will appear in red circle near Junior. Write this letter down. Repeat this method for each symbol in the message.

LITTLE ORPHAN ANNIE'S NEW DRINK ... ICE COLD OVALTINE
HERE'S MY ICE-COLD "SHAKE-UP" DRINK FOR HOT DAYS AN' MY OWN RECIPE FOR MAKIN' IT—
"SHAKE UP" WAS ANNIE'S IDEA, BUT MY RECIPE HAS ICE CREAM IN IT TOO— TRY IT RIGHT NOW, WILL YUH?
HAROLD GRAY
THIS IS HOW ANNIE MAKES ICE-COLD OVALTINE—HER OWN RECIPE
THIS IS HOW JOE MAKES ICE-COLD OVALTINE—HIS OWN RECIPE
WHICH DO YOU LIKE BEST?
VOTERS BUTTON FOR JOE CORNTASSEL
VOTERS BUTTON FOR LITTLE ORPHAN ANNIE
PRE-FLIGHT TRAINING KIT!
HOW TO FLY
LOOK WHAT KIT CONTAINS!
1. PILOT TRAINER
2. FLIGHT MANUAL
3. CORPS WINGS
4. OFFICIAL INSIGNIA
5. CUB PILOT CORPS NEWS
GET THIS KIT
WITH PURCHASE THESE TWO PKGS.
WHEATIES
Get these TARZAN GIFTS FREE
SAVE THIS COLOR CHART
The Tarzan Gift Statues are TWICE as large as shown in these Pictures
Mail this FREE GIFT OFFER BLANK
BUCK ROGERS FREE OFFER
STAGE-SCENERY-CHARACTERS 25TH CENTURY INVENTIONS Given away without cost
Complete details and pictures on pages 2-3-4
BUCK ROGERS CUT-OUT ADVENTURE BOOK
BUCK ROGERS IN THE TWENTY-FIFTH CENTURY
POP!
How to get the most fun from your 25th CENTURY Helmet and Rocket Pistol
HOW TO ASSEMBLE YOUR HELMET
BUCK ROGERS
Orphan Annie Circus
THE ALL-STAR ACTION SHOW
Captain Midnight's FLIGHT PATROL REPORTER
SPRING OPENS UP FOR AVIATION FUN
SPARTAN SCHOOL TRAINS YOUTHS IN AIR MECHANICS
A 3-Cent Stamp Brings You Plans for Spartan Bomber
HERE'S THE BIG SPARTAN BOMBER!
Farming From the Air
BUCK ROGERS
Buck Rogers
CAPTAIN MARVEL CLUB
MEMBERSHIP CARD
HEADQUARTERS Captain Marvel Club
CAPT. MARVEL CLUB
WHIZ COMICS
Captain Marvel
ON SALE AT ALL NEWS-STANDS
The CAPTAIN MARVEL MAGIC LIGHTNING BOX
SHAZAM
BILLY BATSON
10¢
BILLY BATSON BROADCASTS!
NO CAPTAIN MARVEL
SHAZAM!
CAPTAIN MARVEL CLUB
CAPT. MARVEL JR.
CAPTAIN MARVEL

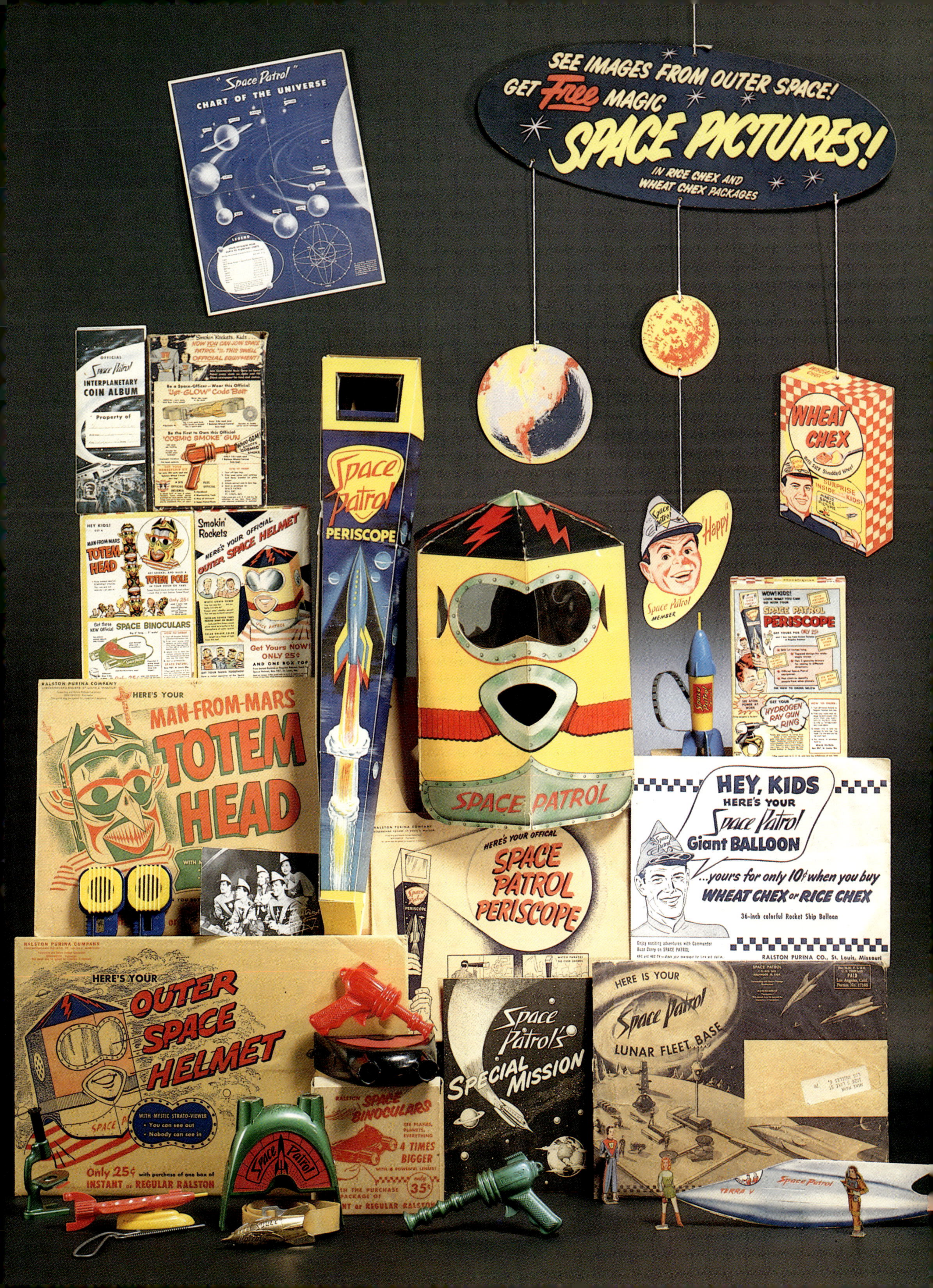

SEE IMAGES FROM OUTER SPACE!
GET Free MAGIC
SPACE PICTURES!
IN RICE CHEX AND WHEAT CHEX PACKAGES
"Space Patrol" CHART OF THE UNIVERSE
OFFICIAL Space Patrol INTERPLANETARY COIN ALBUM
Space Patrol PERISCOPE
WHEAT CHEX
"Happy"
Space Patrol MEMBER
Smokin' Rockets HERE'S YOUR OFFICIAL OUTER SPACE HELMET
MAN-FROM-MARS TOTEM HEAD
SPACE BINOCULARS
SPACE PATROL
HERE'S YOUR MAN-FROM-MARS TOTEM HEAD
HERE'S YOUR OFFICIAL SPACE PATROL PERISCOPE
HEY, KIDS
HERE'S YOUR Space Patrol Giant BALLOON
...yours for only 10¢ when you buy WHEAT CHEX or RICE CHEX
36-inch colorful Rocket Ship Balloon
RALSTON PURINA CO., St. Louis, Missouri
HERE'S YOUR OUTER SPACE HELMET
WITH MYSTIC STRATO-VIEWER
• You can see out
• Nobody can see in
Only 25¢ with purchase of one box of INSTANT or REGULAR RALSTON
RALSTON SPACE BINOCULARS
4 TIMES BIGGER
Space Patrol's SPECIAL MISSION
HERE IS YOUR Space Patrol LUNAR FLEET BASE
Space Patrol
TERRA V

Captain Marvel

GET VALUABLE
GIFTS Free
with BOX TOPS
from QUAKER PUFFED WHEAT
and QUAKER PUFFED RICE
Amazing! Absolutely NEW!
DICK TRACY
ROCKET PLANE
Rockets up high
Opens wings
Lands automatically.
GIVEN FOR 5 BOX TOPS OR 1 BOX TOP AND 10¢
BEAUTIFUL
MONOGRAM RING
Your Own Two Initials In
24-Carat Gold Plate Letters!
Fits Any Finger.
GIVEN FOR 5 BOX TOPS OR 1 BOX TOP AND 10¢
OFFICIAL
DICK TRACY FLASHLIGHT
Send Secret Messages At Night!
Compact! Powerful! Complete!
GIVEN FOR 5 BOX TOPS OR 1 BOX TOP AND 10¢
GIVEN FOR 10 BOX TOPS OR 1 BOX TOP AND 20¢
3-POWER
POCKET SIZE TELESCOPE
More Powerful! Brings Distant
Objects Closer! Handy Pocket Size!
GIVEN FOR 5 BOX TOPS OR 1 BOX TOP AND 10¢
YOUR OWN
SECRET TELEPHONE
Send and hear whispered
messages up to 100 feet!
and other Gifts too!
Send your BOX TOPS to the
QUAKER OATS CO. BOX L, CHICAGO
MAKERS OF QUAKER PUFFED WHEAT and QUAKER PUFFED RICE

BOYS! GIRLS!
AIR SPEED
TURN AND BANK
CAPT. SPARKS AIRPLANE COCKPIT
GET Capt. Sparks'
AIRPLANE PILOT
TRAINING COCKPIT
and 16 PAGE INSTRUCTION BOOK..
COME IN
for
FREE ORDER BLANK

HI-YO ...
SILVER HAS A SON!
NAME HIM
and
WIN THIS COLT*
OR
$1,000.00
IN CASH
1,050 ADDED PRIZES!
50 SCHWINN-BUILT
DE LUXE BICYCLES
OR
UNDERWOOD DE LUXE LEADER
TYPEWRITERS
(YOUR CHOICE)
1,000 EVEREADY CAMP-TYPE
FLASHLIGHTS
FOLLOW THESE SIMPLE RULES:
KiX
2 Pkgs.
20¢

JOIN UP!
CUB
PILOT
CORPS
LISTEN TO
JACK ARMSTRONG
STATION
FOR FULL DETAILS!
WHEATIES
2 PKGS.
¢
GET YOUR PIPER CUB PRE-FLIGHT KIT!
HOW TO FLY
A PRACTICAL FLIGHT MANUAL FOR MEMBERS OF CUB PILOT CORP
CUB PILOT CORPS NEWS
Win a Cub! Learn to Fly!
SEND TWO WHEATIES BOX TOPS AND 10¢ TO JACK ARMSTRONG, DEPT. 80, MINNEAPOLIS 15, MINN.
1. Pilot Trainer comes ready-cut out of strong cardboard all set to assemble. When you move controls, little plane moves into positions for dive, bank, climb, etc.—just like a real plane!
2. Flight Manual. Cub Pilot Corps Manual "How to Fly"—24 pages of real pilot instruction. Over 50 step-by-step photos show just how planes fly!
3. Corps Wings. Sturdy paper-board wings to put on your sweater, jacket, etc. Shows you're a member of CUB PILOT CORPS.
4. Official Insignia. Two sizes—hot iron transfers! Snappy emblems for shirt or jacket.
5. CUB PILOT CORPS News. Special Issue of official Aviation Publication gives you complete details about the big NAME YOUR PLANE CONTEST!
$11,760* IN FLYING SCHOLARSHIPS IN BIG PLANE NAMING CONTEST!
GRAND PRIZE - - - A REAL PIPER AIRPLANE!
Separate contest in each of 48 states and District of Columbia!
13 prizes of Free Flight Instruction in each State!
Full information in each Pre-flight Kit. Send for your Kit today!
* 1,176 hours of flying instructions in the air with competent instructor, at current rate of $10.00 per instruction hour. Contest entries must be postmarked on or before July 1, 1945.
WHEATIES
Breakfast of Champions
Product of General Mills, Inc.

Cheerios
A nourishing cereal made from
FAMILY SIZE
Cheerios
an OAT cereal ready to eat
Valuable Silverware Coupon Inside
Queen Bess Pattern
Oneida Community
Get a complete set... easy!
NET WT. 10½ OZ.
Cheerios
OFFICIAL LONE RANGER DEPUTY BADGE
Cheerios
ADVENTURES OF JACK ARMSTRONG THE ALL-AMERICAN BOY
JACK RESCUES CAST-AWAY CREW!
SPECIAL MAGAZINE OFFER!
WHEATIES
Breakfast of Champions
Kellogg's
RAISIN BRAN
FLAKES
CEREAL with FRUIT
Look for WALT DISNEY "JOINIES"
NET WEIGHT 10 OUNCES
ADVENTURES OF JACK ARMSTRONG THE ALL-AMERICAN BOY
ATTACKED BY AN ENRAGED TIBETAN EAGLE
SPECIAL MAGAZINE OFFER!
WHEATIES
Breakfast of Champions
QUAKER PUFFED WHEAT
QUAKER Puffed Wheat
SPECIAL OFFER! GET 2
"Challenge of the Yukon"
DOG PICTURE CARDS
inside this package
NEW! Collect 35 Amazing, Official DOG CARDS like these!
World's "Biggest" Dog!
World's "Smallest" Dog!
World's "Fastest" Dog!
YOURS...at no extra cost!
QUAKER Puffed Wheat
INSIDE THIS PACKAGE ARE 2 DOG PICTURE CARDS IN FULL COLORS!
WEIGHT 4 OZ. NET
The Quaker Oats Company
WHEATIES
"Breakfast of Champions"
Sensational Offer!
8 Walt Disney COMIC BOOKS
248 PAGES OF COMICS IN SET
Only 15¢ PLUS WHEATIES BOX TOP
LOOK FOR ALL THE WALT DISNEY FUN MASKS
4 DIFFERENT SETS
ORDER TODAY!
GET ALL 4 SETS—A, B, C, AND D
ADVENTURES OF JACK ARMSTRONG THE ALL-AMERICAN BOY
JACK FINDS PHANTOM SUBMARINE HIDE-OUT
SPECIAL MAGAZINE OFFER!
WHEATIES
Breakfast of Champions
"BIG AS LIFE" the Lone Ranger or Tonto
25" x 75" (Over six feet tall!)
FULL COLOR... LIFE-SIZE POSTERS OF THE PICTURES YOU SEE HERE!
ORDER NOW
WHEATIES
"Breakfast of CHAMPIONS"
YAHOO! I'M FIREBALL TWIGG!
Post's
GRAPE-NUTS
FLAKES
Get "The Explorer's Ring" THAT TELLS TIME
See back of package
12 Ounces—Net Weight—340 Grams
Post Cereals
GRAPE-NUTS FLAKES
Try these Delicious Recipes!
YAHOO! Kids... IT'S TERRIFIC!
The most sensational ring offer ever made...
The new "EXPLORER'S RING" that tells time!
Everybody's gettin' em!
YOURS for ONLY 25¢ and the BOX TOP from this PACKAGE
GRAPE-NUTS FLAKES
Post Cereals
snap! crackle! pop!
Kellogg's RICE KRISPIES
Kellogg's
RICE KRISPIES
SNAP! CRACKLE! POP!
snap! crackle! pop!
Kellogg's PEP
Aluminum Wing Inside Package
Kellogg's PEP WHOLE WHEAT FLAKES
THUNDER-JET
"TURBO-JET PLANE"
Kellogg's PEP
Boys and Girls! BEANIE CAP
Kellogg's PEP
Kellogg's
PEP
WHOLE WHEAT FLAKES
"TURBO-JET PLANE"
Kellogg's PEP
SEND FOR YOUR
Lone Ranger HIKE-O-METER
ONLY 50¢
WHEATIES "Breakfast of CHAMPIONS"
HIKE-O-METER
WHEATIES

CAPTAIN MARVEL CLUB
SHAZAM
SHAZAM CAPTAIN MARVEL CLUB
SUPERMAN
SUPERMAN-TIM CLUB
LET'S 'LECT LUM EDWARDS FOR PRESIDENT
SUPERMEN OF AMERICA
AMERICAN EAGLE DEFENDERS
BUCK ROGERS in the 25th CENTURY
THE SHADOW OF FU MANCHU
I AM A SPY SMASHER
BLACK FLAME HI-SPEED EXPLORER
CAPTAIN MARVEL
ELLERY QUEEN CLUB MEMBER
Space Patrol
BLOOD BOOSTERS
SKIPPY RACER CLUB
SERGEANT PRESTON OF THE YUKON
JOE CORNTASSEL
I'M FOR HOWDY DOODY
HOWDY DOODY
H-BAR-O RANGERS CLUB
Dorothy Hart
SUNBRITE JUNIOR NURSE CORPS
RED RYDER
LITTLE BEAVER
TERRY AND THE PIRATES
CANADA DRY
MEMBER I·S·P Speed Gibson PLEZOL SUNFED BREAD
SPEED GIBSON SECRET POLICE I.S.P.
I HAVE ENTERED THE RED RYDER PONY CONTEST
KAYO CLUB
KAYO
CHOCOLATE
MEMBER
THE LONE RANGER
CISCO KID RANCHER
S·S·S·S
KERN'S CISCO KID
SAFETY
SCHOLARSHIP
STRENGTH
"TRIPLE-S" CLUB
SIGNAL TARZAN CLUB
Tarzan
SAFETY CLUB
THE LONE RANGER
SPACE CADET
MEMBER
LONE RANGER SAFETY CLUB
ROCKY JONES
SPACE RANGER
SILVERCUP BREAD

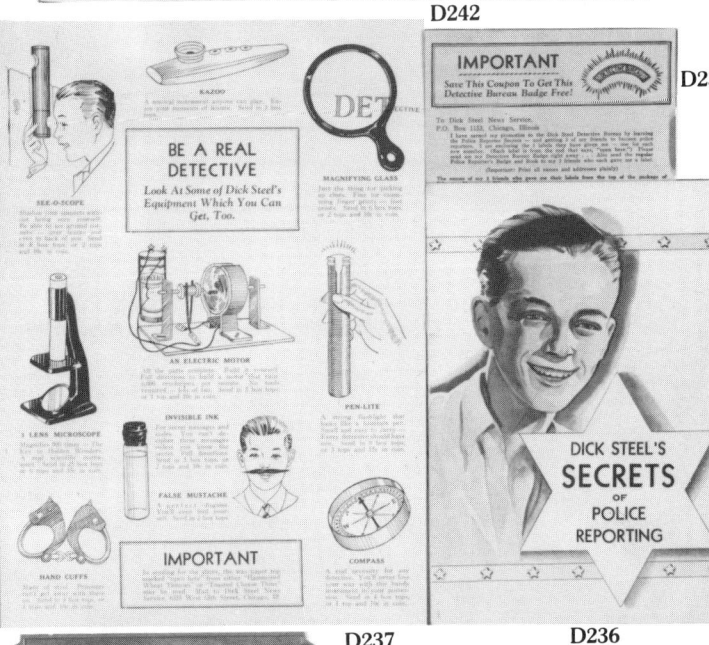

DICK STEEL, BOY POLICE REPORTER

"Dick Steel" was a promotion of Educator Hammered Wheat Thinsies, presumably a breakfast cereal in the early 30's. The manual is an interesting example of the times and encouraged kids to start their own neighborhood newspapers. Dick Steel projected an appeal to kids of better intelligence with electric motors, microscopes, and an encouraged them to write for the fun of it. This seemed to be a major contribution to the sponsored product. How could any intelligent kid ask their mom to buy a product named Educator Hammered Wheat Thinsies?

		Good	Fine	Mint
D233	Cast Photo	5	10	15
D234	Membership Badge, steel	5	10	15
D235	Detective Bureau Advancement Badge, steel	5	10	15
D236	Manual, Dick Steel's Secrets of Police Reporting	10	20	30
D237	Premium Offer Sheet	5	10	15
D240	Membership Badge, brass	10	17	25
D242	How to Start Your Own Newspaper w/sample newspaper	10	20	30
D243	Whistle	6	9	15

DICK TRACY

Dick Tracy had a difficult time transferring his popularity from newspaper and comic books to radio ... or at least holding a steady sponsor and network time slot. The first run began in 1935, on Mutual, moved to NBC in 1937, and was cancelled at the end of the 1939 season. Like Buck Rogers, he was only on the network a couple days a week. The two-a-week format never seemed to work out for juvenile adventure serials. It just wasn't enough exposure to maintain interest. Part of the problem may have been character changes imposed on the radio version. Writers tried to make him an aviator air detective in the 30's and a war hero during the war years. The best surviving broadcasts, however, are shows in which he is portrayed as a top metro police detective. Most premiums stick to the image created by Chester Gould. The show ran in syndication and perhaps some new episodes were written before the show left the air in 1948.

"Dick Tracy" has the distinction of requiring a kid to eat the most boxes of cereal to get the top premium - his Inspector General badge. Even though badges of other ranks were awarded along the way kids had to eat 39 boxes of Quaker Puffed Wheat or Rice to get the top badge, as follows - initial membership 2 box tops, 5 more for promotion to Sergeant, then 7 additional to become a Lieutenant, 10 more to achieve the rank of Captain, and a final 15 additional box tops to achieve the highest rank of Inspector General. If they spent 12 box tops to become a Patrol Leader, along the way, then they would have had to eat a total of 51 boxes of cereal.

		Good	Fine	Mint
D250	Detective Club Belt Badge, leather pouch back	10	19	35
D253	Detective Club Shield Badge	10	18	30
D260	Enameled Hat Ring	25	35	60
D261	Rubber Band Gun	10	20	32
D265	Family Fun Book	3	8	12

1938

Code	Item			
D275	Secret Service Patrol Secret Code Book	20	35	50
D276	Member Pinback	6	12	20
D277	Certificate for Posting Promotion Stickers	10	14	18
D278	Sergeant Badge	15	25	35
D279	Lieutenant Badge	20	35	60
D280	Captain Badge	30	50	100
D281	Inspector General Badge	40	75	150
D282	Patrol Leader Bar Pin	8	12	16
D285	Lucky Bangle Bracelet	20	45	95
D287	Secret Detecto Kit	40	55	75
D288	Aviation Wings	15	25	35
D290	Siren Plane	30	55	85
D291	Air Detective Badge	10	18	24
D292	Air Detective Cap	15	32	45
D293	Air Detective Ring	25	65	90
D294	Wing Bracelet	30	40	50
D295	Secret Compartment Ring	35	55	100

1939

Code	Item			
D300	1939 Manual & Code Book	35	45	60
D301	Brass Member Badge	10	15	20
D302	Second Year Member Badge	10	18	25
D303	Girl's Division Badge	10	18	25
	Radio Play Adventure Scripts:			
D308	Vol. I - The Invisible Man	10	30	50
D309	Vol. II - Ghost Ship	10	30	50
D315	Pocket Flashlight	15	25	35
D316	Siren Code Pencil	15	22	30
D317	Private Telephones	30	35	44
D318	Flagship Rocket Plane	35	40	65
D325	Secret Detective Methods & Magic Tricks Manual	10	18	25

1942

Code	Item			
D330	Detective Club Tab	10	18	35
	Crime Detection Folio (D335-D338)			
D335	Decoder	10	25	40
D336	Puzzle	10	18	25
D337	Mystery Sheets, set of 3	8	12	15
D338	Notebook	5	8	10
D339	Paper Pop Gun	8	10	25

1944

Code	Item			
	Detective Kit (D340-D346)			
D340	Manual	12	25	40
D341	Badge, paper	5	10	15
D342	Membership Certificate	6	10	15

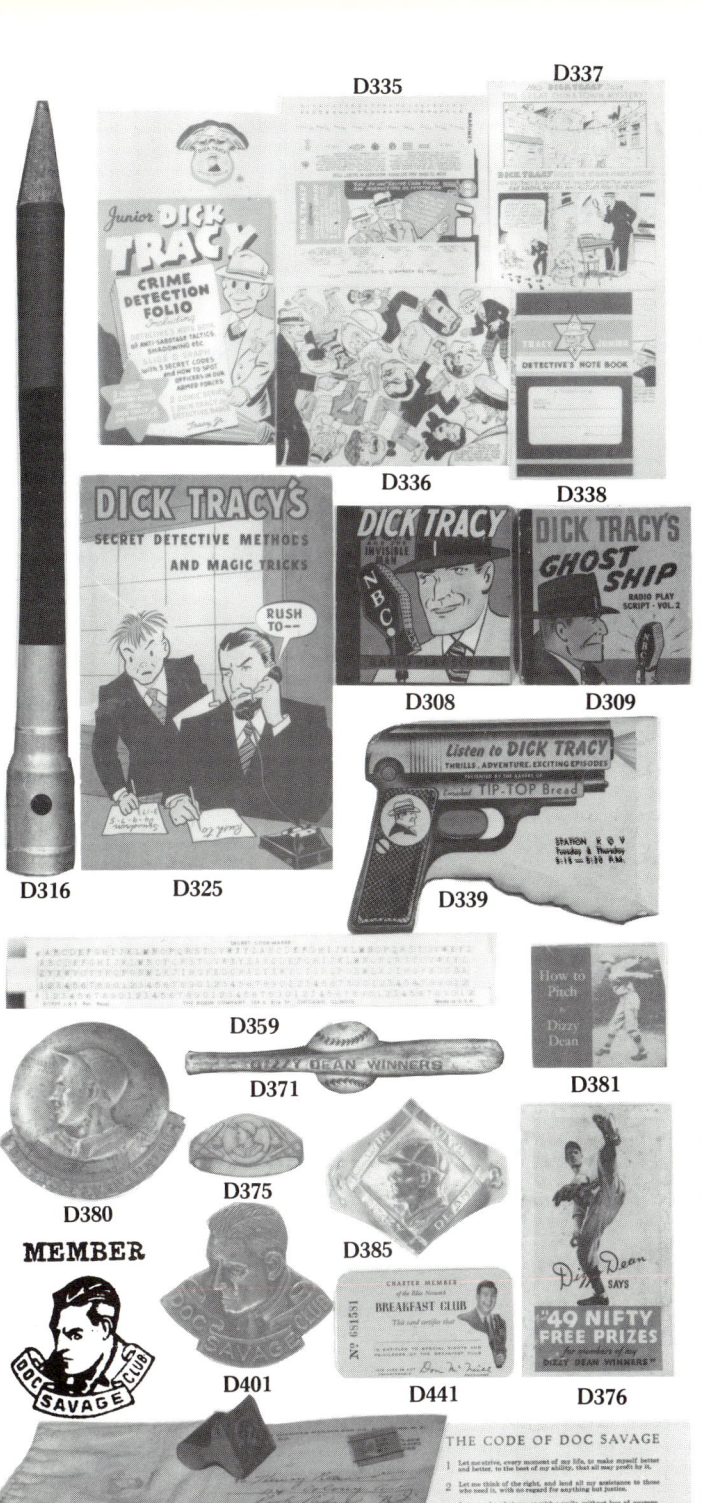

D343	Secret Code Dial	35	50	80	
D344	Suspect Wall Chart	5	8	12	
D345	File Cards	2	4	6	
D346	Tape Measure	2	3	4	

After 1940

D348	Red & Green Post Cereal Decoder Cards, each	3	5	8
D359	Detective Kit w/wood decoder, pot metal badge, etc., 1961	10	15	20

DIZZY DEAN WINNERS CLUB

The "Winner's Club" was another Post cereal non-radio campaign built on the reputation of the personable St. Louis Cardinal pitcher. Post Cereals either wanted to avoid higher costs of radio sponsorship or felt the media wasn't as good as the Sunday comics . . . which were the backbone of the Dizzy Dean and other real-life personality promotions. Most of these 30's promotions lasted only two or three years.

		Good	Fine	Mint
D371	Bat & Ball Pin	6	10	15
D372	Lucky Piece	10	20	30
D373	Autographed Photo, 8 x 10	6	10	15
D375	Dizzy Dean Winner's Ring	15	25	40
D376	Premium List Folder	5	10	15
D380	Member Pin	6	8	12
D381	How To Pitch Booklet	6	8	12
D385	Win With Dizzy Dean Ring	15	25	38

DOC SAVAGE

Doc Savage, (Clark Savage, Jr.) surgeon and perfectionist, known as the "Man of Bronze," was primarily a pulp magazine hero . . . although reportedly he had a brief flight on the radio in the 30's. Along with his cadre of assistants: William Harper Littlejohn (Johnny), world's greatest living expert on archeology and geology; Col. John Renwick (Renny), engineer; Lt. Col. Andrew Blodgett Mayfair (Monk), foremost scientist; Maj. Thomas J. Roberts (Long Tom), genius at electricity; and Brig. Gen. Theodore Marley Brooks (Ham), lawyer, "they would go anywhere, fight anyone, dare everything - seeking excitement and perilous adventure." There was literally nothing Doc Savage and his men couldn't accomplish.

		Good	Fine	Mint
D400	Color Illustration, bust	20	35	50
D401	Bronze Membership Pin	50	100	160
D402	Membership Card & Creed	10	20	30
D404	Color Illustration, reclining figure	20	35	50
D410	Medal of Honor	70	180	300
D414	Member's Rubber Stamp	25	85	125

DON McNEILL'S BREAKFAST CLUB

In the early 30's NBC had a morning program called "The Pepper Pot." The show was doing poorly so in 1933, the network hired Don McNeill to see what he could do to turn things around. The key to success was to eliminate the script and to start reading listeners' mail on the air. From then on until the show left the air on Dec 27, 1968 - one of radio's longest running programs - McNeill catered to listener involvement. And that included premiums. The annual yearbooks are of greatest interest to collectors. These were probably issued each year with the possible exception of some war years. The volumes were called various names such as Family Albums, Don's Other Life and finally Yearbooks. Years of known publication are mentioned.

59

		Good	Fine	Mint
D439	Membership Folder	5	8	10
D440	Breakfast Club Family Album 1942	4	5	7
D441	Membership Card	2	3	6
D442	Don's Other Life 1944	4	5	7
D446	Breakfast Club 1948 Yearbook	3	4	5
D447	Breakfast Club 1949 Yearbook	3	4	5
D448	Breakfast Club 1950 Yearbook	3	4	5
D451	Twenty Years of Memory Time, 1952	4	5	6
D453	'54 Don McNeill's Breakfast Club Yearbook	5	7	10
D455	20 Years of Corn	5	9	14
D456	Kiddy Party Ideas (Fritos)	3	6	10

DON WINSLOW OF THE NAVY

"Don Winslow of the Navy" was an adventure series that began on the NBC Blue network in 1937, and seemed to disappear about the time World War II ended. Under the sponsorship of Kellogg's Wheat Krispies, Don and his right-hand man, Red Pennington, battled the Scorpion, but promoted "peace - not war."

Post Toasties took over the series in 1942. Later in the run the show was also sponsored by Red Goose Shoes.

		Good	Fine	Mint
1938				
D510	Good Luck Coin	10	16	25
1939				
D520	Squadron of Peace: Creed, Manual, & Membership Card	30	55	80
D521	Ensign Pin	15	20	30
D522	Lt. Commander Pin	50	80	120
D523	Member Ring, serial number on top	55	100	250
D524	Membership Card for ring	10	15	20
D525	Periscope	25	45	70
1940				
D530	Photo of Don and Red	8	12	16
D531	Code Sheet	15	20	25
D540	Rubber Stamp - Anchor w/ listener's initials	20	28	35
1942				
D545	Catapult Bomber	20	40	60
D548	Undercover Deputy Certificate	8	16	24
D549	Golden Torpedo Decoder	30	60	90
D550	Creed w/cast photo	25	45	55
1943-44				
D560	Red Goose Shoe Coloring Picture	2	5	8

DOROTHY HART, SUNBRITE JR. NURSE CORPS

Dorothy Hart was the featured character for Sunbrite's Jr. Nurses Corps.

This girl oriented program was sponsored by Sunbrite Cleanser and Quick Arrow Soap Flakes. Available information indicates the program aired in 1937 and 1938. Dorothy was a teenage nursing student who's Aunt Jane was a professional nurse. Listeners were encouraged to hold their own Jr. Nurse meetings and learn first aid. Pat Gass, an old prospector/Indian guide type character, provided comic relief and somehow interwove historical story telling such as events surrounding the Lewis and Clark expedition. There was a manual type catalog offering a large selection of interesting premiums.

Redeeming premiums was extremely complicated for Dorothy Hart offers. Sunbrite was a leading cleanser in the 30's. Swift and Company also made Quick Arrow Soap Flakes, a new, unknown brand. They tried to push Quick Arrow by requiring a combination of Sunbrite and Quick Arrow labels and box tops for each item. In 1938 three Sunbrite labels could be substituted for one Quick Arrow box top. That gives you some idea of how the promotion was going and why it disappeared after the June 1, 1938 deadline for ordering premiums. The Dorothy Hart premium promotion was one of the finest ever produced. It failed because the sponsor's desire to require more than a premium program could produce.

		Good	Fine	Mint
D600	Catalog	10	20	30
D601	Official Armband Patch	10	20	30
D602	First Aid Cabinet	15	25	35
D603	Notebook	10	20	30
D604	Official Uniform, including Junior Nurse Corps Badge, complete	20	50	75
D604A	Membership Badge only	7	15	22
D605	Sewing Kit	7	15	24
D606	Hand Towel	10	20	30
D607	Official Service Set, including nurse's chart, button bandaids and unguentine, complete	20	40	60
D607A	Nurse Chart or Button, individually	7	15	25
D608	Identification Wristlet	10	25	40
D609	Ring	25	50	75
D610	Dorothy Hart Doll	12	24	36
D611	First Aid Kit	15	25	35
D612	Supervisor's Badge	10	20	30
D613	Handbrush	5	10	15
D614	Picture of Dorothy Hart	5	10	15
D615	Picture of Aunt Jane	4	8	12
D616	Picture of Sa-ca-ja-wea Cast	5	10	15
D617	Graduate Jr. Nurse Pin	10	20	30
D618	Toothbrush	5	10	15
D619	Brush & Comb Set	8	16	24
D620	Handkerchief	5	10	15
D621	Picture of Sa-ca-ja-wea	4	8	12
D622	Picture of Pat Gass w/Aunt Jane & Dorothy	5	9	14

61

DUFFY'S TAVERN

"Duffy's Tavern, where the elite meet to eat, Archie the manager speakin', Duffy ain't here - oh, hello, Duffy" was the intro which welcomed listeners to each episode. Duffy never was in. Ed Gardner, the producer of the show, played Archie. He first created the character in 1939, but the program wasn't fully developed until 1941 when it debuted on CBS. It changed sponsors and networks several times before it faded from the airwaves in 1951. The focus of the show was big name star guests dropping by to be subjected to Archie's fractured English and embarrassing questions. There were few premiums. The most interesting is the Reader. It's still funny today.

		Good	Fine	Mint
D900	Fan Photo of Ed Gardner as Archie	5	10	15
D905	Duffy's First Reader	10	20	30

EDGAR BERGEN & CHARLIE McCARTHY —
See Charlie McCarthy

EDDIE CANTOR

Eddie Cantor was a top star in the 30's with a prime time adult show for Chase & Sanborn Coffee. His annual publication offered a test of his popularity, a chance to show off his facial gymnastics in photo spreads, and last but not least, an opportunity to show him drinking and plugging the sponsor's coffee. Pebeco Toothpaste became his sponsor for the 1935 season and created his magic club to involve more kids. Cantor remained on the air until 1950, but the Pebeco experience seemed to discourage further premium use.

		Good	Fine	Mint
Chase & Sanborn Photo Albums of Eddie:				
E100	1932	3	4	5
E101	1933	2	3	4
E102	1934	2	3	4
E104	Book of Magic	8	16	24
E105	Cantor's Comics	8	16	24
E106	Magic Club Pin	2	3	4
E107	Secrets of Master Magic	8	16	25
E108	Master Card Mysteries	8	16	25

ED WYNN, THE FIRE CHIEF

Ed Wynn was billed as the Perfect Fool in vaudeville, but the power of radio changed his image overnight to the Texaco Fire Chief. His radio popularity rose rapidly after the show first aired in 1932. It continued until 1935. The face mask premium was used to promote the program at the 1933 Chicago World's Fair.

E110	Face Mask	15	20	25

ELLERY QUEEN

CBS introduced "Ellery Queen" on June 18, 1939. The radio series was based on a character created by Frederic Manfred Lee. The format was designed to appeal to armchair detectives and had a celebrity panel which listened to the program along with the audience. Before Ellery Queen revealed the solution to the evening's presentation the celebrity guests were asked their solution to the mystery. There were changes in the format, sponsors and networks over the years before it left the air in 1948. The character was later seen on television and promotional Ellery Queen 5-minute mysteries were syndicated for local radio sponsorship. Here again the clues were quickly unfolded and the audience was left to ponder the solution while a 60-second commercial aired. These were available around the 60's.

E500	Ellery Queen Club Member Pinback	15	25	40

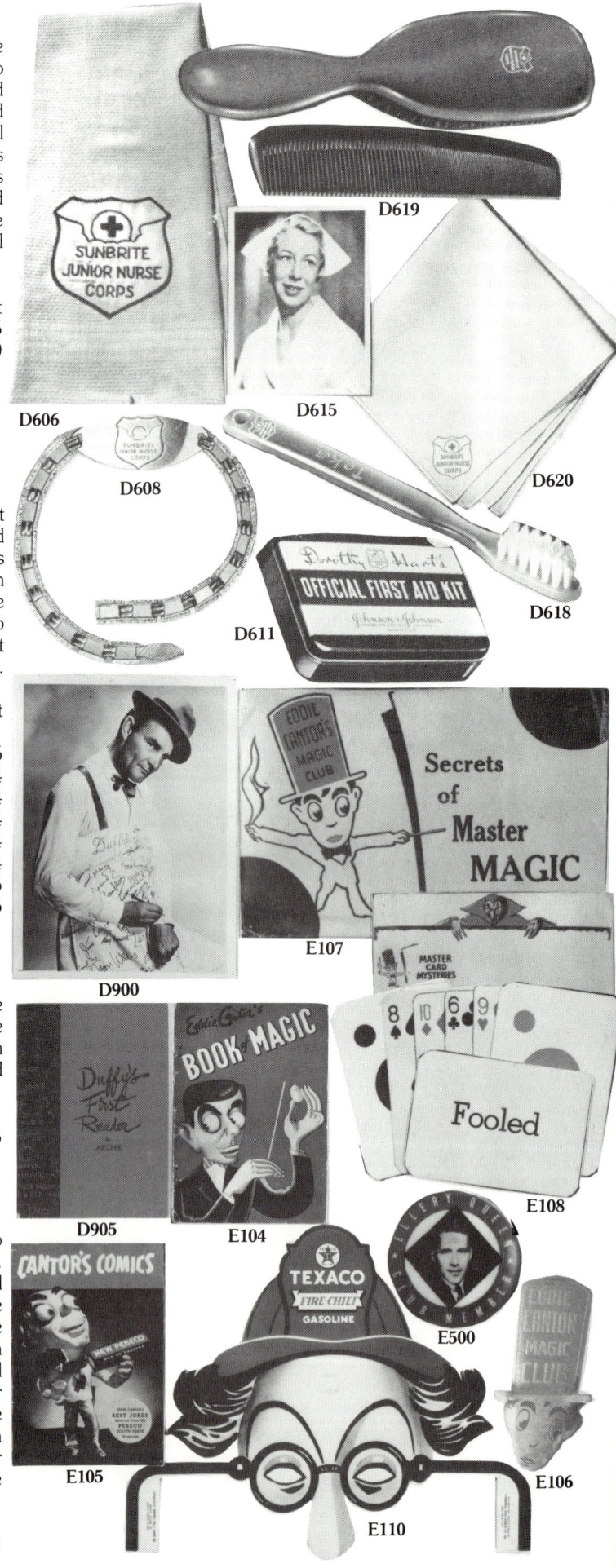

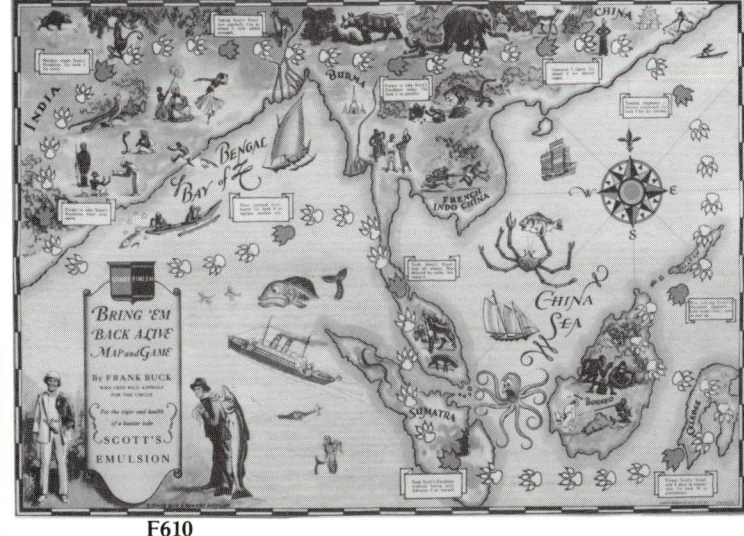

FIBBER McGEE AND MOLLY

One of radio's all-time popular comedy series, "Fibber McGee and Molly", aired weekly from the late 30's to the early 50's with Johnson's Wax as sponsor. In real life Jim and Marian Jordan were a happily married couple and despite all the carrying on, the overloaded hall closet and some of the craziest neighbors Hollywood has ever produced, it was this genuine loving charm which won over the listening audience. But for all McGee's wild inventions, there were few true premiums. Many collectors fill the void with the "The Merry Game of Fibber McGee and the Wistful Vista Mystery." This Milton Bradley game is a radio script with blanks. Players draw word or phrase cards and read them into the blanks. At least four different editions of the game exist. The water commissioner of Wistful Vista was Thratmorten P. Gildersleve, later to spin off as "The Great Gildersleve."

		Good	Fine	Mint
1936				
F300	Fibber Spinner	15	25	50
F301	Molly Spinner	15	25	50
F310	Wistful Vista Game (not premium — many versions available)	5	10	15
1941 - Conclusion				
F330	Cast Photo	8	12	15
F335	Pet Milk Recipe Folder	1	3	5

FLYING FAMILY - THE HUTCHINSONS

Col. George Hutchinson, his wife Blanche, daughters Kathryn and Janet and their "famous mascot", the flying lion cub "Sunshine", flew to every U.S. state, plus Greenland as one of this nation's first flying families. Cocomalt sponsored a radio series in 1932 retelling their adventures. A jigsaw puzzle was distributed free with every can of Cocomalt, but you had to send in for the other premiums received in conjunction with membership as a Flying Cub. The offer folder to become a Flight Commander was a forerunner of the one for the Buck Rogers Cut-Out Adventure Book. It required the applicant to drink Cocomalt for 30 days straight and have the form signed by their parents.

		Good	Fine	Mint
F500	Jigsaw Puzzle w/illustrated envelope	5	10	18
F504	Flying Cub Membership Pin	10	20	30
F506	Flight Commander Offer Folder	10	20	30
F507	Cub Flight Commander Pin	20	35	50
F508	The History of Notable Flights and Flyers Book	5	12	18

FRANK BUCK

Frank Buck was a real-life animal trainer who built a reputation on bagging his own animals and the slogan, "Bring "Em Back Alive." The radio show was sponsored by Pepsodent for apparently just one season in 1934. There were also two Ivory Soap premiums from a special 1939 promotion. The Explorers Sun Dial Watch was a Wheaties premium advertised on the Jack Armstrong radio program.

		Good	Fine	Mint
1934-38				
F600	Adventure Club Handbook	20	45	80
F601	Adventure Club Pinback	5	10	18
F602	Lucky Piece	10	18	30
F603	Black Leopard Ring	80	200	350
F604	Lariat	20	25	30
F605	Jungle Neckerchief	30	45	60
F610	Bring 'Em Back Alive Map & Game (Scott's Emulsion)	40	80	150
F620	Black Flag Jungle Game	25	32	45

1939

F650	Genuine Ivory Initial Ring	40	85	150
F651	Ivory Knife	30	35	50

1949

F660	Explorers Sun Dial Watch (offered by Jack Armstrong)	15	22	28

FRED ALLEN

"Allen's Alley" was a leading night-time comedy program for 17 years (1932-49). True to form of the big prime time programs, premiums were generally a no-no. Fan mail came rolling in anyway. Any mention of a free offer to millions of listeners had the potential of tying up an army of people and could easily get out of hand. The one exception is the Donut Book which was probably distributed in stores.

F700	Donut Book	3	4	8

FU MANCHU

Sax Rohmer's famous villian, Fu Manchu "the prince of darkness, master scientist, and evil genius" was the subject of the CBS series premiering for one season beginning Sept 26, 1932. Earlier it was dramatized as a 12-chapter radio serial which was syndicated in 1929. An on-going 15-minute serial was also syndicated in 1939. A premium puzzle of interlocking keys is believed to be from the radio show.

		Good	Fine	Mint
F900	Key Puzzle	40	80	120
F901	The Shadow of Fu Manchu Button	80	150	220

GABBY HAYES

George "Gabby" Hayes played comic relief to Roy Rogers on radio and many other western heroes in the movies. He hosted a TV show for Quaker Cereals which unreeled old B westerns on a serial basis. Gabby told a few tales and plugged the products. He used a large cannon to shoot Quaker Puff Wheat and Rice right into the camera's eye (and hopefully into viewers homes). We were cautioned to "stand back away from your TV sets now." Gabby always made a big deal about shooting off the cannon and naturally it eventually ended up as a ring. It vies with the Sky King Teleblinker Ring as the largest such premium rings ever to be produced.

The show had one of the most unusual arrangements in the history of premium giveaways. Quaker also sponsored Sgt. Preston on radio and for a time in the early 50's the identical premiums were offered on both programs. Perhaps Quaker was testing which medium would pull the most response. Items known to be offered on both programs are marked with an asterisk.

		Good	Fine	Mint

1951

G100	Shooting Cannon Ring	25	60	95

64

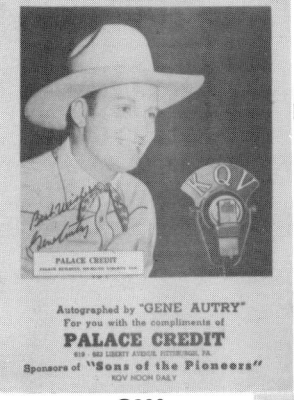

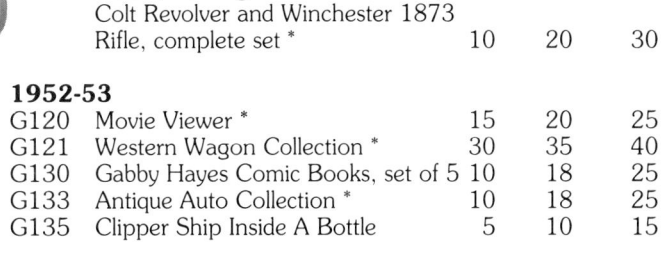

G105	Western Gun Collection, 6 - "Peacemaker" six shooter, Buffalo Rifle, Flintlock Dueling Piston, Remington Breech-Loader, Colt Revolver and Winchester 1873 Rifle, complete set *	10	20	30

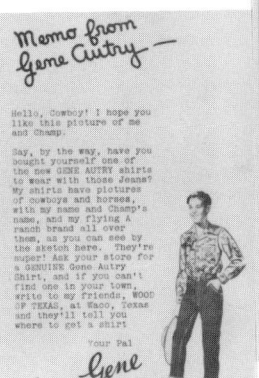

1952-53

G120	Movie Viewer *	15	20	25
G121	Western Wagon Collection *	30	35	40
G130	Gabby Hayes Comic Books, set of 5	10	18	25
G133	Antique Auto Collection *	10	18	25
G135	Clipper Ship Inside A Bottle	5	10	15

GANGBUSTERS

"Gangbusters" dramatized real stories of the law cracking down on criminals. At the end of each program the description of individuals wanted by the law were broadcast. In the first few years alone over 500 fugitives were brought to justice as a result of the program. It first aired in 1936 and continued into the 50's.

		Good	Fine	Mint
G200	Stop Thief Game	25	35	55
G250	Phillips H. Lord Badge, blue and gold litho	5	15	25

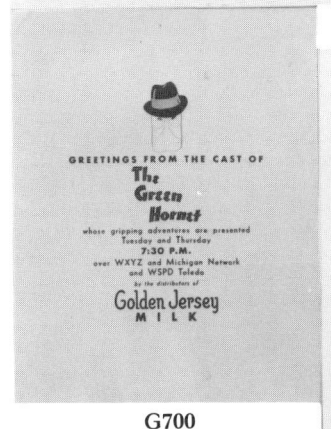

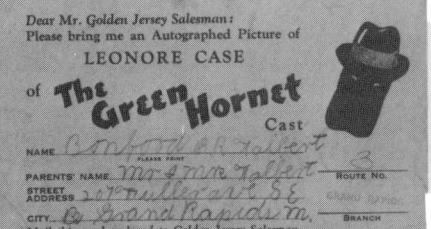

GENE AUTRY'S MELODY RANCH

Gene Autry was around radio for over ten years before he "was back in the saddle again" each week over CBS. His once-a-week show always aired on a Saturday or Sunday evening. Wrigley's Gum sponsored the entire run - featuring their Doublemint brand predominantly. Gene reached more of a family audience. Perhaps the sponsor wanted to avoid the premiums that were always associated with the kids' adventure programs. Whatever the reason, few premiums were made available before or during the network years. Most were photos of Gene. The most American Flag and American Eagle rings were received for subscribing to a year of Gene Autry comics from Dell Publications.

		Good	Fine	Mint
G300	Photo (pre-network)	3	5	8
G320	Photo	2	4	6
G330	Photo	2	4	6
G350	American Eagle Ring (Dell)	15	50	85
G351	American Flag Ring (Dell)	15	50	85
G355	Premium Comics, set of 5	10	15	24
G360	Flying A Wings	10	20	30
G361	Flying A Horsehoe Nail Ring (store item)	15	25	45
G362	Flying A Photo & Letter (Wood Mfg.)	5	10	15
G365	Bread End Seal Map/Poster, complete	20	60	110
G365A	Bread End Seal Map/Poster, no end seals	10	25	40

GOLDBERGS, THE

"The Goldbergs" was an ethnic serial based on the life and writings of Gertrude Berg. It began on NBC Nov 20, 1929 and ran until 1934. It was revived in 1937 and again in 1941 in a 15-minute daytime version until 1945. The 1949 TV version was one of the new media's earliest successes. Gertrude Berg produced, wrote, directed and played the starring role of Molly Goldberg. She was so identified with the role everyone called her Molly. The lone premiums from this historic broadcasting gem are two puzzles from the 30's.

		Good	Fine	Mint
G400	Puzzle	10	15	20
G401	Puzzle	10	15	20

65

GREEN HORNET, THE

The Green Hornet (Bret Reid) was a blood descendant of the Lone Ranger's nephew, Dan Reid. Fran Striker and the creative staff of WXYZ, Detroit, wrote both shows. Reportedly the "Hornet" was Striker's favorite of the two. The show was first broadcast in Jan 1936 on the Michigan Network sponsored by Golden Jersey Dairies. It converted with the change to Mutual in 1936 and lasted until 1952. General Mills became the sponsor in the 40's and offered the famous Secret Seal Ring from Cereal Trays in 1947. It was later seen on TV in 1966.

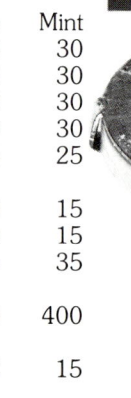

		Good	Fine	Mint
G700	Photo of Bret Reid, 8x10	10	20	30
G701	Photo of Kato	10	20	30
G702	Photo of Leonore Case	10	20	30
G703	Photo of Mike Oxford	10	20	30
G704	Photo	5	15	25
G705	Postcard to order Michigan Network photos, each	5	10	15
G706	Membership Card	5	10	15
G708	Photo Postcard	15	25	35
G719	Secret Compartment Glow-In-The-Dark Seal Ring	110	250	400
G720	Seal Ring, green & orange plastic, 1966	4	12	15

GREEN LAMA, THE

The Green Lama was primarily a comic book hero created in 1944. The 1945 membership kit depicts victory over the Axis enemy leaders World War II. A "Green Lama" radio show was later heard on CBS in 1949 with the characterization changed to one of a mystic from Tibet righting the wrongs of the world from his New York base. No premiums are known from the radio show.

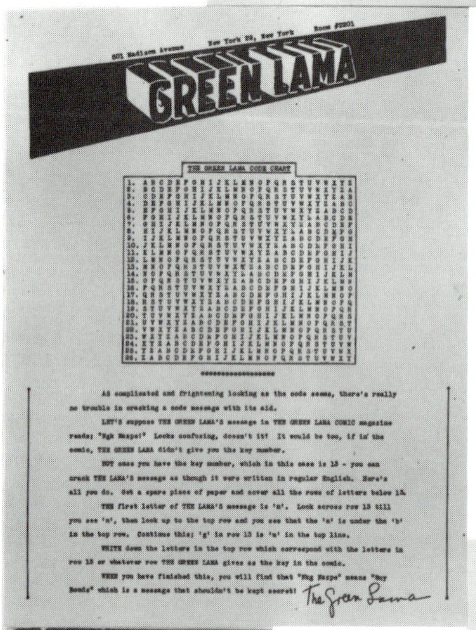

		Good	Fine	Mint
G780	Membership Card	10	20	30
G781	Green Lama's Escape Trick	20	40	60
G782	Letter w/Code Chart	18	35	50

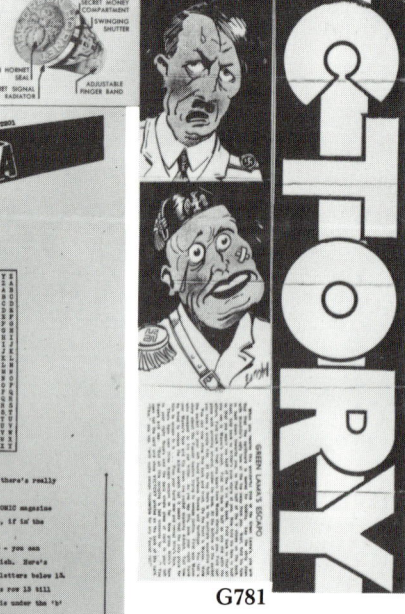

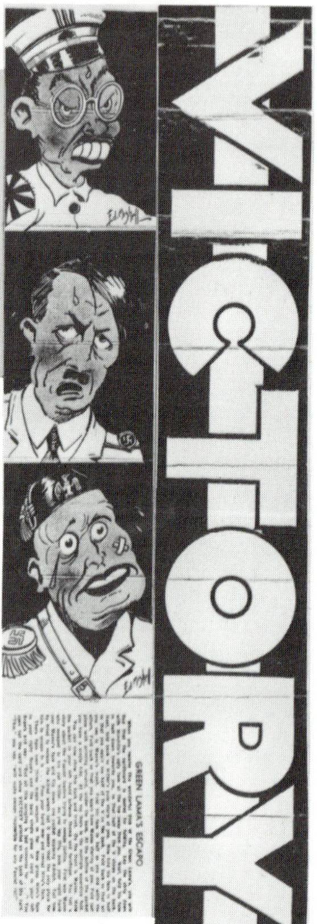

GUMPS, THE

The Gumps in Radio Land mentions the program in the back of the Daisy rifle type premium booklet. It's the only premium found from the show, if indeed it actually came to pass. Popular books on old radio do not mention the program.

| G900 | The Gumps in Radio Land Book | 10 | 20 | 30 |

HERMIT'S CAVE, THE

One of radio's blood and gore mystery shows, the gravel voice hermit spun spine chilling yarns of gory deaths under the most bazaar circumstances. Dismemberment, crushing and slashing were enhanced by sound effects designed to create horror in the mind. The illusion was largely broken by the booklet premiums employed to satisfy the morbid curiosity of listeners who wanted to see what they were hearing.

| H200 | Olga Coal Folder | 5 | 12 | 18 |

HOBBY LOBBY

"Hobby Lobby" was an early audience participation program where listeners would join the host to tell about their hobby. Each guest received the Hobby Lobby charm which is now part of a newer hobby - collecting the giveaways from old radio shows.

| H250 | Hobby Lobby Charm | 4 | 6 | 10 |

HOOFBEATS — See Buck Jones

HOP HARRIGAN

"Hop Harrigan" (1942-1948) was a relatively short-lived aviation "also flew" as the number of surviving premiums will attest. A number of Hop Harrigan program transcriptions have been preserved for posterity. The quality of writing and production are good. The list of premiums are largely comic book related. Since the show didn't get off the ground until the fall of 1942, war materials shortages undoubtedly restricted premium manufacture, so he never had the opportunity to offer anything really keen. When the war was over the character and program were out of style.

		Good	Fine	Mint
H304	Membership Card	5	12	20
H305	Flight Wings	8	18	35
H306	Flying Club Patch	10	15	20
H307	Observation Corps Patch	10	15	20
H310	Para-Plane Kit	10	25	45
H312	Bomber	10	25	45

HOPALONG CASSIDY

During the 40's, as the story goes, William Boyd realized the coming impact of television and bought the rights to most of his Hopalong Cassidy B-western movies. His TV show began in 1948 and by 1950 low-cost TV sets were in mass production. Hoppy had the programming new TV stations needed and his show hit like a tidal wave right along with the new video phenomenon. There was a flood of retail store character merchandise. Premium promotions were licensed for a variety of product categories including tie-ins with milk, bread, potato chips, savings institutions and a host of other companies. TV had still not totally replaced radio's children adventure programs, so for a brief time Hoppy also had a radio show sponsored by Post cereals. Post premiums came in cereal boxes for the most part.

There were a number of other offering companies. Hoppy's "Frontier Town" was life size and was constructed by Savings and Loans across the U.S. Want to bet some of those dismantled towns are still in storage somewhere?

Hoppy premiums all date from 1950-53 and are best categorized by the endorsed product - bread, milk, cereal or savings club. A smaller version of the Tenderfoot Savings Club badge was mailed by some S&L's on a Christmas postcard.

		Good	Fine	Mint
BREAD				
H500	Wallet Size Color Photos, each	3	6	9
H510	Postcard Size Color Photos, each	4	8	12
H518	8-1/2" x 11" Color Photos, each	5	9	12
H519	Bread End Seals, each	1	3	5
H520	End Seal Hang Up Album	10	20	30
H525	Book Cover	4	8	12

67

CEREAL

H530	In-Pack Radio Show Announcement Photo	5	10	15
H531	Western Collector Cards, 36, set	20	50	90
	Hoppy Cards, each	3	5	7
	Other Cards, each	1	2	4
H535	Western Hero Tabs - Hoppy	5	9	15
	Other Hero Badges	1	3	4
H540	Comic Book	6	10	20
H550	Compass Hat Ring w/hat	50	100	175
	(This ring was selling in the $300 range until a substantial quantity was found.)			

MILK

H560	Harmony Farms & Similar Buttons	5	12	20
H561	Milk Cartons (various sizes)	1	2	3

SAVINGS CLUBS

H570	Members Certificate	10	20	30
H571	Bank, plastic	4	8	12
H572	Tokens, many different	2	5	10
H573	Photo	2	4	8
	Membership buttons for different savings levels:			
H574	Tenderfoot (small size)	2	4	10
H575	Tenderfoot	1	2	8
H576	Wrangler	2	4	10
H577	Bulldogger	4	6	14
H578	Bronc Buster	6	8	18
H579	Trail Boss	10	15	20
H580	Straw Boss	20	25	30
H581	Bar 20 Foreman	25	35	45
H582	Teller Button	25	35	45
H583	Letter and Envelope	8	15	25
H584	Premium Folder	8	15	25
H585	Wallet	20	35	50
H586	Club Invitation Mailer	10	20	30

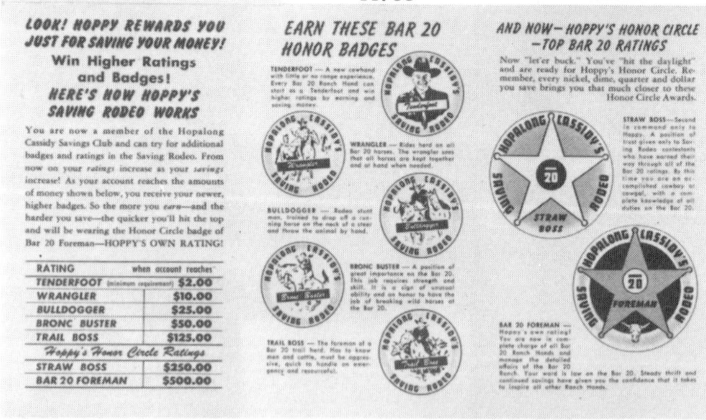

OTHER

H590	Spunny Spread Poster	10	20	30

HOWDY DOODY

"Howdy Doody" first aired in 1947. In the beginning it was both a radio and TV program. The puppet star underwent drastic "plastic surgery" only six weeks after the first viewing. The radio show may have been scrapped at that time. Howdy will best be remembered in his clean cut new image. Little is written about the radio days, perhaps due to the program's success as a TV phenome-

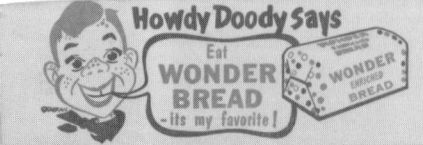

68

non. Somehow the show always seemed to be filled with mystery and excitement without really having much plot. The kids who packed the Peanut Gallery would sing the Howdy Doody song, laugh endlessly at the antics of Clarabell the (horn honking) Clown, and hang on every word of Buffalo Bob Smith - the show's creator and host.

Besides Howdy other familiar puppets in Doodyville were Dilly Dally, Flub-a-Dub, and Phineas T. Bluster. Other human types introduced to the show included Lanky Lou and Doctor Singasong, but none could match the impact of Princess Summer-Fall-Winter-Spring joining the cast. The show last aired on network TV in 1960. The program was a source of premiums, but there was an important difference. Whereas the kids' programs of radio days had a single sponsor, the high cost of TV required participating sponsorships of many non-competing products. Major sponsors and sources of premiums included Wonder Bread, Poll-Parrot Shoes, Ovaltine, Royal Pudding, Nabisco Shredded Wheat, Welch's Grape Juice and Mars Candies. Where dating is possible it has been noted; however, premiums have been grouped according to sponsor in the sequence that made the best sense. Miscellaneous items are listed after items of known sponsorship.

		Good	Fine	Mint
WONDER BREAD				
H740	Flip-up Paper Badge	5	12	20
H741	Paper Hat	5	12	20
H742	Bread End Seals, Series One, each	1	3	5
H747	Album for Series One End Seals	5	12	18
H748	Bread End Seals, Series Two, each	1	3	5
H749	American History End Seal Album	6	14	22
H750	Howdy Puppet w/bread	6	12	20
H751	Character Puppets, larger w/o bread, each	5	11	18
POLL-PARROT SHOES				
H770	3-D Character Face Masks, 6, each	10	22	35
H775	Howdy Doody's Comic Circus Animals	20	40	70
H777	Puppets, each	10	22	35
H778	Newspaper, No. 1, May 1950	8	16	25
H779	Howdy for President Flip-up Badge	5	12	18
H780	Coloring Book	10	18	25
H782	Jumble Joy Book, 1955	10	18	25
H783	Flasher Ring	15	25	40
H784	Comic Books	5	10	20

WELCH'S
H790	Juice Bottle Cap w/Howdy	4	8	12
H791	Jelly Jar/Glasses - Series One, each	3	6	10
H792	Jelly Jar/Glasses - Series Two, each	3	6	10
H793	Label w/Howdy	8	16	25
H794	Jar Lid w/Howdy	4	6	12
H795	Cook Book, 1952	6	12	20

OVALTINE
H800	Shake-up Mug	6	15	30
H801	Drinking Mug	5	14	22

MARS
H810	Howdy Animated Puppet	5	12	18
H811	Clarabell Animated Puppet	5	12	18
H814	Magic Kit	5	12	18

ROYAL
H820	Package Back Trading Cards, each	1	3	5
H821	Package Back Coloring Cards, each	1	4	6
H825	Masks	4	8	15

OTHERS
H827	Miniature TV viewer (Colgate)	12	22	35
H828	Prize Doodle List	4	8	12
H830	Twin-Pop Jackpot of Fun Comic,	4	8	12
H831	Frozen Dessert Bags, each	1	3	5
H832	Wheaties Masks	4	8	12
H833	Corn Flakes Dangle-Dandies, each	5	10	18
H834	Palmolive Stand-up	4	9	15
H835	Howdy String Climber	10	17	25
H836	Periscope	15	35	55
H837	Christmas Coloring Book	5	10	15
H838	Nabisco Divider Cards, Canadian, each	1	3	5
H840	Howdy Flashlight Face Ring	30	60	95
H841	Clarabell Horn Ring	30	80	150

HOWIE WING

Howie Wing was a Jimmie Allen-type character and a leader in the Cadet Aviation Corps. The program aired during the 30's on U.S. and Canadian stations sponsored by Kellogg's cereals and was probably owned by them. In keeping with a British flavor, Howie had a sidekick named Typhoon Tootel.

		Good	Fine	Mint
H850	Wings	5	6	7
H851	Membership Card	3	4	5
H852	Membership Certificate	1	3	5
H853	Handbook	10	17	25
H854	Weather Forecast Ring	15	25	45
H855	Rubberband Gun	8	12	16
H856	Cadet Aviation Corp Newspapers, each	8	15	25
H857	Chart - Adventures on the Canadian Lakes	15	30	45
H858	Mystery Message Decoder	20	40	60
H860	Movie Viewer	20	32	50
H865	Typhoon Tootel Vent Dummy	20	30	45
H870	Aluminum Good Luck Coin	12	14	20
H871	Official Flying Shirt	15	25	40
H872	Model Plane Kits, each	10	20	30
H873	Cadet Aviation Corps Flying Guide Chart	15	25	40

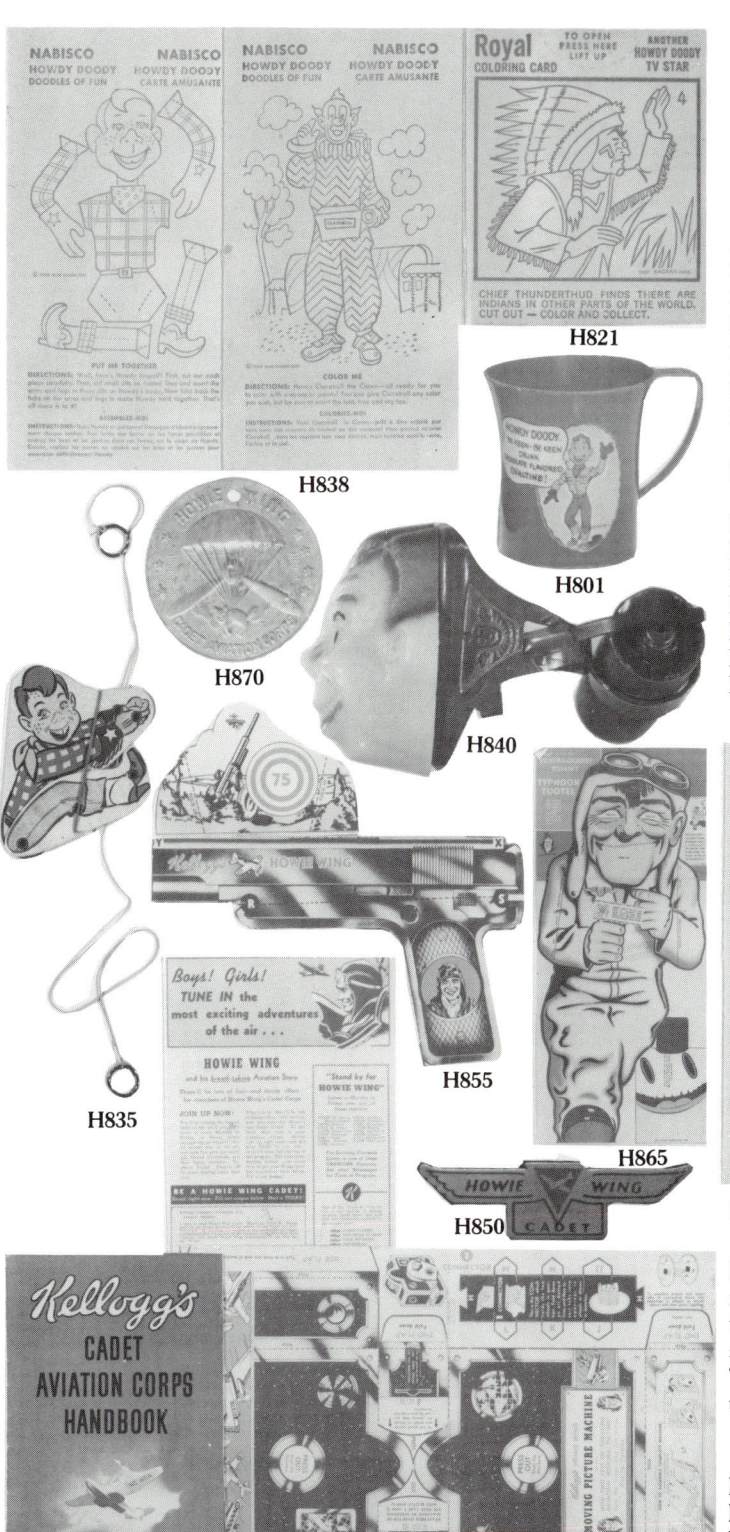

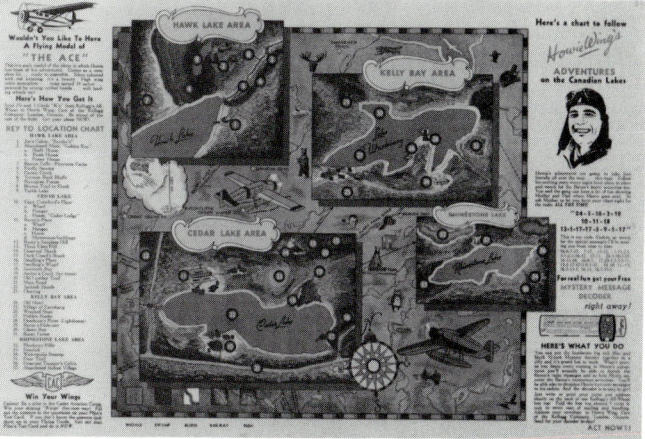

INSPECTOR POST

Inspector Post was a 1932 character created by General Foods. He was promoted on Post cereal packages and Sunday newspaper comic sections into 1933. This was Post's earliest effort to compete with children's radio programs. The manuals are substantial and interesting reading for prospective junior detectives. The badges for each promotional level were among the most uninteresting produced.

		Good	Fine	Mint
Post's Junior Detective Corps				
I500	Manual No. 1 for Detectives	5	10	15
I501	Detective Badge	2	5	10
I502	Manual No. 2 for Detective Sergeants	5	10	15
I503	Sergeant Badge	2	5	10
I504	Manual No. 3 for Lieutenants	7	12	18
I505	Lieutenant Badge	3	6	10
I506	Manual No. 4 for Captains	7	12	18
I507	Captain Badge	3	6	10
I510	Inspector Post Case Book	10	15	20

JACK ARMSTRONG — THE ALL-L-L-L AMERICAN BOY

"Jack Armstrong" was one of the longest running radio adventure serials . . . and one of the most prolific issuers of premiums. The secret to his longevity was probably his extreme flexibility. Jack could do everything - and often did. More importantly he successfully changed with the times. He was a high school football hero . . . and equally at home speaking a few words of Zulu in deepest Africa. No one knew where Jack's next adventure would take him and it kept the audience interested.

The show first aired in 1933 as a daily 15-minute serial. At first Jack was the classic high school hero . . . a strong optimist who helped many a youth cope with the Depression. Times improved and so apparently did Jack's production budget. His adventures went worldwide during the middle and late 30's. During the war years he spearheaded patriotic efforts on the home front while outsmarting spies and saboteurs.

In 1947, Jack and his eternal friends, Billy and Betty Fairfield, said farewell to "Uncle Jim" and cast their lot with Vic Hardy and the Scientific Bureau of Investigation. The show soon went to a half-hour complete story format and was renamed "Armstrong of the SBI." It was Jack's first mistake in the 13 years it took him to get through high school. Like Radio Orphan Annie's Capt. Sparks, Vic Hardy held a higher rank. The show dwindled and finally left the air in 1951. Premiums all but disappeared in the mid-40's.

		Good	Fine	Mint
1933				
J090	Photo of Johnny Weismuller	10	20	30
J100	Shooting Propeller Plane Gun (Daisy)	20	40	60
J105	Photo of Jack on his Horse Blackster	5	9	12
J106	Babe Ruth Flip Movie "How to Hit a Home Run"	25	50	75
J107	Grip Developer, unmarked	5	10	15
1934				
J120	Photo of Jack, Betty and Arrow Champ	6	9	12
J121	Photo of Jack	6	9	12
J122	Photo of Betty	6	9	12
J124	Package Back Photo of Jack, baseball	10	15	25
J125	Hike-O-Meter, sports figures on rim	12	20	35
J128	Wee-Gyro	15	25	40
J129	Stamp Offer Folder	10	15	20
1935				
J137	Package Back Photo of Jack, baseball	10	15	25

72

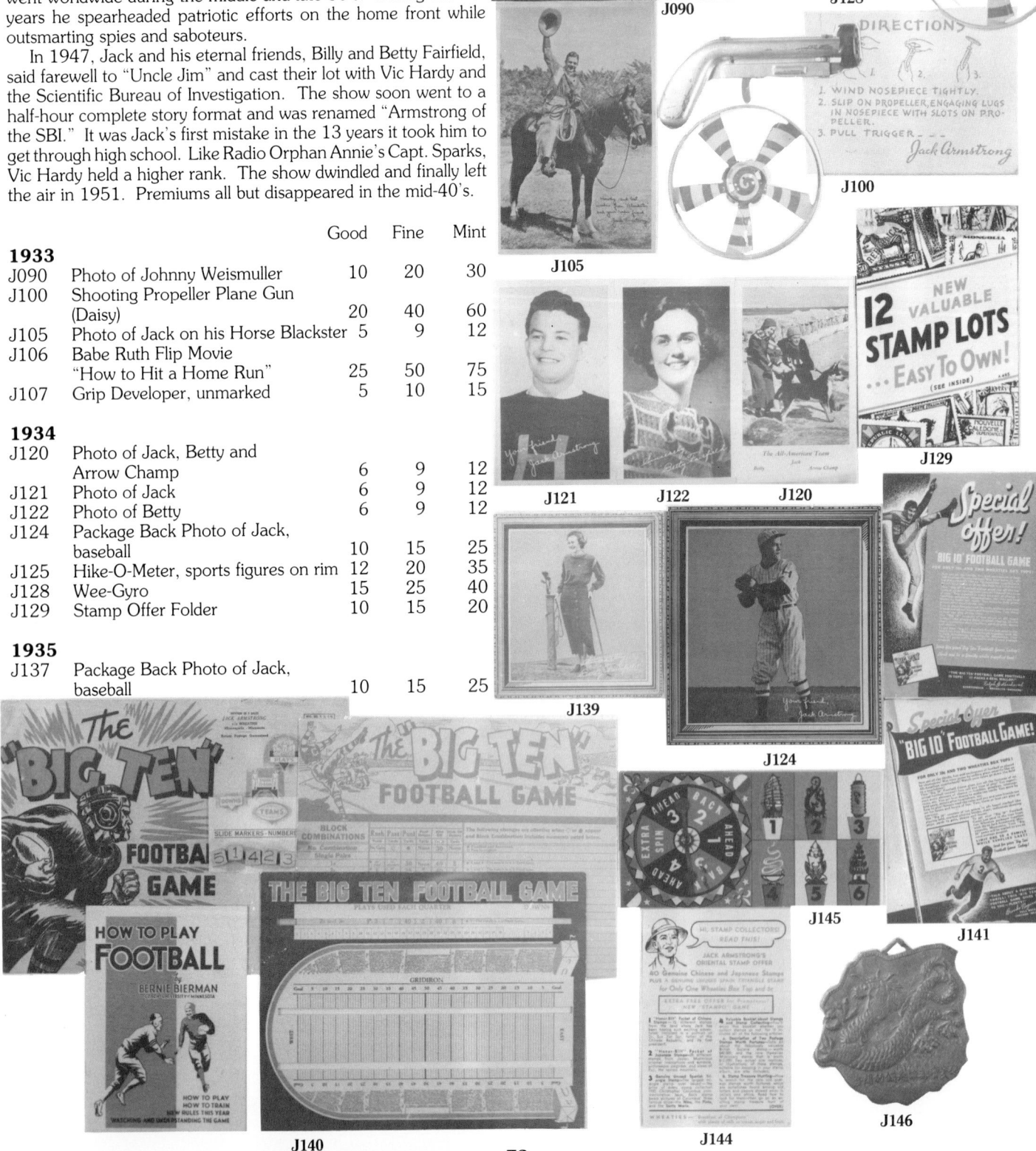

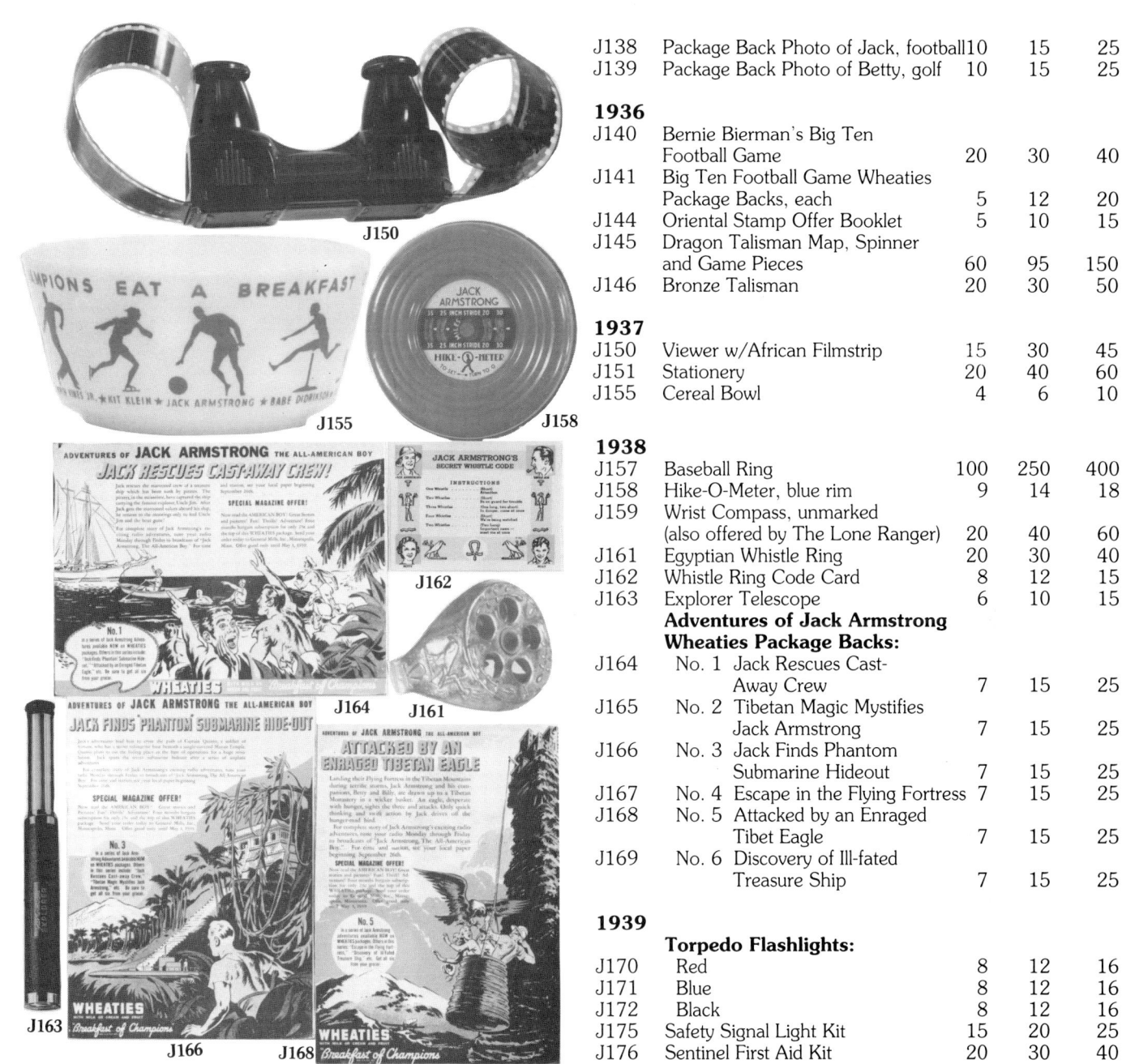

J138	Package Back Photo of Jack, football	10	15	25
J139	Package Back Photo of Betty, golf	10	15	25

1936

J140	Bernie Bierman's Big Ten Football Game	20	30	40
J141	Big Ten Football Game Wheaties Package Backs, each	5	12	20
J144	Oriental Stamp Offer Booklet	5	10	15
J145	Dragon Talisman Map, Spinner and Game Pieces	60	95	150
J146	Bronze Talisman	20	30	50

1937

J150	Viewer w/African Filmstrip	15	30	45
J151	Stationery	20	40	60
J155	Cereal Bowl	4	6	10

1938

J157	Baseball Ring	100	250	400
J158	Hike-O-Meter, blue rim	9	14	18
J159	Wrist Compass, unmarked (also offered by The Lone Ranger)	20	40	60
J161	Egyptian Whistle Ring	20	30	40
J162	Whistle Ring Code Card	8	12	15
J163	Explorer Telescope	6	10	15

Adventures of Jack Armstrong Wheaties Package Backs:

J164	No. 1 Jack Rescues Cast-Away Crew	7	15	25
J165	No. 2 Tibetan Magic Mystifies Jack Armstrong	7	15	25
J166	No. 3 Jack Finds Phantom Submarine Hideout	7	15	25
J167	No. 4 Escape in the Flying Fortress	7	15	25
J168	No. 5 Attacked by an Enraged Tibet Eagle	7	15	25
J169	No. 6 Discovery of Ill-fated Treasure Ship	7	15	25

1939

Torpedo Flashlights:

J170	Red	8	12	16
J171	Blue	8	12	16
J172	Black	8	12	16
J175	Safety Signal Light Kit	15	20	25
J176	Sentinel First Aid Kit	20	30	40

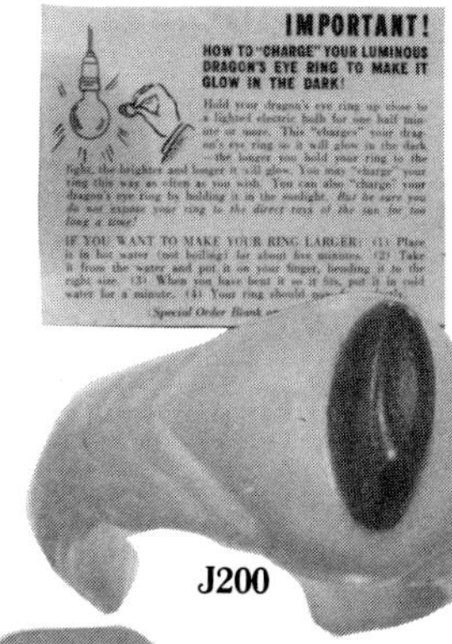

J180	Catapult Plane		30	45	60
J185	Treasure Hunter Stamp Offer		4	6	8
J186	Emergency Signaling Mirror		15	25	35
J187	Pedometer, silver aluminum rim		10	12	15

			Good	Fine	Mint
1940					
J199	Magic Answer Box		15	22	30
J200	Dragon's Eye Ring, crocodile design, green stone		75	150	250
J201	Listening Squad Certificate (Test)		15	28	35
J202	Lieutenant Listening Squad Whistle Badge		100	200	300
J203	Captain Listening Squad Whistle Badge (none distributed)		—	—	500
J205	Sky Ranger Airplane		20	24	28
J209	Luminous Gardenia Brooch				
J210	Betty's Luminous Gardenia Bracelet		50	100	150
1941					
J216	Flashlight Pistol		30	90	100
J217	Sound Effects Kit		15	35	65
J218	Crocodile Whistle		200	400	600
1942					
J220	Secret Bombsight, w/3 bombs		75	100	135
J225	Write a Fighter Corp Kit, complete w/stars, stencil, etc.		30	60	100
J225A	Write a Fighter Corp, manual only		20	35	50
1943					
J230	Future Champions of America Manual, Patches and Transfer Stars		20	35	50
J231	Future Champions of America Cloth Patch		10	14	18
1944					
J234	Aviation Goggles, unmarked		20	40	60
	Tru-Flite Model Airplanes:				
J235	Set A - Curtis P-40 Flying Tiger				
J236	and Jap Mitsubishi Zero		10	12	18
J237	Set B - Supermarine Spitfire V				
J238	and Focke Wulf 190		10	12	18
J239	Set C - Grumman Hellcat FGF				
J240	and Jap Nakajima		10	12	18
J241	Set D - Fairey Fulmar				
J242	and Heinkel He. 113		10	12	18
J243	Set E - Thunderbolt P-47				
J244	and Russian Yak I-26		10	12	18
J245	Set F - American Bell P-39 "Airacobra"				
J246	and Russian IL-2 "Slormovik"		10	12	18
J247	Set G - Mustang Fighter				
J248	and AICHI Dive Bomber		10	12	18

Super color reproductions of all 14 Jack Armstrong Tru-Flite airplanes are now available for $2.50 each or $25.00 for all 14 from: Saf-Flite Models, P.O. Box 62, Roseville, MI 48066. Add $1.00 for postage and handling on all orders. Great fun to build these planes once again.

		Good	Fine	Mint
Tru-Flite News-Newspapers:				
J249	Vol. 1, No. 1	6	8	12
J250	Vol. 1, No. 2	6	8	12
1945-46				
Pre-Flight Training Kit:				
J255	How to Fly Manual	8	14	20
J256	Pre-Flight Trainer Model	16	32	50

74

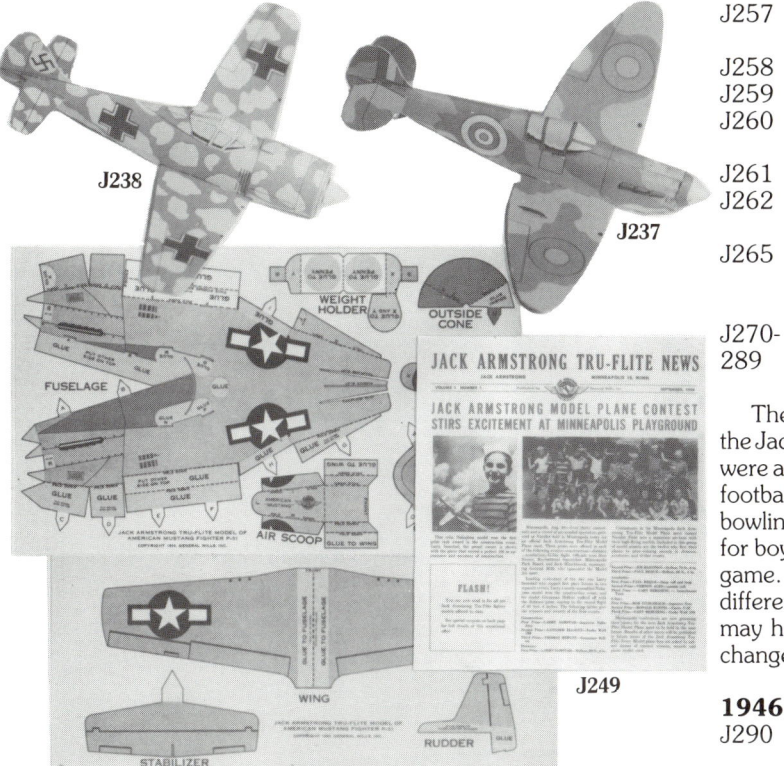

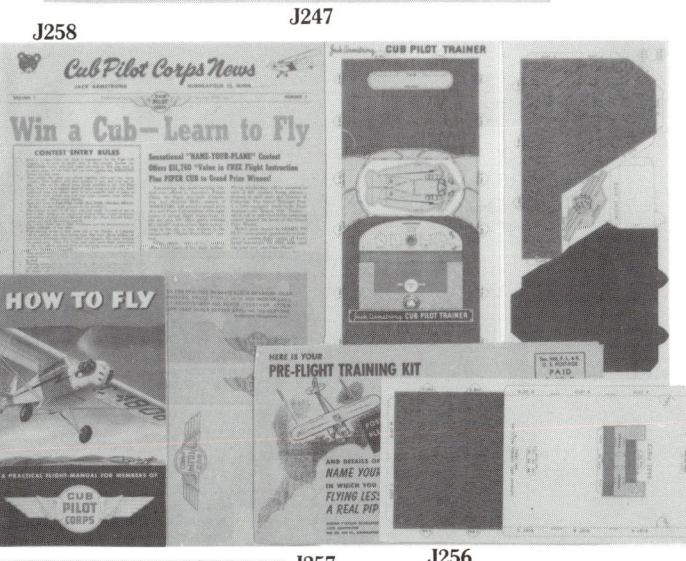

J257	Cub Pilot Corps Hot Iron Transfer Ensemble		10	14	18
J258	Cub Pilot Corps, News Vol.1, No. 1		8	12	16
J259	Store Envelope		8	14	20
J260	Cub Pilot Corps News Vol.1, No. 2 2 learn to Fly Contest		8	14	20
J261	Cub Pilot Corps News Vol. 1, No. 3		8	14	20
J262	G.I. Identification Tag included w/J261		10	14	20
J265	Airplanes of World War II (Tru-Flite Airplanes re-offered on Wheaties Packages), set of 10		10	25	40
J270-289	Library of Sports Books, each		4	6	8

The Wheaties' *Library of Sports* booklets were first offered on the Jack Armstrong program and in comic book ads in 1945. There were apparently 18 different titles covering such sports as baseball, football, basketball, golf, tennis, track and field, softball, swimming, bowling and home and neighborhood games. Some titles were just for boys or girls. Others covered just the offense or defense of the game. In 1946, many titles underwent major revisions (note the two different covers on the baseball books pictured). Additional titles may have been added at this time. The books underwent many changes over the many years they were offered.

1946

J290	Parachute Ball	12	25	40

1949

Sun Watch (See Frank Buck, F660)

1973

J295	Radio Broadcast Record	6	12	18

JACK BENNY

A headliner superstar and radio king, Jack Benny was tighter with premiums than his radio portrayal was with money. However, that was the norm with prime-time comedy programs. The exception is an interesting Jell-O cookbook featuring character drawings of Jack and his wife, Mary Livingston. Jack and Mary were featured in advertisements, often along with Jack's chauffeur, Rodchester, or the show's spokesman. Jack's Maxwell, played by the sound effects men, was also a favorite "character" with the audience.

		Good	Fine	Mint

1937

J300	Jell-O Recipe Book	2	4	5

JACK WESTAWAY'S UNDER SEA ADVENTURE CLUB

Jack Westaway's signature was printed on the membership card received with the diving helmet shaped badge sent to members of his Under Sea Adventure Club. His creed appeared on the back of the card. These were the usual guidelines to become an ideal kid ... the last advising to start each day "with a breakfast of warm Malt-O-Meal" so you were always "Ready for Adventure." These seem to be the only premiums offered and give a clue to the source.

		Good	Fine	Mint
J375	Membership Badge	7	12	20
J376	Membership Card	5	10	15

JIMMIE ALLEN, AIR ADVENTURES OF

Lindbergh soloed across the Atlantic in 1927 and firmly entrenched a goal in young boys to become heroes of the skyways. Many companies recognized the promotional value of identifying with a young man's desire to fly. One of the first radio programs to do so featured Jimmie Allen, a teenage aviator who started offering flying lessons in 1934. Unlike other premiums you got through the mail, Jimmie Allen premiums were picked up at your neighborhood gasoline station, grocery store or other retail outlet. The program was syndicated out of Kansas City to radio stations who sold the sponsorship mostly to gasoline and bread companies patterned after the show's early sales successes. As a result there were numerous different versions of the most successful premiums. Some flight lessons were in folders. Others were simply reproduced on 8-1/2" x 14" paper. The basic flight wings, for example, came in at least seven different variations. Some local sponsors saw fit to toss in an extra premium now and then. There are examples where Jimmie Allen was merchandized on blotters, whistles, newspapers, road maps and other giveaway items. All traces of new Jimmie Allen episodes disappeared when the writing team switched over to Captain Midnight ... even though the transcribed adventures were re-broadcast with new sponsors and premiums to 1940 or so.

		Good	Fine	Mint
1934				
J400	Photo of Jimmie	4	6	8
J404	Photo of Speed Robertson	3	5	7
J405	Action Photo	4	6	8
J406	Action Photo	4	6	8
J407	Jimmie Allen Membership Cards	2	5	10
J410	Jimmie Allen Stamp Album	10	20	30
J420	Flying Lesson 1, various brands	3	5	8
J421	Flying Lesson 2, various brands	3	5	8
J422	Flying Lesson 3, various brands	3	5	8
J423	Flying Lesson 4, various brands	3	5	8
J424	Flying Lesson 5, various brands	3	5	8
J425	Chart of Flying Maneuvers	10	12	15
J430	Air Battles Book	10	20	30
J433	Skelly Airplane Pin	8	10	20
Flying Cadet Flight Wings:				
J440	Skelly-Type I	3	7	12
J441	Skelly-Type II	3	7	12
J445	Hi-Speed - Type III	4	8	15
J447	Blue Flash - Type III	4	8	15
J450	Richfield - Type IV	4	8	15
J453	Richfield - Type V	4	8	15
J455	Colonial - Type V	3	5	10
J457	Log Cabin - Type V	3	5	10
J459	Certified - Type V	3	5	10
J460	Debus - Type V	3	5	10
J461	Cleo Cole - Type V	3	5	10
J462	Town Talk Bread	3	5	10
J463	Rainbo Gas - Type V	3	5	10
J465	Duplex - Type V	3	5	10
J470	Weather Bird - Type V	3	5	10
J473	Sawyer - Type V	3	6	12
J474	Certified - Type V	3	7	12

J475	Butter-Nut - Type V		3	6	12
J490	Pilots Creed		5	12	18
J491	Blue Flash Paper Monoplane		10	20	30

1935

J500	Jimmie Allen Skelly Album		20	25	30
J501	Road Maps, various states, brands and years		5	8	12
J503-514	Jimmie Allen Club Newspapers, 12 issues, each		4	6	8
J520	Kansas City Air Races Bracelet		12	18	24
J522	Transfer		5	10	15
J535	I.D. Bracelet (Richfield)		12	18	24
J536	I.D. Bracelet (Weather Bird)		12	18	24

1936-39

J550	Whistle, brass		15	22	30
J553	Knife		15	25	40
J560	Weather Bird Manual		8	15	25
J561	Weather Bird Patch		8	15	23
J562	Blotter		1	3	5

JOE E. BROWN CLUB

The "Joe E. Brown Club" was one of several Post cereal attempts to compete with radio via newspaper and on-pack promotion. Others were Capt. Frank Hawks, Dizzy Dean and Melvin Purvis. None of these succeeded for over two or three years. The Bike Club was a bicycle company promotion in 1934.

		Good	Fine	Mint
1934				
J615	Bike Club Button	15	20	25
J616	Book	10	15	20
1936				
J650	Manual and Premium List	8	12	16
J651	Membership Pin	5	6	7
J652	Sergeant's Bar, green enamel star	1	2	3
J653	Lieutenant's Bar, red enamel, 2 stars	2	3	4
J654	Captain's Bar, blue enamel, 3 stars	3	4	5
J655	Membership Ring	12	17	25
J656	Autographed Photo	4	6	8

JUNIOR JUSTICE SOCIETY OF AMERICA, THE

The Junior Justice Society was first formed for the readers of All Star Comics in 1942 and consisted of such super heroes as Wonder Woman, The Flash, Hawkman, The Spectre, The Green Lantern, Dr. Fate, The Sandman, and Johnny Thunder. The Society had one of the more active comic book clubs, second only to Captain Marvel. Wonder Woman served as Secretary.

		Good	Fine	Mint
J800	Membership Certificate	10	16	25
J801	Membership Pin	20	65	85
J805	Letters to Members, several, each	5	10	20
J810	Paper Decoder	15	32	50
J811	Patch	17	38	55

KATE SMITH

Kate Smith was just a gal from Virginia with a booming contralto voice and a folksy charm listeners believed in. In short, a spokesperson who could sell products on the radio. She did a series of successful Broadway shows in the mid-20's, but tired of the "fat" jokes to which she was always subjected. Her manager, Ted Collins, redirected her talents to recording and radio in 1930. In 1931 she began what would be a 16-year association with CBS doing a variety of different format programs of songs and conversation. General Foods was her sponsor from 1937 through 1947. During this time only she and Jack Benny had the only non-cancellable contracts in radio. Her friendship with Irving Berlin resulted in an exclusive arrangement to sing "God Bless American", one of the many songs with which she became personally identified. A number of recipe books were produced as premiums to take advantage of her tremendous popularity.

		Good	Fine	Mint
K200	Monthly Recipe Mailers, each	3	6	10
K205	Recipe Books, each	5	10	15

KAYO

The comic book character Kayo was used to merchandise a chocolate drink in the 40's or 50's. The Kayo Club was founded as part of the promotion.

K225	Membership Button	15	25	35

KUKLA, FRAN, AND OLLIE

Many of the early TV shows featured puppets - Howdy Doody, Snarley Parker, Rootie Kazootie. The first, beginning Oct 13, 1947, was "Kukla, Fran, and Ollie." Fran was Fran Allison, the Aunt Fanny of "Breakfast Club" fame. All the other Kuklapolitans were hand puppets.

Burr Tillstrom had been a puppeteer since age 4 and in 1936 created an unnamed puppet he used wherever he could get booked in the Chicago Area. One day he stuck the puppet into the dressing room door of a Russian ballerina and she said, "Ah, Kukla", her native word for doll. The name stuck and many players were added by the time the show went on the air. Ollie the Dragon was the chief instigator of mayhem. Other characters included Madame Ooglepuss, Colonel Crackie, Fletcher Rabbit and Buelah Witch. The show was early enough to offer a few premiums; newspapers at first and a year book once the circulation past 200,000.

		Good	Fine	Mint
K900	Kuklapolitan Courier Newspapers, each	4	8	12
K908	Kuklapolitan Courier Year Book	10	15	20

LASSIE

Lassie's major claim to fame was as a movie star until it premiered on TV in 1955. The canine outlasted four complete cast changes and managed a couple neat premiums reminiscent of days gone by.

		Good	Fine	Mint
L100	Ring	25	35	50
L101	Photo Membership Folder	5	12	20
L110	Color Photo w/Robert Bray	10	15	20

LIGHTNING JIM (MEADOW GOLD ROUND-UP)

"Lightning Jim" was a regional western adventure program sponsored by Meadow Gold productions in the 30's. Jim's sidekick's name was Whitey Larsen. Apparently there was little to distinguish the program from the competition and it quickly faded. There were at least three premiums.

		Good	Fine	Mint
L210	Membership Card	3	6	10
L211	Membership Badge	4	8	12
L212	Photo	3	6	10

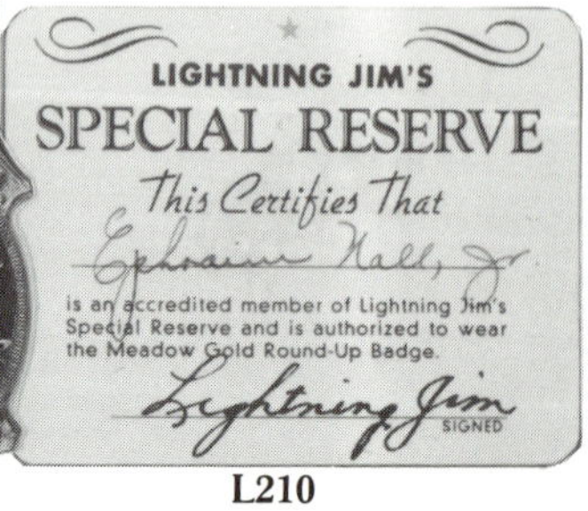

LITTLE ORPHAN ANNIE —
See Radio Orphan Annie

LONE RANGER, THE

"The Lone Ranger" first aired on WXYZ Detroit on Jan 30, 1933. It was not only the birth of one of the most successful radio programs of all time, but the beginning of the Mutual Radio Network as well. (See "How It All Began")

The characters created for radio eventually went on to films and TV. The program began on the Michigan Radio Network. In addition to the items listed here, a published survey on the WOR (New York) Lone Ranger Club reported the following events for program listeners: "Free theatre parties, admission to aviation meets, visits to U.S. Battleships, etc. Occasionally there was an offer of theatre tickets to the first fifty non-members who applied for membership."

The masked rider of the plains enjoyed tremendous success from the very beginning. But early on there appeared to have been some reluctance to offer more premiums tied directly to the character. Perhaps this was due to the producer and his desire to keep the Lone Ranger's image of perfection, idealism and Americanism apart from the business of selling products. More likely it was the number of different sponsors in a growing number of cities prohibited unified offerings.

Things began to change in 1934 when Silvercup Bread issued the first Lone Ranger badge. Then in 1938 a major Lone Ranger merchandising blitz began. Radio premium activity was minute compared to the usage of the character on toys, games, food products, watches and a wide assortment of other merchandise. From 1939-1941 regional bread companies continued to offer premiums (which varied according to each company) under the banner of The Long Ranger Safety Club. In 1941 General Mills became the national sponsor in all but the 7 states where Merita Bread retained their franchise. General Mills identified their states as Lone Ranger territory. The same premiums were often offered in a Whistling Jim version in the Merita territory. In some cases the same art was used with the mask removed. It's for this reason The Lone Ranger is rarely mentioned on mailers or instruction charts. Merita Bread continued to offer Lone Ranger premiums into the 50's.

The most interesting of the syndicated "Safety Club" premiums was a map produced to cover the Ranger's disappearance while Earle Graser, the voice of the Lone Ranger, was on vacation in Europe. (No tape recording back then.) For the nine weeks thereafter listeners followed the map as Tonto and Cactus Pete searched for the missing masked man. Not long after his return Graser was killed in an auto accident. Brace Beemer, an announcer at the station, was selected to replace Graser and played the radio role until the show left the air.

General Mills used the program to promote Kix, then Cheerios and finally, in the 50's, Wheaties. It was a long association which continued well into the TV version run.

One of the program's most spectacular premiums was conceived as part of the show's 15th anniversary promotion - The Long Ranger Frontier Town. It came in four sections. When assembled the base maps covered about nine square yards of floor space. To get each section required a Cheerios box top and a dime. Additional buildings came on the backs of nine different Cheerios cereal boxes.

For weeks the radio episodes centered in and round Frontier Town. Listeners could play along on their own Frontier Towns to better visualize what was happening.

Then for one proud day - June 30, 1948 - the name of Cheyenne, Wyoming was officially changed to Long Ranger Frontier Town. Of course the Ranger was on hand to wave to the crowd which "lined the streets for miles" according to the Wyoming State Tribune. The Ranger cooperated with the Treasury Dept. to sell War Bonds in the 40's and 50's.

From the very beginning the spirited "William Tell Overture"

79

trumpeted the masked rider's coming. We gladly returned with announcers Brace Beemer and later Fred Foy to those thrilling days of yesteryear when out of the past came the thundering hoofbeats of the great horse Silver. The Lone Ranger, along with his faithful Indian companion, Tonto, did indeed ride again . . . and again . . . and again. We didn't mind each show was molded in an iron-clad success formula. The character was so good, the production so stirring and the message so strong to dislike it would have been un-American. The last radio program in the series aired May 27, 1955. Clayton Moore and Jay Silverheels played the Lone Ranger and Tonto on TV from 1948 to 1961. The Good Food Guys is a supermarket promotion syndication around Clayton Moore in 1969.

A 1982 movie, The Legend of the Lone Ranger, produced an interesting membership kit even though the movie's concept of the great Mask Man was not successful.

		Good	Fine	Mint
1933				
L290	Michigan Network Photo	10	20	30
1934-38				
L300	How The Lone Ranger Captured Silver Booklet, 7 chapters	10	20	30
L301	Safety Club Pledge Letter	5	9	12
L302	Silvercup Bread Safety Scout Membership Badge	6	10	15
L303	Chief Scout Badge	25	60	90
L304	Lone Ranger Photo	4	7	10
L305	Tonto Photo	3	6	8
L306	Chief Scout 1st Degree Postcard	2	7	12
L307	Chief Scout 2nd Degree Postcard	3	8	15
L308	Chief Scout 3rd Degree Postcard	4	11	20
L309	Chief Scout 4th Degree Postcard	5	12	25
L310	Miami Maid Safety Club Badge	12	20	35
L311	Chief Scout Commission	7	12	20
L312	Safety Club Pinback	10	15	20
L313	Merita Safety Club Pinback	10	15	20
L314	Merita Mask	6	10	15
1938-40				
L315	Photo (sepia)	8	10	12
L316	Lone Ranger Secret Writing Manual	15	20	25
L317	Photo, four-color	5	10	15
L318	Blotter	3	5	8
L320	Good Luck Token	5	7	12
L323	Bond Bread Postcard	4	10	15
L325	Safety Club Certificate	3	5	8
L326	Safety Club Letters, many different, each	2	5	9
L328	Ho Ling's Recipes	10	18	25
L329	Silvercup Color Photo	6	12	18

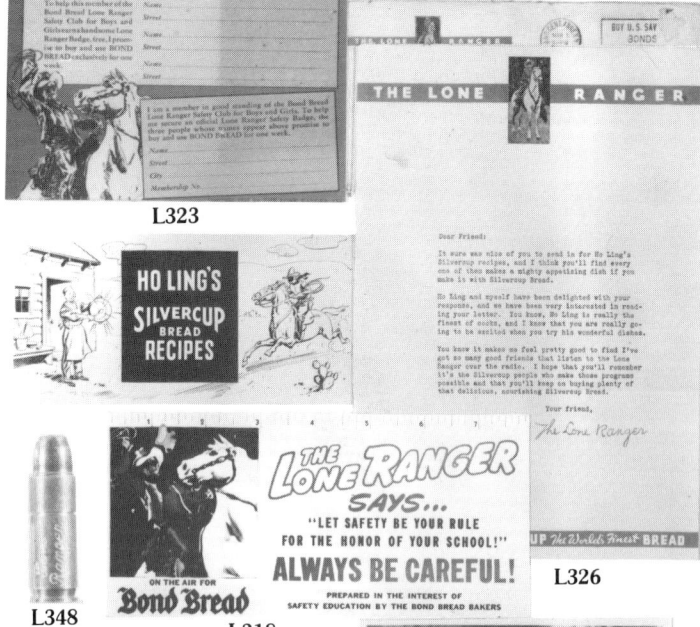

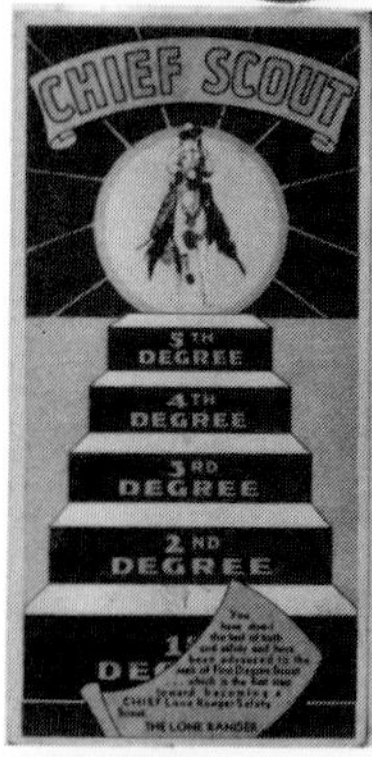

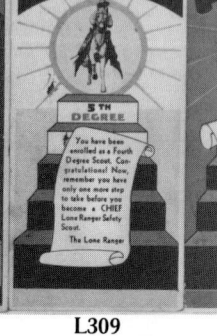

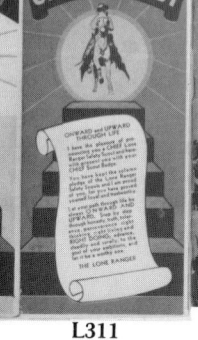

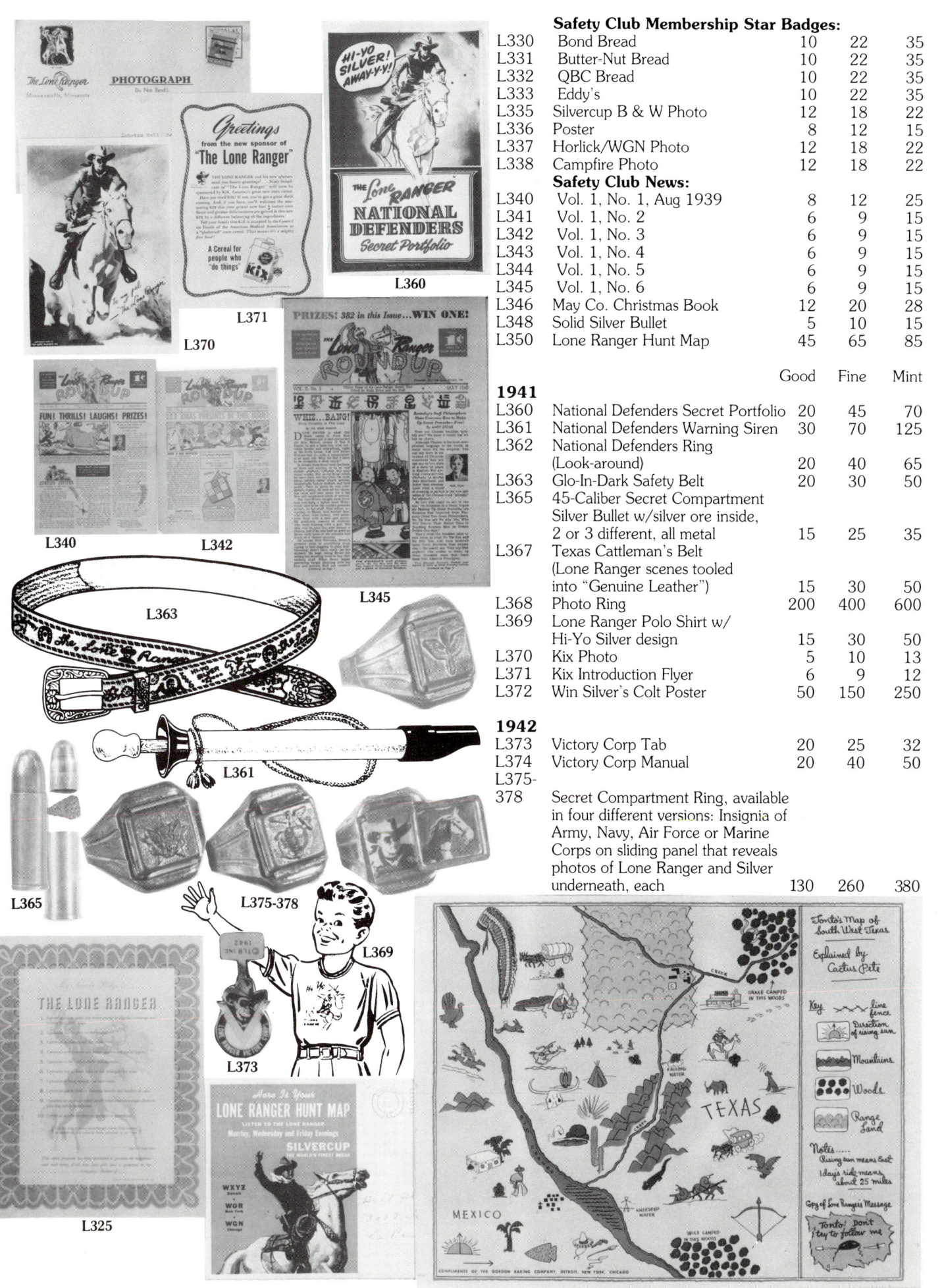

Safety Club Membership Star Badges:

L330	Bond Bread	10	22	35
L331	Butter-Nut Bread	10	22	35
L332	QBC Bread	10	22	35
L333	Eddy's	10	22	35
L335	Silvercup B & W Photo	12	18	22
L336	Poster	8	12	15
L337	Horlick/WGN Photo	12	18	22
L338	Campfire Photo	12	18	22

Safety Club News:

L340	Vol. 1, No. 1, Aug 1939	8	12	25
L341	Vol. 1, No. 2	6	9	15
L342	Vol. 1, No. 3	6	9	15
L343	Vol. 1, No. 4	6	9	15
L344	Vol. 1, No. 5	6	9	15
L345	Vol. 1, No. 6	6	9	15
L346	May Co. Christmas Book	12	20	28
L348	Solid Silver Bullet	5	10	15
L350	Lone Ranger Hunt Map	45	65	85

		Good	Fine	Mint
1941				
L360	National Defenders Secret Portfolio	20	45	70
L361	National Defenders Warning Siren	30	70	125
L362	National Defenders Ring (Look-around)	20	40	65
L363	Glo-In-Dark Safety Belt	20	30	50
L365	45-Caliber Secret Compartment Silver Bullet w/silver ore inside, 2 or 3 different, all metal	15	25	35
L367	Texas Cattleman's Belt (Lone Ranger scenes tooled into "Genuine Leather")	15	30	50
L368	Photo Ring	200	400	600
L369	Lone Ranger Polo Shirt w/ Hi-Yo Silver design	15	30	50
L370	Kix Photo	5	10	13
L371	Kix Introduction Flyer	6	9	12
L372	Win Silver's Colt Poster	50	150	250
1942				
L373	Victory Corp Tab	20	25	32
L374	Victory Corp Manual	20	40	50
L375-378	Secret Compartment Ring, available in four different versions: Insignia of Army, Navy, Air Force or Marine Corps on sliding panel that reveals photos of Lone Ranger and Silver underneath, each	130	260	380

81

			Good	Fine	Mint
L379	Victory Corp Stationery, 8 different, test premiums, set		40	80	120
L380	Combat Insignia Album & Stamps		10	20	35
L381	Victory Corp Gun		35	70	100
L382	Military Pin, unmarked		10	20	30
L383	Billfold		20	40	60
L384	Blackout Kit		15	30	55

1943-46

		Good	Fine	Mint
L391	Paper Decoder (Weber's Bread)	25	50	75
L395	Kix Airbase	30	60	90
L400	Tattoo Decals, 1944	15	20	25
L401	Mask	20	30	40
L410	Album of Victory Battles of 1942-45	5	10	18
L415	Weather Ring	20	37	55
L420	War Bonds Pinback	5	12	20
L421	War Bonds Membership Card	5	10	15

1947

		Good	Fine	Mint
L430	Atom Bomb Ring	20	35	50
L436	Silver Bullet w/Compass and Secret Compartment	20	30	40
L437	Six Shooter Ring	20	35	50

1948

		Good	Fine	Mint
	Frontier Town (four sections) mint price is for unpunched section			
L440	Northeast Section	25	75	150
L441	Northwest Section	25	75	150
L442	Southeast Section	25	75	150
L443	Southwest Section	25	75	150
L444-452	Frontier Town Package Backs, each	10	20	35
L455	Flashlight Ring	20	35	50
L458	Pedometer, aluminum rim	10	15	20

		Good	Fine	Mint

1949-50

		Good	Fine	Mint
L462	Flashlight Gun w/Secret Compartment Handle	25	55	90
L463	Movie Film Ring, no film	20	25	30
L463A	Movie Film Ring, w/8mm Marine Corps film	25	50	70
L464	17th Anniversary Coin (Luck Piece)	5	9	15
L465	Bandana	18	24	30
L466	Shirt & Mask Neckerchief	20	40	60
L467	Secret Compartment Deputy Badge, 1949	10	18	25
L468	Deputy Secret Folder, 1949	15	22	28
L469	Safety Club Kit, 1950 (Merita), letter, photo & card	40	60	80

82

L442

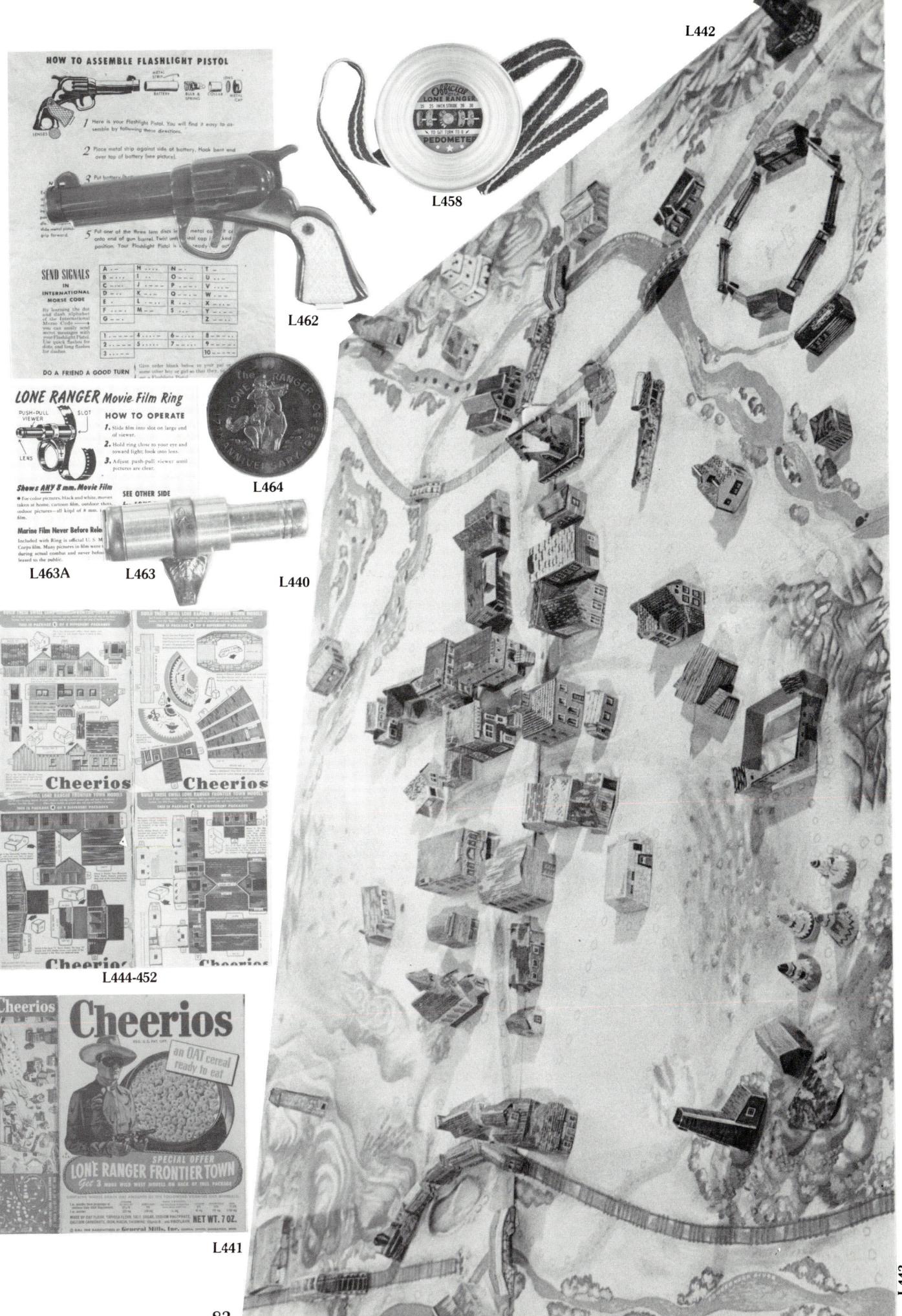

L458

L462

L464

L463A L463 L440

L444-452

L441

L443

83

1951-56

L470	Filmstrip Saddle Ring, w/16mm Lone Ranger scenes used to expose images in glow-in-dark surfaces	35	75	120
L471	Coloring Contest Drawing, from package back, each	5	10	15
L472	Contest Postcard, color Giveaway Comics, 1954			
L473	The Story of Silver	3	5	7
L474	His Mask and How He Met Tonto	3	5	7
L475	"How To Be A Lone Ranger" (Merita), 1954	10	20	30
L477	Jr. Deputy Kit, card, tin badge, and plastic mask	15	25	35
L478	Charter, Deputy Club	10	20	30
L481	Wheaties Hike-O-Meter	8	10	12
L482	Lone Ranger and Tonto Health and Safety Book (Merita), 1955	10	20	30
L485	Wheaties Mystery Backs, 10, each	3	7	10
L486	Branding Iron Initial Stamper, unmarked	8	15	25
L490	Wheaties Masks, 8			
	Lone Ranger and Tonto, each	10	20	30
	Others, 6, each	5	14	20
L491	Lone Ranger Ranch Fun Book	5	12	20
L492	Tonto Leather Beaded Belt	15	20	25
L493	Lone Ranger Cut-Outs (Merita)	20	45	85
L494	Coloring Book (Merita)	5	10	15

1957-82

L505	Life Size Posters of Lone Ranger and Tonto, pair	100	200	300

84

L508	Rapid Fire Revolver		10	20	30
L509	Map of Old West		10	20	30
L510	Tonto Indian Head Dress and Bead Set, 1964		10	18	25
L511	Movie Ranch Wild West Town Plastic Figures		20	40	60
L515	Target Pistol and Targets		15	20	45
L519	Tab, 1969 (Good Food Guys)		10	15	20
L520	Legend Booklet, 1969, (Good Food Guys)		5	10	15
L521	Movie Membership Kit		5	10	15

L486

L490

L491

L508

L492

L494

L511

L519

L520

L515

85

L493

L505

LONE WOLF TRIBE

The "Lone Wolf Tribe" dramatized stories based on the American Indian way of life with emphasis on Indian virtues and ideas. It was presented by Wrigley's gum from 1931 to 1933. Premiums were obtained for "wampum" (actually outer Wrigley gum wrappers) you traded with Chief Wolf Paw. Marked premiums have the imprint of a wolf's paw.

1932

		Good	Fine	Mint
L600	Tribe Book, manual	30	40	50
L601	Arrowhead Member's Pin	7	9	13
L602	Tom Tom, unmarked	10	15	20
L603	Arrowheads, unmarked (like any arrowhead)			
L604	Navajo Blanket Rugs, unmarked	?	?	?
L605	Tribe Bracelet	30	45	60
L606	Tribe Ring, sterling silver	25	38	55
L607	Beaded Rabbit's Foot, unmarked	?	?	?
L608	Fetish Stone, unmarked	?	?	?
L609	Thunder Bird Brooch	15	28	40
L610	Tribe Arrowhead Necklace	16	20	28
L611	Tribe Watch Fob	18	24	30
L612	Steer Head Tie Holder, unmarked	2	4	8
L613	Jacket	?	?	?

LUM AND ABNER

Before radio the post office and the general store were the places where you found the news. Two young actors capitalized on this basic communications idea and created "Lum and Abner." The country was still agrarian enough to enjoy its back-home humor, a flavor that lives on in the print premiums offered by this comedy show.

		Good	Fine	Mint
L750	Photo of Lum and Abner, in and out of makeup	4	5	6
L753	Drink Shaker (maybe commercial)	15	30	45
L755-757	Pine Ridge News (Newspapers), first issue Nov 1933 and ran several volumes through the 30's	3	4	6
L768	1936 Walkin' Weather Prophet Badge	9	11	13
L769	Horlick Malted Maker	12	20	25
L770	1936 Family Almanac	3	5	8
L771	1937 Family Almanac	3	5	8
L772	1938 Family Almanac	3	5	8
L775	Let's 'lect Lum Button	2	3	4

MA PERKINS

Virginia Payne became Ma Perkins on Aug 14, 1933 when it was locally produced in Cincinnati, Ohio. Procter & Gamble transferred the show to Chicago and NBC on Dec 4, 1933. Just 23 years old when the show began, Virginia Payne never missed any of the 7,065 broadcasts which aired until Nov 25, 1960. Oxydol has never been the same since. The show was so popular the same show aired with two hours separation on both NBC and CBS for over six years from 1942 to 1948.

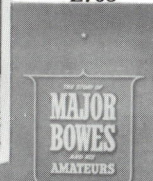

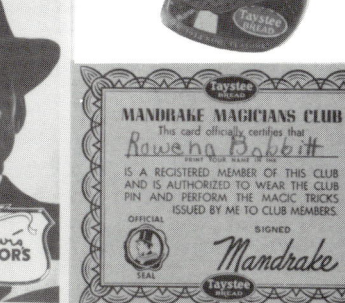

		Good	Fine	Mint
M150	Photo	5	10	15
M151	Recipe Book	2	4	6
M154	Seed Packets, each	2	5	8

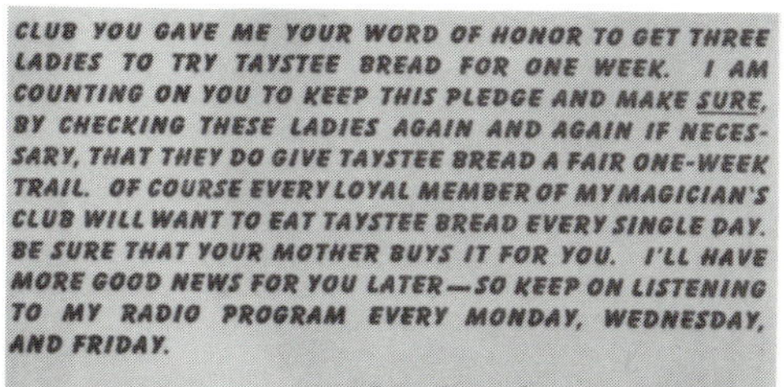

MAJOR BOWES ORIGINAL AMATEUR HOUR

"In New York dial Murray Hill 8000. You out-of-town listeners vote for the amateur of your choice by sending a postcard to P.O. Box 200, Radio City Station, New York..." and millions did. They also wanted to see what the winners looked like so various publications were attempted to fill the void.

		Good	Fine	Mint
M200	Practice Microphone w/decal, wood	10	25	40
M205	Winners Folders, various years	1	3	5
M220	Newspapers, various years	1	3	5

MANDRAKE THE MAGICIAN

Based on the King Features Syndicate adventure comic strip, "Mandrake the Magician" aired as a 15-minute syndicated juvenile adventure serial from 1940 to 1942. Adventures centered around Mandrake, Lothar and the beautiful Princess Narda. He evoked his magic powers to thwart the evils of domestic, as well as war criminals. His "house of Mystery and many secrets" was particularly stimulating to the listener's imagination. The premiums offered have a copyright date conflict, but are believed to be from the radio period.

		Good	Fine	Mint
M250	Magic Club Pin, 1934	15	40	70
M251	Membership Card	10	15	20
M252	Message Card	5	7	18
M253	Sheet of Special Magic Tricks	10	20	30
M254	Magic Club Pinback	20	50	90

MEADOW GOLD ROUND-UP — See Lightning Jim

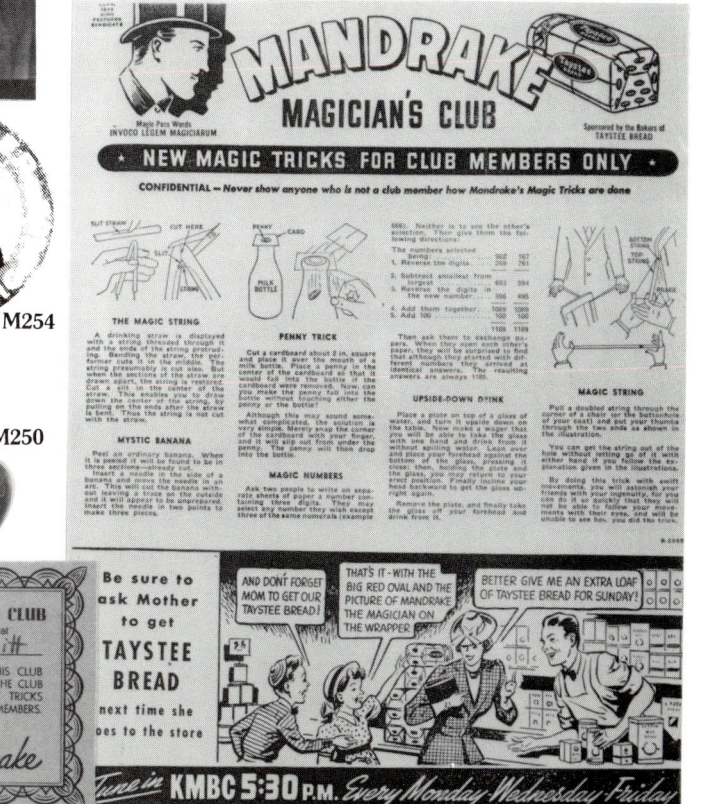

MELVIN PURVIS

"Melvin Purvis" was probably Post Cereals' most successful cereal box, newspaper and magazine-promoted personality designed to compete with the radio serials. Purvis was a true-life hero; the FBI man who supposedly ended the crime careers of many of the nation's top-wanted fugitives. Contrary to information published, Joe Pinkston of the John Dillinger Museum, Nashville, Indiana, relates that Purvis (whom he knew), did not kill Dillinger, was fired from the FBI because J. Edgar Hoover didn't like sharing the publicity, and didn't die until 1960 . . . a suspected suicide.

		Good	Fine	Mint
1936 - Junior G-Man Corps				
M300	Manual of Instructions	12	18	25
M301	Identification Card	3	5	8
M302	Junior G-Man Badge	5	6	8
M303	Roving Operative Badge	6	7	9
M304	Roving Operative Commission	7	8	10
M305	Chief Operative Badge	7	8	10
M306	Chief Operative Commission	8	9	11
M308	Girls' Division Badge	8	9	12
M310	Junior G-Man Ring	15	25	35
M312	Melvin Purvis Fingerprint Set	10	20	30
M315	Pistol Flashlight	10	18	24
1937 - Law and Order Patrol				
M330	Secret Operators Manual	12	18	25
M331	Secret Operators Badge	5	6	8
M332	Lieutenant Secret Operators Badge	6	7	9
M333	Inner District Pass	7	8	10
M334	Captain Secret Operators Badge	7	8	10
M335	Captain Certificate of Appointment	8	10	12
M337	Shoulder Holster	10	14	18
M340	Melvin Purvis Knife	10	20	30
M343	Finger-Print Detection Tape & Transfer Card	5	6	8
M344	Finger-Print Powders	2	3	4
M345	Secret Operators Magnifying Glass & Handwriting Study	3	4	5
M346	Melvin Purvis Pencil	6	10	15
M347	Purvis Combination Pen & Pencil	10	20	35
M349	Autographed Photo of Melvin Purvis	5	10	15
M350	Secret Operators Law & Order Patrol Ring	15	25	35
M352	Secret Operators Key Ring	5	7	10
M353	Official Identification Wallet & Card	10	14	16
M354	Secret Operators Note Book	10	14	16
M355	Girls' Division Secret Operators Badge	3	5	8

NICK CARTER, MASTER DETECTIVE

"Nick Carter, Master Dectective" originated as a pulp magazine gumshoe. Solving murders continued to be his stock in trade when he began a twelve year stint on Mutual in 1943. The Nick Carter Club, however, was connected to the Street and Smith pulps of the early 30's.

		Good	Fine	Mint
N300	Membership Badge	50	75	100
N301	Membership Card	10	20	30
N302	Stickers for S&S pulp, each	5	10	15
N305	Fingerprint Kit	20	40	60

OG, SON OF FIRE

It's hard to image primitive cave people fighting dinosaurs on radio, but Libby Foods bought the concept for airing in the mid-30's. The premiums include an interesting set of metal figures and a colorful map. A game, books, and other store items were other outgrowths of the character.

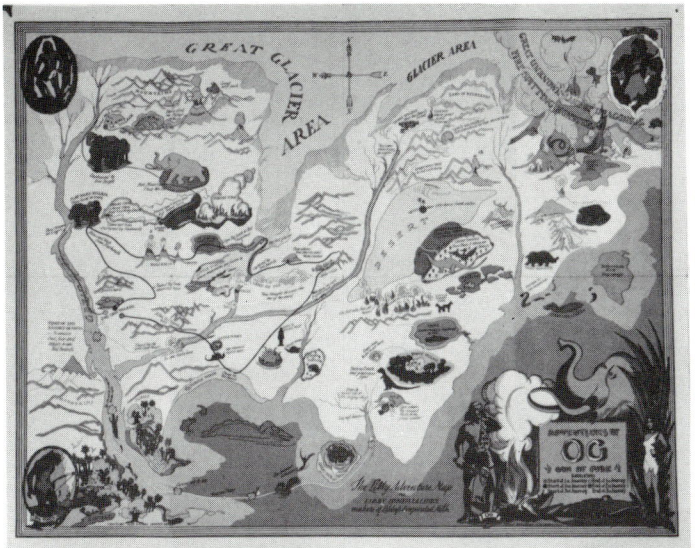

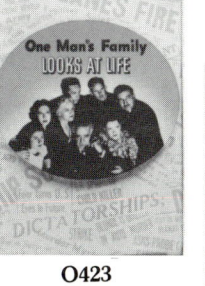

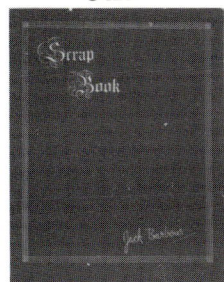

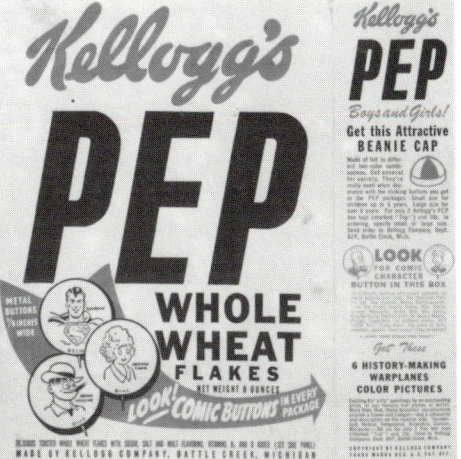

		Good	Fine	Mint
O300	Figures of Og, Ru, Nada, and a black caveman, each	5	12	20
O301	Figure of Three Horned Monster and Other Dinosaurs, each	10	18	30
O302	Map	20	45	80

ONE MAN'S FAMILY

There may be a lesson in the fact radio's most successful and longest running soap opera issued more and better premiums than other daytime hard-luck dramas. The premium offers seemed to increase listener involvement with staged photographs that further dramatized the illusion that the characters were "real" people. Scrapbooks, family trees, photo recaps of the year's adventures added believability to the program and sincerity to the request that the listeners try the Standard Brands products being pushed.

		Good	Fine	Mint
O420	1935 One Man's Family History	3	5	8
O421	1936 Jack Barbour's Scrapbook	4	6	9
O422	1937 Teddy Barbour's Diary	4	6	9
O423	1938 One Man's Family Looks at Life	4	6	9
O424	1939 One Man's Family Looks at Life	4	6	9
O425	1940 Fanny Barbour's Memory Book	3	5	8
O426	1941 I Believe in America	3	5	8
O431	1946 Barbour Family Scrapbook	3	5	8
O436	1951 Barbour Family Album	3	5	8
O437	1952 20th Anniversary Souvenir Cookbook	5	8	12
O438	1953 Father Barbour's "This I give . . ."	3	5	8

OPERATOR #5

Jimmy Christopher, Operator 5 of the United States Secret Service, dedicated his life to battling subversive enemies of our country here and abroad. A pulp hero of 48 novels beginning in 1934, he became "America's Secret Service Ace" and created an organization called The Secret Sentinels of America. You joined by mailing in 25¢. In return you got a ring. It resemble the poison gas ring used by Operator 5, but was quite harmless.

O500	Ring	150	300	500

ORPHAN ANNIE — See Radio Orphan Annie

PEP CEREAL PINS

Beginning around 1943 Kellogg's PEP inserted small litho tin pinback buttons into each package. Each of the first two series were comprised of 18 military insignias and four larger World War II airplanes. Line drawing variations exist for the second four planes. In 1945 the first comic characters series was issued. New series were added periodically over the next two years until a total of 86 different characters appeared. Both the military and comic sets were advertised on the Superman radio show. There were five series of 18 pins each.

Prices for early series and preferred comic characters command higher prices. Popeye $15 to $20; Phantom and Felix the Cat $9 to $15 each; Flash Gordon, Orphan Annie, Dick Tracy and Gravel Gertie $8 to $10 each; Abretha Breeze, Denny, Henry, Herby, Little King, Mama DeStross, Punjab, Sandy, Vitamin Flintheart, Warbucks and Winnie's Twins $5 to $8. All others $3 to $6. Superman was included with every series and there are probably more of him than any other, but the pin still routinely brings $4 to $8.

Comic Character Pins (86)

P250 Abretha Breeze	P265 Daisy	P279 Harold Teen	P293 Maggie	P307 Phantom	P322 Tess Trueheart
P251 Andy Gump	P266 Denny	P280 Henry	P294 Mama De Stross	P308 Popeye	P323 Tilda
P252 Auntie Blossom	P267 Dick Tracy	P281 Herby	P295 Mama Katzenjammer	P309 Pop Jenks	P324 Tillie the Toiler
P253 Barney Google	P268 Don Winslow	P282 Inspector	P296 Mamie	P311 Punjab	P325 Tiny Tim
P254 Beezie	P269 Emmy	P283 Jiggs	P297 Ma Winkle	P312 Rip Winkle	P326 Toots
P255 Blondie	P270 Fat Stuff	P284 Judy	P298 Min Gump	P313 Sandy	P327 Uncle Avery
P256 B.O. Plenty	P271 Felix the Cat	P285 Junior Tracy	P299 Moon Mullins	P314 Shadow	P328 Uncle Bim
P257 Brenda Starr	P272 Fire Chief	P286 Kayo	P300 Mr. Bailey	P315 Skeezix	P329 Uncle Walt
P258 The Captain	P273 Flash Gordon	P287 Lillums	P301 Mr. Bibbs	P316 Smilin' Jack	P330 Uncle Willie
P259 Casper	P274 Flattop	P288 Little Joe	P302 Nina	P317 Smitty	P331 Vitamin Flintheart
P260 Chester Gump	P275 Fritz	P289 Little King	P303 Olive Oil	P318 Smokey Stover	P332 Warbucks
P261 Chief Brandon	P276 Goofy	P290 Little Moose	P304 Orphan Annie	P319 Snuffy Smith	P333 Wilmer
P262 Cindy	P277 Gravel Gertie	P291 Lord Plushbottom	P305 Pat Patten	P320 Spud	P334 Wimpy
P263 Corky	P278 Hans	P292 Mac	P306 Perry Winkle	P321 Superman	P335 Winnie's Twins
P264 Dagwood					P336 Winnie Winkle

Military Insignias

- P200 2nd Bomb Sq.
- P201 17th Bomb Sq.
- P202 25th Bomb Sq.
- P203 27th Fighter Sq.
- P204 24th Bomb Sq.
- P205 41st Bomb Sq.
- P206 44th Fighter Sq.
- P207 53rd Bomb Sq.
- P208 56th Bomb Sq.
- P209 70th Bomb Sq.
- P210 94th Pursuit Sq.
- P211 96th Bomb Sq.
- P212 99th Bomb Sq
- P213 385th Bomb Sq.
- P214 424th Bomb Sq.
- P215 431st Bomb Sq.
- P216 VB-13
- P217 VO-3
- P222 29th Bomb Sq.
- P223 48th Bomb Sq.
- P224 103rd Observation Sq.
- P225 306th Bomb Sq.
- P226 370th Bomb Sq.
- P227 391st Bomb Sq.
- P228 402nd Bomb Sq.
- P229 471st Bomb Sq.
- P230 Marine Bomb Sq. 433
- P231 Marine Fighter Sq. VMF-224
- P232 Marine Torpedo Bomb Sq. 232
- P233 Navy Bomb Fight. Sq. 12
- P234 Navy Bomb Sq. 11
- P235 Navy Cruiser Scot Sq.-2
- P236 Navy Patrol Sq.-23
- P237 Navy Stagron-14
- P238 Navy Torpedo Sq.-3
- P239 Navy Torpedo Sq.-32

Airplanes (8)

- P218 P-47 Thunderbolt
- P219 P-38
- P220 B-24 Liberator
- P221 B-29
- P240 Hellcat
- P241 B-26 Marander
- P242 B-25 Mitchell
- P243 PB2Y-3 Coronado

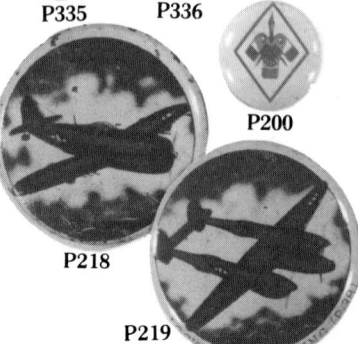

PHANTOM PILOT PATROL

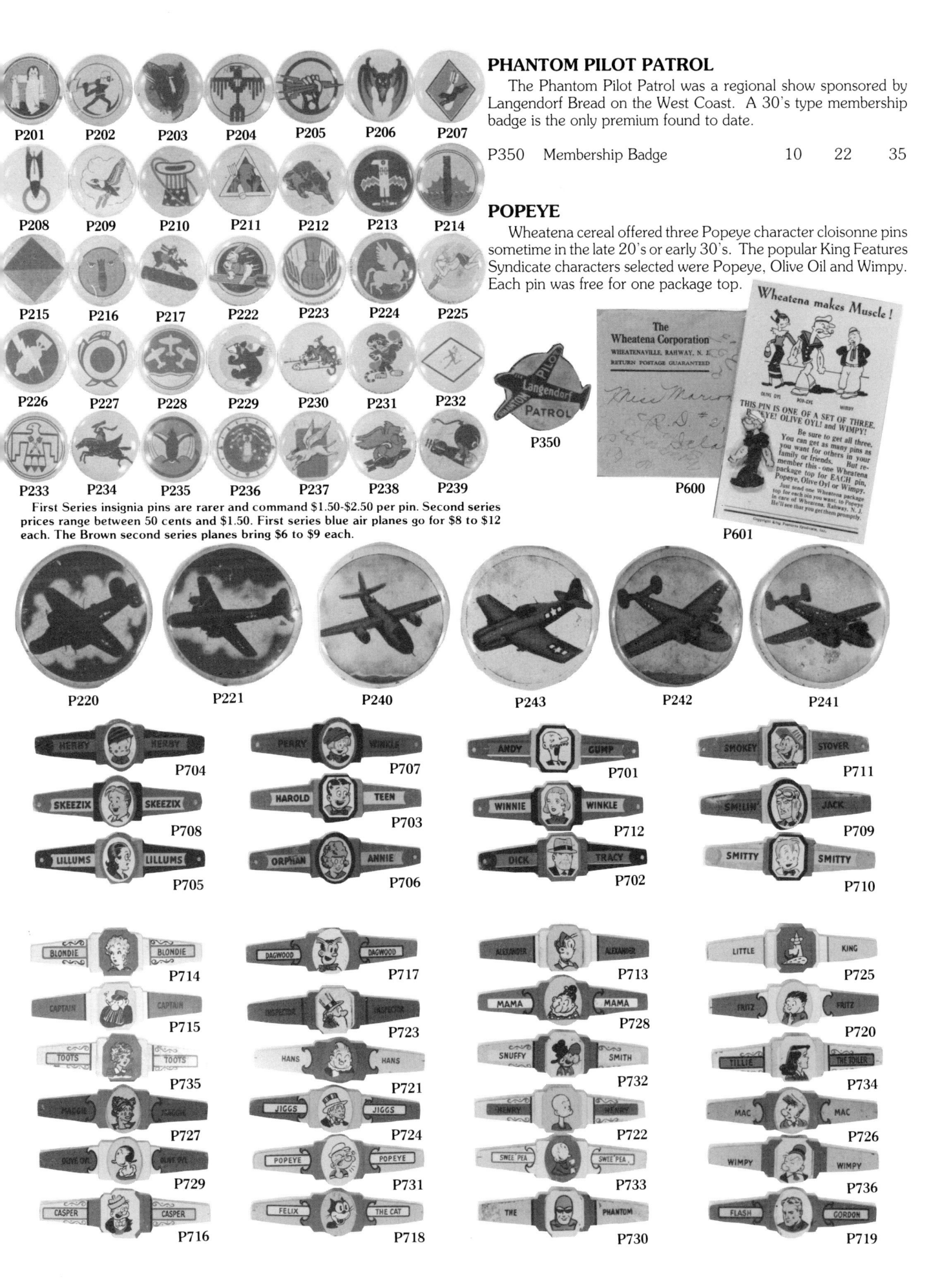

The Phantom Pilot Patrol was a regional show sponsored by Langendorf Bread on the West Coast. A 30's type membership badge is the only premium found to date.

P350   Membership Badge   10   22   35

POPEYE

Wheatena cereal offered three Popeye character cloisonne pins sometime in the late 20's or early 30's. The popular King Features Syndicate characters selected were Popeye, Olive Oil and Wimpy. Each pin was free for one package top.

First Series insignia pins are rarer and command $1.50-$2.50 per pin. Second series prices range between 50 cents and $1.50. First series blue air planes go for $8 to $12 each. The Brown second series planes bring $6 to $9 each.

91

		Good	Fine	Mint
P600	Pin on card, Popeye, Olive Oil or Wimpy, each	50	75	100
P601	Pins only, each	10	25	50

POST COMIC RINGS

These litho tin rings were inserted in Post Raisin Bran cereal packages in 1948 and Post Toasties Corn Flakes boxes in 1949. There were 36 in all. Only Sweet Pea and Alexander were characters that hadn't previously appeared in the highly successful Kellogg's PEP pinback button set.

		Good	Fine	Mint
1948 - Raisin Brand Rings, 12				
P701	Andy Gump	3	6	10
P702	Dick Tracy	8	15	20
P703	Harold Teen	3	6	10
P704	Herby	4	7	10
P705	Lillums	2	5	7
P706	Orphan Annie	6	15	20
P707	Perry Winkle	3	6	8
P708	Skeezix	3	6	8
P709	Smilin' Jack	5	10	12
P710	Smitty	4	7	9
P711	Smokey Stover	4	7	12
P712	Winnie Winkle	3	6	8
Post Toasties Corn Flakes Rings, 24				
P713	Alexander	4	7	10
P714	Blondie	4	7	10
P715	Captain	4	7	10
P716	Casper	3	6	8
P717	Dagwood	5	8	10
P718	Felix the Cat	6	15	20
P719	Flash Gordon	6	15	20
P720	Fritz	4	7	10
P721	Hans	4	7	10
P722	Henry	4	7	10
P723	Inspector	4	7	10
P724	Jiggs	5	8	10
P725	Little King	4	7	10
P726	Mac	3	6	8
P727	Maggie	5	8	10
P728	Mama	4	7	10
P729	Olive Oil	4	7	10
P730	The Phantom	6	15	20
P731	Popeye	5	12	20
P732	Snuffy Smith	3	6	8
P733	Swee' Pea	4	7	10
P734	Tillie the Toiler	4	7	10
P735	Toots	3	6	8
P736	Wimpy	5	11	14

QUIZ KIDS

The show, starring Jack Kelly as quizmaster, started on NBC on June 28, 1949 and eventually aired on every network except Mutual. It left radio after the 1952-53 season on CBS for several successful seasons on TV. Listeners supplied the questions and child prodigies answered them. Anyone sending in a question received an acknowledgment postcard. The lineup of kids changed as each grew out of the child stage. The postcards differ in design, as well as the kids pictured.

Q400-410	Postcards, 10 different seen, each	2	4	6

RADIO ORPHAN ANNIE

"Radio Orphan Annie" (ROA) was the first kids' program to last more than a few seasons. Like all others of the 1930 vintage, it was

92

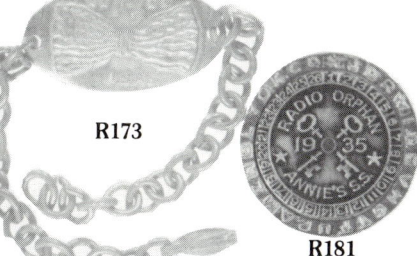

syndicated on a regional basis, but unique in that Ovaltine was the sponsor wherever the show aired. As a result there was an eastern cast in Chicago and a western cast in Los Angeles until 1933 when the program went network. During this period premiums were offered at different times and in different versions. In 1934 the number of premiums accelerated as the hard-luck waif conned kids into drinking more and more Ovaltine. The radio show was quite a departure from the comic strip. New characters were Joe Corntassel plus Ma and Pa Silo. Action centered around the small town of Simmons Corner. Annie stuck more to kids her own age and Daddy Warbucks was conspicuous mainly by his absence from most episodes.

		Good	Fine	Mint
1930-31				
R110	Uncle Wiggily Mug - Type I	8	12	20
R110A	Uncle Wiggily Mug - Type II, w/Ovaltine sign on house	8	12	20
R113	Election mailer	10	20	50
R114	Card for Button	20	30	40
R115	Annie Button	30	70	175
R116	Joe Button	20	50	85
R117	Shake-up Mug - Type I	10	14	20
R118	Shake-up Game Letter	5	8	10
R119	Sheet Music	5	8	10
1932				
R125	Annie Ceramic Mug	12	20	35
R127	Annie Photo, Shirley Bell	8	10	14
R128	Joe Photo, Allan Baruck	8	10	14
R129	Annie Dress Photo, Shirley Bell	8	10	14
1933				
R135	Beetleware Mug - Type I	6	10	20
R137	Orphan Annie Mask	20	30	45
R138	Treasure Hunt Game, w/ships uncut	12	20	40
R138A	Treasure Hunt Gameboard only	5	12	20
R140	Tucker County Race Puzzle	25	30	35
1934				
R150	Manual	30	37	45
R151	Secret Society Pin, bronze	4	7	10
R152	Silver Star Pin	6	10	15
R157	Lucky Piece	10	18	22
R158	Silver Star Manual	10	14	20
R160 -165	Adventure Book Mailings (Shake-up contest), 6 different books, each	5	10	15
R160A	Contest Letter/Winners List	5	10	15
R168	Bandana	20	30	40
R169	Orphan Annie Face Ring	10	16	30
R173	Identification Disc, bracelet	15	20	25
1935				
R180	Manual	25	37	48
R181	Round Decoder Pin	10	18	28
R184	Magic Transfer Pictures	20	30	45
R185	Beetleware Mug - Type II	15	20	25
R186	Silver Star Manual	15	20	25
R187	Shake-up Mug - Type II	10	15	20

R168
R184
R160A
R160-165
R191
R169
R187
R185
R190
R192
R197
R194
R195
R198
R196

94

1936

R190	Manual	20	28	35
R191	Silver Star Ring, crossed keys on star	15	30	50
R192	Secret Compartment Decoder Pin	8	10	15
R193	Silver Star Manual	15	20	25
R194	Birthstone Ring	15	28	45
R195	Map of Simons Corners	25	40	55
R196	Circus Action Show	30	45	75
R197	Book About Dogs	20	28	36
R198	Glassips	10	15	20

1937

R200	Manual	22	30	38
R201	Sunburst Decoder Pin	9	12	16
R202	Silver Star Secret Message Ring (Numbers on top) The decoded message reads "I Am A Silver Star Member of Orphan Annie's Secret Society and belong to the circle of her special friends."	20	27	35
R203	Silver Star Manual	15	25	35
R212	Foreign Coin Folder	18	30	40
R215	Talking Stationery Set	25	40	60
R217	Christmas Card Set	10	24	40
R219	Two Initial Signet Ring	14	22	35

1938

		Good	Fine	Mint
R220	Manual	30	45	60
R221	Telematic Decoder Pin	14	20	26
R222	Silver Star Triple Mystery Secret Compartment Ring	50	200	400
R223	Silver Star Manual	22	30	40
R224	School Pin	15	20	30
R225	Shake-up Mug - Type III, dancing w/milk	18	25	33
R227	Snow White Book (Whitman book in ROA mailer), thinner paper than cardboard store version	45	75	100
R229	Photo Stamps	12	18	24
R230	Sun Watch	14	18	22
R232	Shadowetts, 6	18	24	30
R233	Silver Plated Fotoframe - plate reads "To My Best Friend"	4	10	20

95

1939

R240	Manual	32	45	60
R241	Mysto-Matic Decoder	12	20	30
R242	Code Captain Secret Compartment Pin	24	35	50
R243	Shake-up Mug - Type IV, brown	12	20	30
R244	Identification Tag Bracelet	15	20	26
R246	Mystic Eye (Look Around) Ring	20	27	34
R247	Goofy Circus	30	45	60
R248-250	Goofy Gazzetts #1, #2, #3, each	10	20	30

1940

R260	Manual	40	60	75
R261	Speedomatic Decoder Pin	15	22	40
R262	Code Captain Belt & Buckle	40	60	85
R263	Code Captain Manual	30	35	40
R265	Shake-up Mug - Type IV, green	20	26	32
R267	Three-Way Dog Whistle, Sandy's Head	15	23	35

Ovaltine dropped "Radio Orphan Annie" in 1941 in favor of the more timely war hero, Captain Midnight. The Annie show was picked up by Quaker Sparkies Puffed Wheat and Rice. The Secret Society was transformed into the Secret Guard in 1941 and the Safety Guard in 1942. In the process Annie gained a new sidekick named Captain Sparks. Annie should have been smarter. His rank was Commander in Chief while Annie was only Lieutenant Commander. His role grew and her's diminished. Within two years the show lost most of its audience . . . and the Age of Radio Orphan Annie was over.

		Good	Fine	Mint
1941				
R270	Secret Guard Handbook	30	50	100
R271	Slidomatic Decoder, paper	30	40	55
R272	Mysto-Snapper Membership Badge (clicker)	8	10	15
R273	Captain's Emblem Glow Wings	45	70	100
R274	Captain's Secret Manual	30	40	50

96

Kellogg's
SUGAR CORN POPS
"YIP-EE!"
LARGE SIZE
Special Offer!
Inside this package
Get 2
"Yukon Adventure"
PICTURE CARDS
COOKS IN 10 SECONDS
Instant RALSTON
HOT WHOLE WHEAT CEREAL
WHEATIES
Quaker Puffed
WRIGLEY'S SPEARMINT
5 10 15 20 25
Ralston
25 20 15 10 5
TAILOR-MADE FOR COLORADO
SKELLY
ROAD MAP
CAPTAIN MIDNIGHT'S
HOW TO PLAY
Little Orphan Annie's
ICE-COLD OVALTINE SHAKE-UP GAME
OVALTINE
Postal Telegraph
SIGNAL SET
INTERNATIONAL SYSTEM
RALSTON STRAIGHT SHOOTERS
TELEGRAPH SET
MAGIC ANSWER BOX
OFFICIAL COMMISSION
SECRET INSTRUCTIONS
Sincerely your friend Capt. Midnight
BOBBY BENSON
STRAIGHT ARROW
Tell your pals about this special offer
INSTRUCTIONS INSIDE
HERE'S WHAT RADIO ORPHAN ANNIE'S VERY OWN LUCKY PIECE MEANS!
A SECRET MESSAGE from CAPT. MARVEL!
POST CARD
Paid
KLONDIKE LAND
CISCO KID
HUMMING LARIAT
ON TELEVISION!
SATELLITE PIONEERS

Welcome to
SIMMONS CORNERS
TUCKER COUNTY
SILO FARM
SUNFIELD
County Fair Grounds
P-61 LITHO. IN U.S.A.

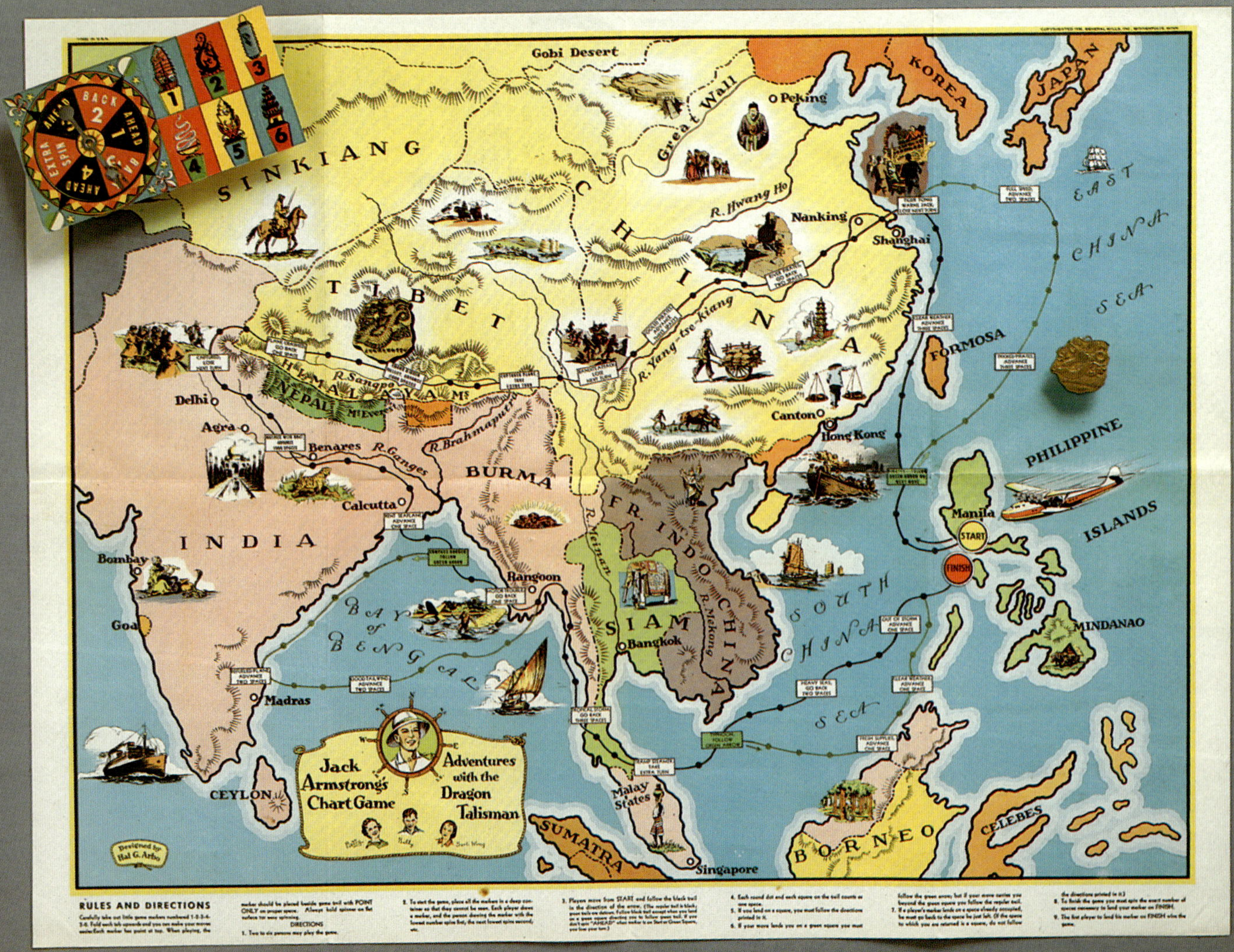

Gobi Desert
KOREA
JAPAN
Peking
Great Wall
SINKIANG
CHINA
R. Hwang Ho
Nanking
Shanghai
EAST CHINA SEA
TIBET
R. Yang-tse-Kiang
FORMOSA
NEPAL
HIMALAYA Mts.
Mt. Everest
R. Sangpo
Delhi
Agra
Benares
R. Ganges
R. Brahmaputra
Canton
Hong Kong
PHILIPPINE ISLANDS
BURMA
FR. INDO CHINA
Calcutta
Manila
START
FINISH
INDIA
Bombay
Rangoon
SIAM
Bangkok
R. Mekong
MINDANAO
Goa
BAY of BENGAL
SOUTH CHINA SEA
Madras
Jack Armstrong's Chart Game
Adventures with the Dragon Talisman
CEYLON
Malay States
SUMATRA
Singapore
BORNEO
CELEBES
Designed by Hal G. Arbo
RULES AND DIRECTIONS
AHEAD
BACK
EXTRA

INDIA
BURMA
CHINA
BAY of BENGAL
FRENCH INDO CHINA
CHINA SEA
SUMATRA
BORNEO
START FINISH
BRING 'EM BACK ALIVE MAP and GAME
By FRANK BUCK
WHO GETS WILD ANIMALS FOR THE CIRCUS
For the vigor and health of a hunter take
SCOTT'S EMULSION
© FRANK BUCK & EDWARD ANTHONY

ARCTIC OCEAN
ARCTIC CIRCLE
ALASKA
FT. YUKON
EAGLE
DAWSON
KLONDIKE RIVER
KLONDIKE GOLD FIELDS
YUKON TERRITORY
NORTHWEST TERRITORY
FT. SELKIRK
LAKE LABERGE
WHITEHORSE
LAKE BENNETT
SKAGWAY
JUNEAU
BRITISH COLUMBIA
MAP OF YUKON TERRITORY

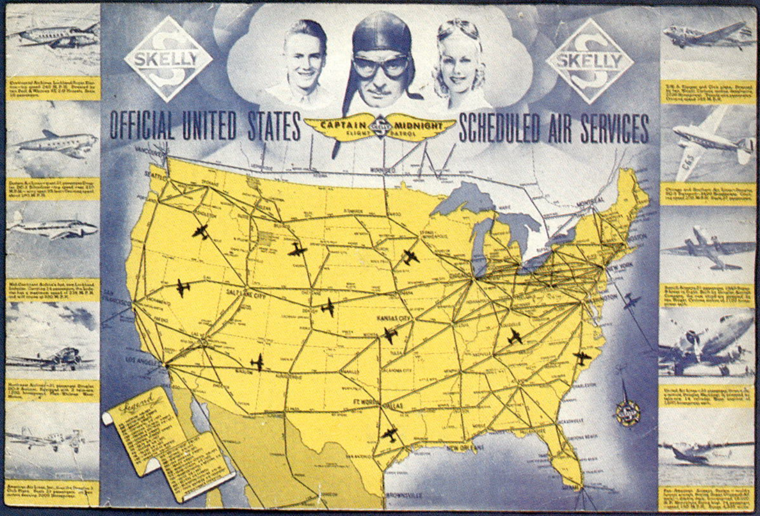
SKELLY
SKELLY
OFFICIAL UNITED STATES
CAPTAIN MIDNIGHT
SCHEDULED AIR SERVICES

NON-RECOIL ONE-WAY ENERGY GUN
UTILIZING THE EARTH'S HEAT
ARCTURUS
VEGA
232 TRILLION MILES FROM THE SUN
PLUTO
ALTAIR
NEPTUNE
NEXT TO FARTHEST PLANET
34,800 MILES DIAM.
ORBIT 165 YEARS
ONE SATELITE
JUPITER
THE GREATEST PLANET
86,500 MILES DIAM.
ORBIT: 12 YEARS
7 SATELITES
BUCK WITH JUMPING BELT
4,200,000,000 MILES FROM SUN
2,791,600,000 MILES FROM SUN
MARS
THE RUDDY PLANET
4,230 MILES DIAM.
ORBIT 687 DAYS
2 SATELITES
URANUS
HERSCHEL'S PLANET
31,900 MILES DIAM.
4 SATELITES
1,781,900,000 MILES FROM SUN
VENUS
THE EVENING STAR
7770 MILES DIAM.
ORBIT 225 DAYS
SUN
DIAMETER OF SUN
864,000 MILES
SATURN WITH 10 SATELITES
THE PLANET WITH THE RINGS
73,000 MILES DIAMETER
ORBIT 29½ YEARS
886,000,000 MILES FROM SUN
MERCURY
THE PLANET NEAREST THE SUN
THE MOON
THE EARTH
OUR OWN PLANET
7,918 MILES DIAM.
ORBIT 365 DAYS
NIAGARA
THE LIGHTNING GUN
TELE-RADIOSCOPE
THE REPELLOR RAY SHIP
DISINTEGRATOR RAY MACHINE
PHASES OF THE MOON
ECLIPSE OF THE MOON
ECLIPSE OF THE SUN
THE SEASONS & THE EARTH'S ORBIT
SPRING
WINTER
SUMMER
AUTUMN
BLACK BARNEY
WILLIE
KILLER KANE

HI-YO SILVER! AWAY-Y-Y!
THE Lone RANGER
NATIONAL DEFENDERS
Secret Portfolio
MESSAGE TO MY FELLOW TRIBESMAN:
HERE'S YOUR OFFICIAL TRIBAL PATCH WEAR IT PROUDLY ON YOUR SHIRT SWEATER CAP OR ARMBAND
IF YOU CAN'T SEW IT ON YOURSELF, ASK YOUR MOTHER OR SISTER TO DO IT. JUST STITCH AROUND THE OUTSIDE EDGE.
Straight Arrow
P.S. SEE OTHER SIDE. LEARN HOW TO BECOME A TRIBAL CHIEF.
THE STORY OF THE UNITED STATES MARINES
By CAPTAIN MIDNIGHT
NOTICE!
HOW TO SIGNAL WITH THIS GREEN HORNET RING
HOW TO LEAVE GREEN HORNET SEAL
Here's your LASSIE FRIENDSHIP RING and wallet size PICTURE of LASSIE and TIMMY
THE CAPTAIN MIDNIGHT INSIGNIA
THIS COUPON IS GOOD FOR ONE "WHIRLWIND" Whistling Ring
JACK ARMSTRONG'S SECRET WHISTLE CODE
STRAIGHT ARROW
KIDS! Wyatt Earp MARSHAL'S RING!
ONLY 25¢
FIGHTING BLUE DEVILS
101ST CAVALRY
B COMPANY
RIN TIN TIN CLUB
Here's your.. TERRY'S OFFICIAL VICTORY AIRPLANE "SPOTTER"
SPOT THAT PLANE
TERRY'S OFFICIAL VICTORY AIRPLANE SPOTTER
SPOT THE PLANE
HOW TO PLAY "SPOTTER"
HOLD HERE
LIBBY McNEILL & LIBBY — CHICAGO, ILL.
Libby's TOMATO JUICE
DICK TRACY SECRET SERVICE PATROL
SECRET CODE BOOK
and SECRET methods of communication
New 1939 REVISED EDITION
DICK TRACY SECRET SERVICE PATROL
SECRET CODE BOOK
and SECRET methods of communication Confidential—For Members Only!
The Quaker Oats Company MAKERS OF PUFFED WHEAT PUFFED RICE PRESENTING DICK DARING
MOVIE ROOM
LIBRARY
SWIMMING POOL
LABORATORY
LIVING ROOM
SECRET TUNNEL
The BLACK FLAME of the AMAZON
CARIBBEAN SEA
VENEZUELA
COLOMBIA
BRAZIL
BOLIVIA
EQUATOR
HAROLD NOICE
PACIFIC OCEAN
ATLANTIC OCEAN
HI-SPEED GAS STATIONS' Educational Map of SOUTH AMERICA featured in The BLACK FLAME of the AMAZON RADIO PROGRAM
TERRY AND THE PIRATES
Adventure of the "RUBY OF GENGHIS KHAN"
GAMES PUZZLES RIDDLES CUT OUTS Party Suggestions Coloring Pages MAZE GAMES PAPER DOLLS
OFFICIAL Roy Rogers RIDERS CLUB COMICS

B
WRANGLER
STRAIGHT TOM MIX
RALSTON SHOOTERS
WRANGLER
STRAIGHT TOM MIX
RALSTON SHOOTERS
WRANGLER
WRANGLER
STRAIGHT TOM MIX
RALSTON SHOOTERS
WRANGLER
STRAIGHT TOM MIX
RALSTON SHOOTERS
WRANGLER
STRAIGHT TOM MIX
RALSTON SHOOTERS
OFFICIAL
JIMMY
ALLEN
SECRET
SIGNAL
WRANGLER
TOM MIX RALSTON
STRAIGHT SHOOTER
WRANGLER
TOM MIX RALSTON
STRAIGHT SHOOTER
DICK STEEL
NEWS SERVICE
FLIGHT COMMANDER
FLYING CUBS
SUPERVISOR
SUNBRITE
JUNIOR NURSE
CORPS
DIZZY DEAN WINNERS
SERGEANT
LIEUTENANT
CAPTAIN
YOUR PERSONAL
NAME & ADDRESS
STAMPING
KIT from Sky King
RANCH BOSS
TOM MIX RALSTON
STRAIGHT SHOOTERS
DASC
Space Patrol
SKY KING
S
K
3970743

Kellogg's
PEP
WHOLE WHEAT FLAKES
SPACE CADET
TRUTH
VIRTUE
Tom Mix
S
SH
SECRET SOCIETY
FORT APACHE
RINTY & RUSTY
ZORRO

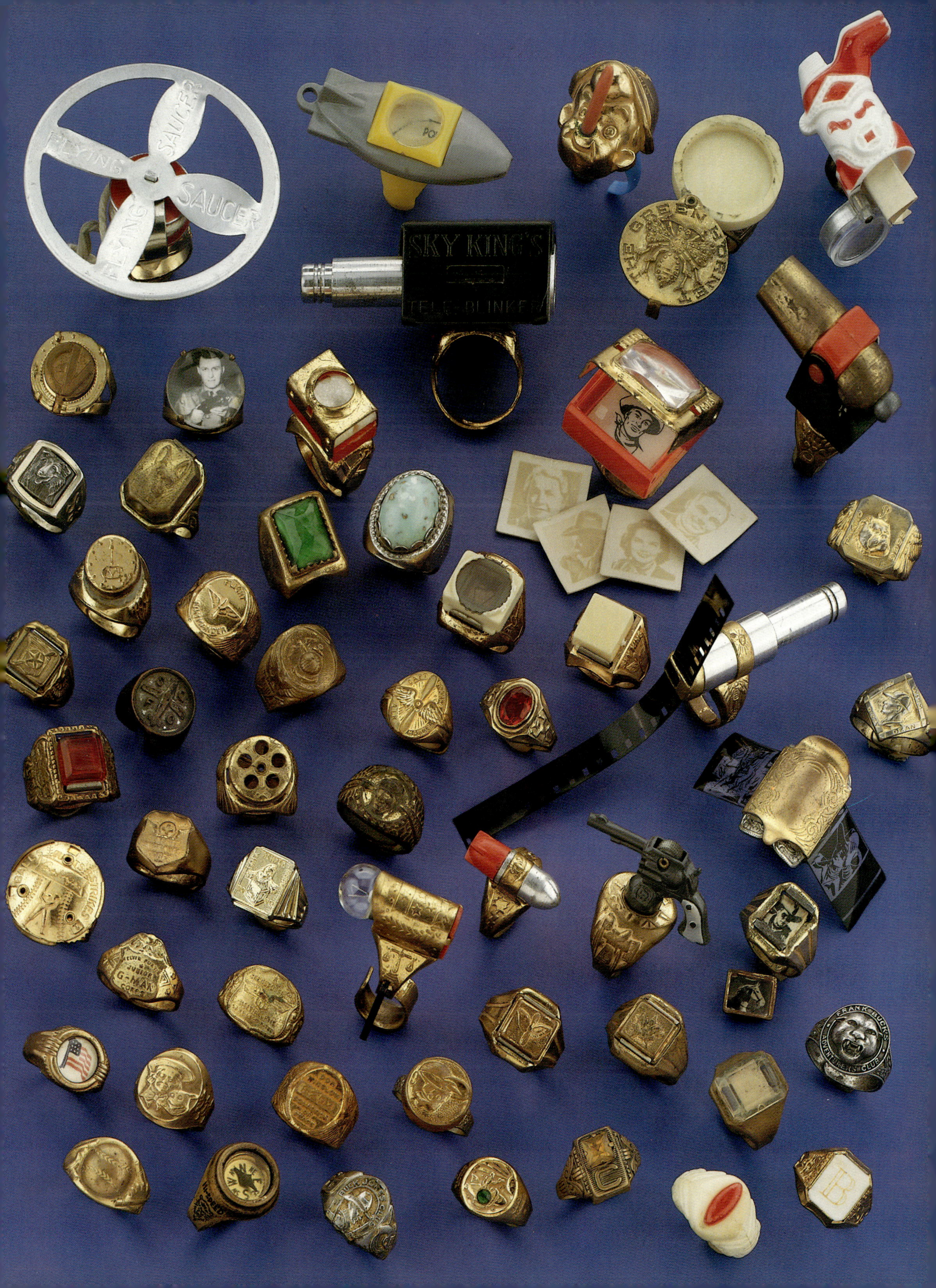
FLYING SAUCER
FLYING SAUCER
SKY KING'S

The Shadow
blue coal
HERE'S YOUR NEW "TALKING" STATIONERY
IT'S So Easy TO HEAT with blue coal
CUDAHY FUEL CO.
YOU, TOO, WILL GET BETTER HEAT AND GREATER COMFORT IF YOU HEAT YOUR HOME THE EASY WAY WITH—
'blue coal'
LLANERCH LUMBER & COAL CO.
blue coal MAKES HOME HEATING Easy as ABC
CUDAHY FUEL CO.
'blue coal'
THIS May BE GOOD?
YOU KNOW THIS IS GOOD!
CUDAHY FUEL CO.
HEATING OUR HOME WAS NEVER SO EASY—WE USE 'blue coal'
THE PEOPLES COAL CO.
NO NEED TO GUESS OR GAMBLE WHEN BUYING FUEL! SAVE AND BE SAFE with 'blue coal'
THE PEOPLES COAL COMPANY
The TARZAN JUNGLE MAP and TREASURE HUNT
OFFICIAL HANDBOOK
Orphan Annie's SECRET GUARD
WARNING!
NEW! 1942 Official Handbook!
SAFETY GUARD
CAPTAIN SPARKS
ORPHAN ANNIE
BIGGER AND BETTER THAN EVER!
THE ADVENTURES OF Little Orphan Annie COMICS
ORPHAN ANNIE AND MR. GUDGE --- ORPHAN ANNIE AND THE GREAT AM --- THE HURRICANE KIDS --- THE ADVENTURES OF CAPTAIN SPARKS --- MAGIC TRICKS, GAMES, PUZZLES!
THE ADVENTURES OF Little Orphan Annie COMICS
ORPHAN ANNIE AND THE KIDNAPPERS MAGIC MORRO THE MYSTERY MAN ADVENTURES OF CAPTAIN SPARKS
THE ADVENTURES OF Little Orphan Annie COMICS
ORPHAN ANNIE AND THE RESCUE MAGIC MORRO THE MYSTERY MAN CAPT. SPARKS' THRILLING ADVENTURES
Tom Mix COMICS
TOM MIX COMICS
RALSTON STRAIGHT SHOOTERS
TOM MIX COMICS
TOM MIX COMICS
TOM MIX COMICS
TOM MIX COMICS
TOM MIX COMICS
TOM MIX COMICS
TOM MIX COMICS
TOM MIX COMMANDOS COMICS
TOM MIX COMMANDOS COMICS
TOM MIX COMMANDOS COMICS

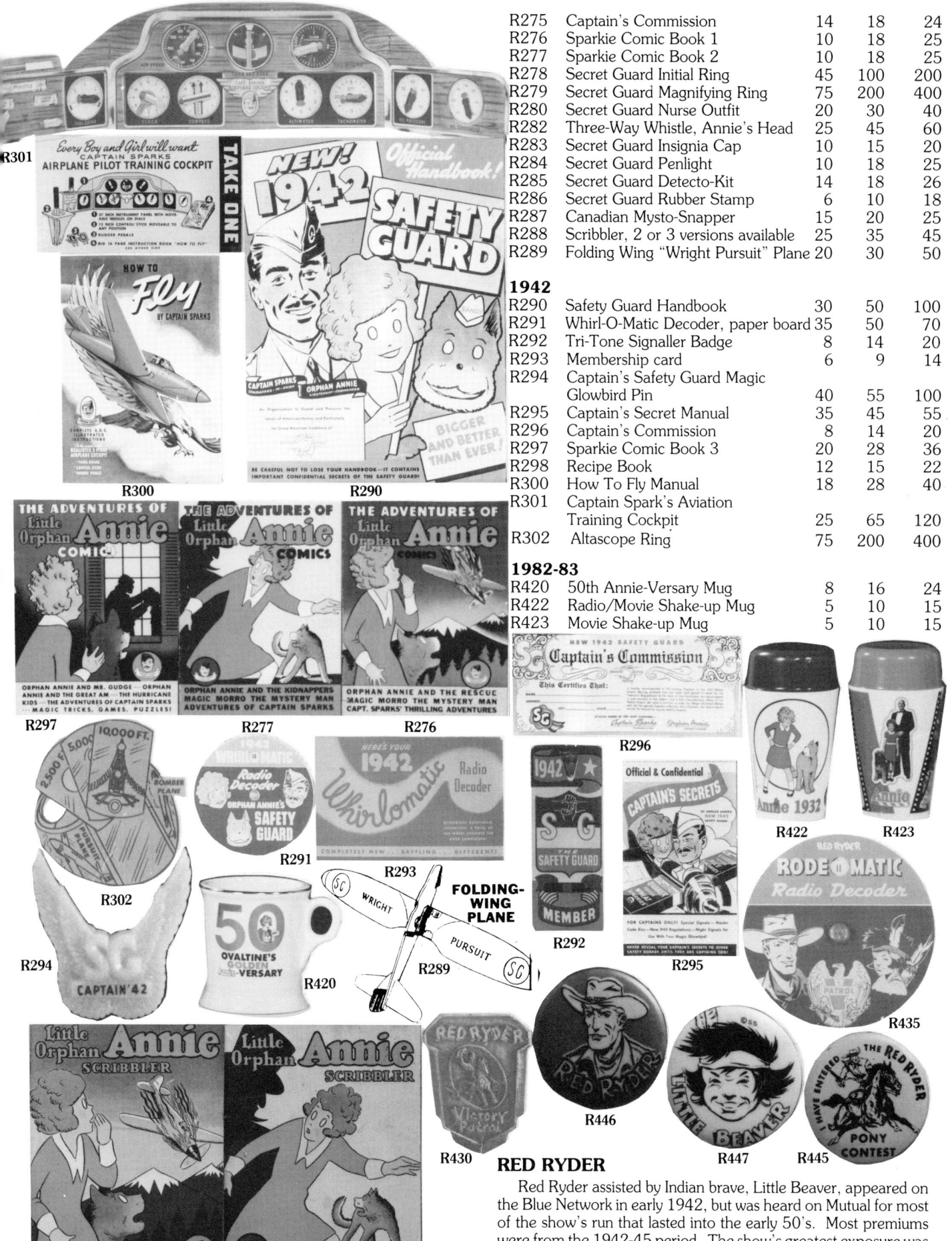

R275	Captain's Commission	14	18	24
R276	Sparkie Comic Book 1	10	18	25
R277	Sparkie Comic Book 2	10	18	25
R278	Secret Guard Initial Ring	45	100	200
R279	Secret Guard Magnifying Ring	75	200	400
R280	Secret Guard Nurse Outfit	20	30	40
R282	Three-Way Whistle, Annie's Head	25	45	60
R283	Secret Guard Insignia Cap	10	15	20
R284	Secret Guard Penlight	10	18	25
R285	Secret Guard Detecto-Kit	14	18	26
R286	Secret Guard Rubber Stamp	6	10	18
R287	Canadian Mysto-Snapper	15	20	25
R288	Scribbler, 2 or 3 versions available	25	35	45
R289	Folding Wing "Wright Pursuit" Plane	20	30	50

1942

R290	Safety Guard Handbook	30	50	100
R291	Whirl-O-Matic Decoder, paper board	35	50	70
R292	Tri-Tone Signaller Badge	8	14	20
R293	Membership card	6	9	14
R294	Captain's Safety Guard Magic Glowbird Pin	40	55	100
R295	Captain's Secret Manual	35	45	55
R296	Captain's Commission	8	14	20
R297	Sparkie Comic Book 3	20	28	36
R298	Recipe Book	12	15	22
R300	How To Fly Manual	18	28	40
R301	Captain Spark's Aviation Training Cockpit	25	65	120
R302	Altascope Ring	75	200	400

1982-83

R420	50th Annie-Versary Mug	8	16	24
R422	Radio/Movie Shake-up Mug	5	10	15
R423	Movie Shake-up Mug	5	10	15

RED RYDER

Red Ryder assisted by Indian brave, Little Beaver, appeared on the Blue Network in early 1942, but was heard on Mutual for most of the show's run that lasted into the early 50's. Most premiums were from the 1942-45 period. The show's greatest exposure was in the West Coast where it was sponsored by Langendorf Bread.

		Good	Fine	Mint
R430	Member Pin	10	14	18
R431	Sliding Decoder, paper	20	35	75
R435	Rodeomatic Decoder, paper	20	35	75
R440	Good Luck Token (J.C. Penney)	2	6	10
R445	Pony Contest Pin	6	8	15
R446	Red Ryder Pinback	10	20	30
R447	Little Beaver Pinback	10	20	30
R450	Daisy Plastic Arrowhead	10	20	30

RENFREW OF THE MOUNTED

"Renfrew of the Mounted" was sponsored by Wonder Bread on CBS from 1936 to 1940. Heard three-times-a-week, "Renfrew" dramatized tales of the Canadian Red Coats and how they always got their man.

		Good	Fine	Mint
R470	Photo of Renfrew	5	7	10
R472	Cello Photo Pinback	2	3	4
R475	Map of Wonder Valley	25	35	55
R478	Handbook for His Friends	20	24	28
R479	Around the Campfire w/Carol & David	15	18	24

RIN TIN TIN

Rin Tin Tin was the silent screen's first canine movie star and was featured on the radio in 1923 and made over 40 movies before his death in 1932. There was a photo and perhaps some other movie premiums from that era. Premiums listed below are from the 1954 to 1956 TV show sponsored by Nabisco. In this version the German shepherd, Rinty, was the constant companion of a boy named Rusty who has been adopted by the Fighting Blue Devils of the 101st Cavalry B Company based at Fort Apache. Other lead characters were Lt. Rip Masters, Sgt. O'Hara and Cpl. Boone. The stories were set around the mid-1800's. Each episode brought new peril to one of our friends only to have Rin Tin Tin save the day. Cheerios did one promotion with three different package back editions to make Fort Apache and a mail-in offer for Marx type plastic figures.

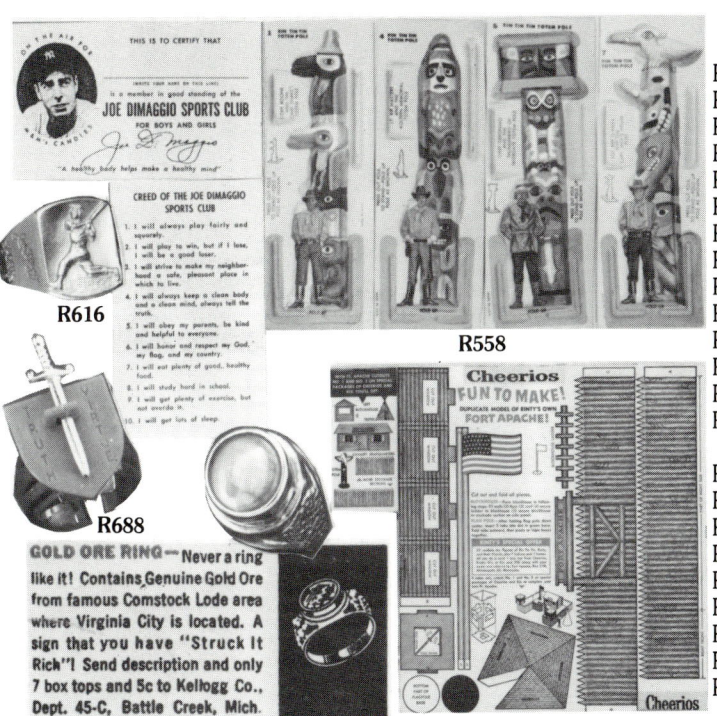

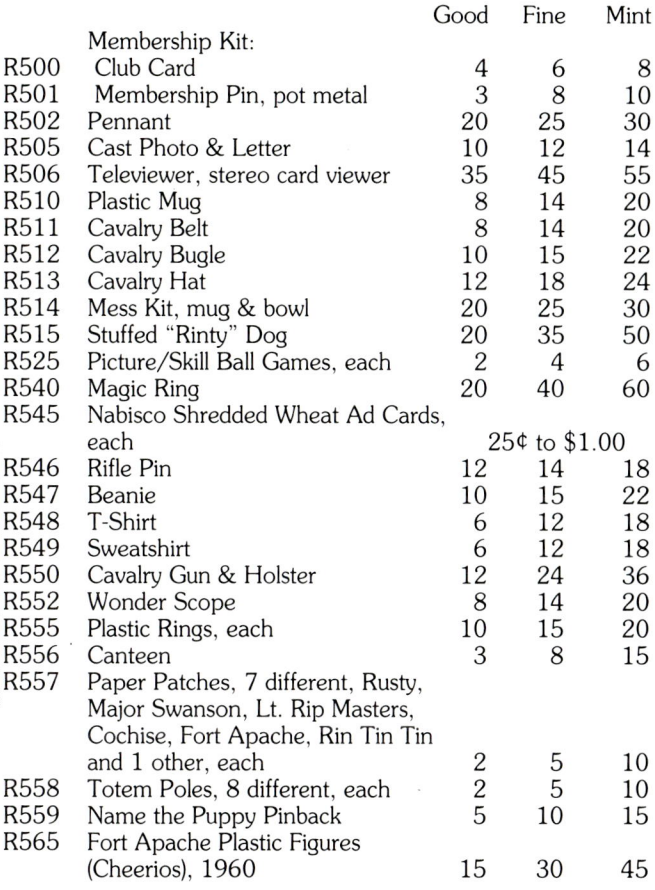

		Good	Fine	Mint
	Membership Kit:			
R500	Club Card	4	6	8
R501	Membership Pin, pot metal	3	8	10
R502	Pennant	20	25	30
R505	Cast Photo & Letter	10	12	14
R506	Televiewer, stereo card viewer	35	45	55
R510	Plastic Mug	8	14	20
R511	Cavalry Belt	8	14	20
R512	Cavalry Bugle	10	15	22
R513	Cavalry Hat	12	18	24
R514	Mess Kit, mug & bowl	20	25	30
R515	Stuffed "Rinty" Dog	20	35	50
R525	Picture/Skill Ball Games, each	2	4	6
R540	Magic Ring	20	40	60
R545	Nabisco Shredded Wheat Ad Cards, each		25¢ to $1.00	
R546	Rifle Pin	12	14	18
R547	Beanie	10	15	22
R548	T-Shirt	6	12	18
R549	Sweatshirt	6	12	18
R550	Cavalry Gun & Holster	12	24	36
R552	Wonder Scope	8	14	20
R555	Plastic Rings, each	10	15	20
R556	Canteen	3	8	15
R557	Paper Patches, 7 different, Rusty, Major Swanson, Lt. Rip Masters, Cochise, Fort Apache, Rin Tin Tin and 1 other, each	2	5	10
R558	Totem Poles, 8 different, each	2	5	10
R559	Name the Puppy Pinback	5	10	15
R565	Fort Apache Plastic Figures (Cheerios), 1960	15	30	45

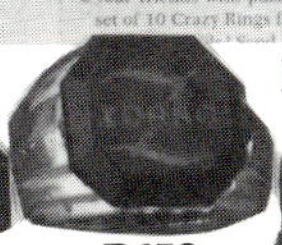

RINGS, MISCELLANEOUS

Premium rings have been the favorite category for collectors. Some of the most interesting rings, however, are not character related or were offered by a character not featured elsewhere in this book. There are even more than those listed, but an effort was made to include many of the major ones.

		Good	Fine	Mint
R602	Gold Ore Ring (Kellogg's) (also used for a Lone Ranger test)	100	200	300
R604	China Clipper	8	15	23
R605	Devil Dogs	20	35	50
R610	Compass Ring, 1947 Nabisco	12	18	24
R615	Ted Williams Baseball Ring, 1948 (Nabisco)	45	75	150
R616	Joe Dimaggio Sports Club (M&M's)	30	60	90
R620	Fireball Twin Explorer, 1948 (Post Grape Nuts)	15	22	30
R625	Roger Wilco Magni-Ray, 1948 (Power House)	12	18	24
R630	Roger Wilco Rescue Ring	15	35	50
R635	Donald Duck "Living Toy", 1949 (PEP)	30	70	150
R640	Andy Pafco Ball/Strike, 1949 (Muffets)	20	35	50
R643	Tim Ring, 1949-50	10	18	25
R645	Saddle Initial Ring	5	10	15
R646	Whistle/Bomb Ring	50	100	150
R650	Lionel Model Railroad Printing Ring	10	20	30
R655	Popsicle Boot Ring, 1951	20	35	50
R657	Zorro Logo Ring	5	10	15
R658	Zorro Big Z Ring	5	10	15
R660	Rocket to Moon Ring w/3 Rockets, 1951 (Kix)	40	85	135

R640
R552
R665
R666
R667
R635
R646
R630
R643
R556
R661
R685
R660
R620
R605
R604
R645
R687
R686
R900-926
R960
R680
R860-895
R951
R851
R814
R815
R927

108

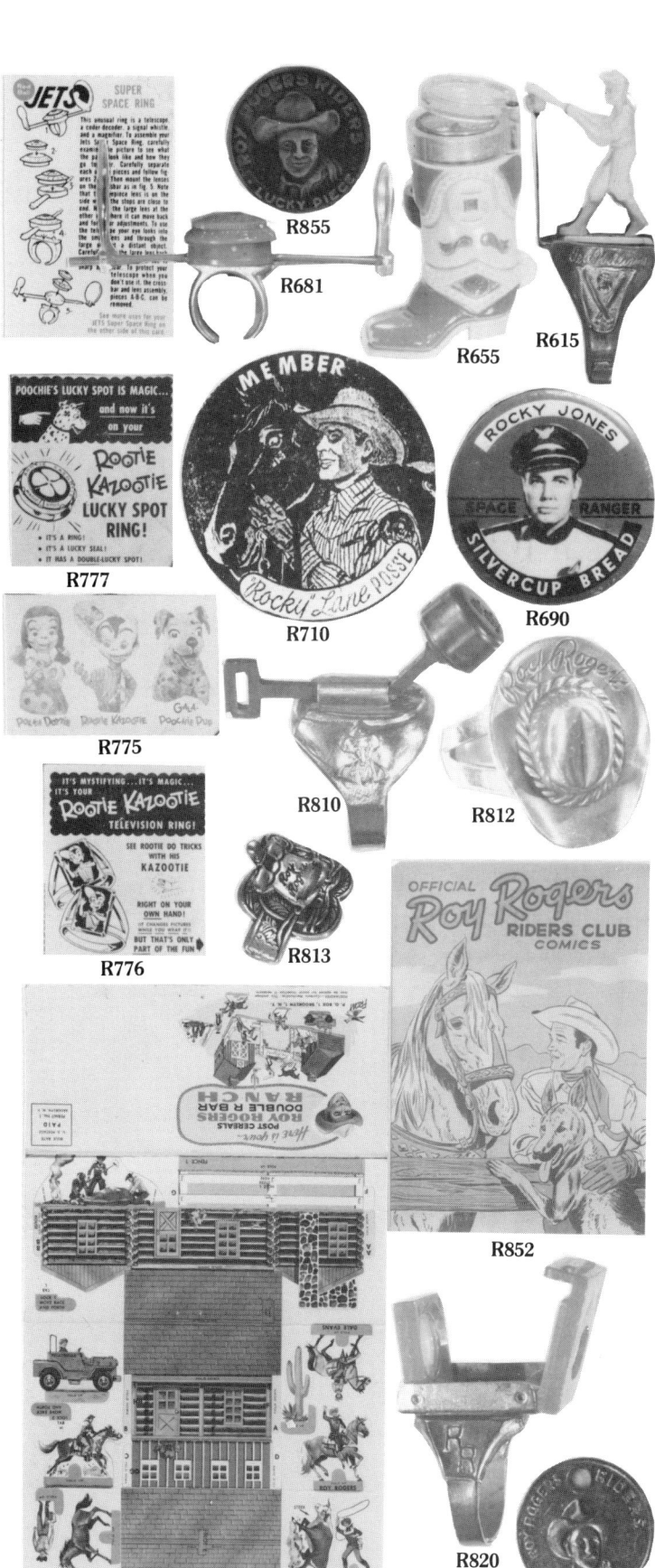

		Good	Fine	Mint
R661	Major Mars Rocket (film) Ring Complete w/film (Popsicle)	50	150	300
R662	Disney Plastic Set, 8 (Sugar Jets), each	5	15	25
R665	Snap Ring (Kellogg's)	50	100	150
R666	Crackle Ring (Kellogg's)	50	100	150
R667	Pop Ring (Kellogg's)	50	100	150
R668	Wyatt Earp Marshall's Ring	5	15	25
R669	Crazy Rings, 10 (Quaker), each	5	10	15
R680	PF Decoder Ring (PF Tennis Shoes)	10	20	30
R681	Red Ball Decoder/Microscore Ring	8	12	20
R685	Davy Crockett Compass Ring	10	22	35
R686	Bazooka Joe Printing Initial Ring	10	20	35
R687	Pinocchio Ring	50	100	150
R688	Sword in Stone (Shoe Polish)	15	25	35

ROCKY JONES, SPACE RANGER

This was a short-lived TV show c.1953. The program is probably best known from the Silvercup Bread pinback button which is fairly common

R690	Membership Pinback	4	8	12

ROCKY LANE

Cowboy star Rocky Lane was the subject of at least two premiums. Both mentioned were offered by Carnation Malted Milk powder. A sundial watch, exactly like the Frank Buck's with the name removed, was also offered.

		Good	Fine	Mint
R705	Sundial Watch, no name	10	20	30
R710	Patch	10	20	30

ROOTIE KAZOOTIE

"Rootie Kazootie" was an early TV puppet show for kids where the puppets were kids dealing with the same types of joy, sadness, and problems the real kids had to face. In addition to Rootie, there was Polka Dottie, Gala Poochie, and El Squeako Mouse. The names may be your first hint the situations weren't exactly played straight.

		Good	Fine	Mint
R775	Membership Card	5	10	15
R776	Rootie Kazootie Television Ring	10	20	30
R777	Rootie Kazootie Lucky Spot Ring	10	20	30

ROY ROGERS

The post-war 40's gave rise to a new age of cowboys. Gene Autry and Roy Rogers sang on radio and in the movies. Hopalong Cassidy boomed into fame in 1950, almost too late for radio. Of the three giants, Roy Rogers and his horse Trigger made the biggest splash as far as radio premiums were concerned. His show first aired in 1944 for Goodyear. The show changed format in 1948 when Quaker Oats took over and began issuing premiums. Post Cereals became sponsor in 1952 and issued many in-pack items. Dodge was the final sponsor in 1955.

		Good	Fine	Mint
1948				
R810	Branding Iron Ring w/black cap	20	40	60
R812	Sterling Silver Hat Ring, signed across the brim	50	100	150
R813	Signed Sterling Saddle Ring	40	80	130
R814	Roy Rogers Contest	5	10	15
R815	Quaker Oats Contest Post Card	4	8	10

109

1949
R820	Microscope Ring	20	30	40
R821	Win Trip to Hollywood Contest Ad	5	10	15

1950
R830	Deputy Star Badge, secret compartment and whistle on back	12	20	30
R833	Plastic Toby Mug of Roy	4	7	10
R834	Plastic Toby Mug of Quaker	2	3	4

1951
R840	Humming Lariat	10	25	40

1952
	Riders Club			
R849	Riders Club Ad	5	10	15
R850	Club Card	6	8	10
R851	Tab	15	25	35
R852	Comic	10	22	30
R853	Color Photo of Roy & Trigger	6	8	10
R855	Lucky Coin, small	4	6	8
R856	Lucky Coin, large	5	7	9

1953-55
R860-895	Post Pop-Out Cards, 36, each	1	3	5
R900-926	Post Raisin Bran Western Medals, 27, each	1	3	5
R927	Roy Rogers Ring, 12, each	5	15	25
R950	Family Contest Ad	5	10	15
R951	Pinback Set, 15, each	3	6	12
R954	Paint-By-Numbers Set	15	30	45
R955	Sugar Crisp 3-D Photo & Glasses, each	10	15	20
R958	Double R Bar Ranch	15	30	50
R960	Bang Gun (cookies)	5	10	15

"SCOOP" WARD

A one-brand character. The promotion must have been a big success because the only badge known is common.

S100	Badge ("Scoop" Ward Official Reporter News of Youth - Ward's Soft Bun Bread)	3	4	5

SECKATARY HAWKINS

Seckatary Hawkins was the leader of a group of good boys who helped the authorities round up bad boys. The program was based on the comic strip of the same name by Robert F. Schulkers. The motto of the Seck Hawkins Club was "Fair and Square." Ralston cereals sponsored the program during the 1932 season with a "food drink" continuing the show for one more year in 1933.

		Good	Fine	Mint

1932
S110	Membership Button	2	3	4
S111	Fair and Square Spinner	10	15	20
S112	Paperback Novel - Ghost of Lake Tapaho	15	22	30
S113	Comic Strip Reprint Booklet - The Red Runners	20	28	35
S114	Good Luck Coin	8	12	16

SECRET THREE, THE

"The Secret Three" was one of radio's earliest shows . . . probably heard weekends only on a regional basis. The sponsor was National's Three Minute Oats cereal. Hence the obvious name

110

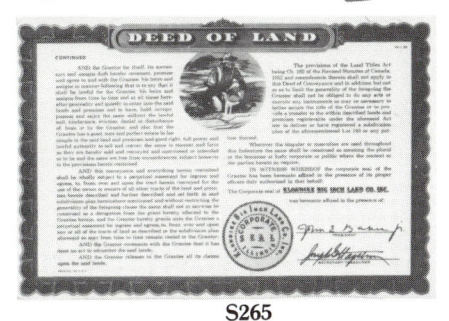

connection. The lead characters were juvenile detectives Ben Potter (Chief), Jack Williams (1st Lt) and Mary Lou Davis (2nd Lt). The premiums included an assortment of disguises and detective equipment.

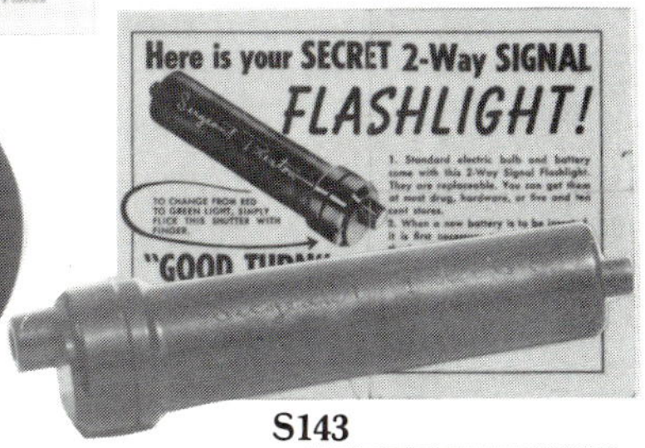

		Good	Fine	Mint
S130	Badge	5	12	20
S131	Handbook	10	15	25
S132	Equipment List	5	10	15
S133	Lieutenant's Special Chevron	5	10	15

SGT. PRESTON (THE CHALLENGE OF THE YUKON)

Sgt. Preston and his wonder dog, King, aired for over ten years beginning in 1947 . . . first on radio and then on TV. The sponsor for nearly the entire run was Quaker Puffed Wheat and Quaker Puffed Rice . . . from 1948 until the show left the radio in 1955. The same WXYZ (Detroit) team that created "The Lone Ranger" and "The Green Hornet" was responsible for developing Sergeant and Yukon King. The formula was almost identical in all three. The classical music chosen to create images of the Yukon Territory was the stirring Donna Diana Overture. The dramatization would then unfold relying on plenty of sound effects to communicate the action. In the end there was the usual "after-the-bad-guys-are-in-jail" chat (and one last bark from King). Certain premiums were identical to those offered on the Gabby Hayes TV show. These are marked with an asterisk. The Quaker Model Farm and other package back cut-outs were advertised on the program, but are not included because they were totally unrelated.

The most successful promotion of the series was the "Deed to One Square Inch of Yukon Land" reported to be in "Gold Rush Country." Some people amassed large holdings of these deeds and tried to consolidate them into a claim in their own name. Actually, it was subsequently reported in the Wall Street Journal the land was never owned by Quaker and not their's to give away. The deeds say as much in the small print. Quaker merely leased the land for 10 years for use in the promotion. A million deeds were packed in cereal boxes and then offered in ads after the supply was exhausted. The deed was also offered along with the Klondike Land Pouch which contained actual dirt.

		Good	Fine	Mint
1949				
S140	Photo, 8-1/2" x 11", b&w	10	15	20
S143	Signal Flashlight	20	30	40
S145	Postcard Size b&w Photo	5	10	15
S150	Yukon Trail - 59 cardboard models from 8 different Quaker Puffed Wheat and Rice boxes, complete, cut-out	100	150	200
	Yukon Trail Package Backs, each	15	25	35
	Adventure Games, package backs:			
S160	Great Yukon River Canoe Race	10	15	20
S161	Sgt. Preston Gets His Man	10	15	20
S162	Dog Sled Race	10	15	20
S163	Dog Card Series 1, Yukon King, Miniature French Poodle, Chihuahua, Saluki, Smooth Fox Terrier, Brussels Griffon, Collie, English Foxhound, Pointer, Doberman Pinscher, Airedale, Cocker Spaniel, Bloodhound, Beagle, Shetland Sheepdog, Dalmatian, Irish Wolfhound, West Highland White Terrier, each			50¢ to $1.00
S164	Dog Card Series 2, Yukon King, Great Dane, Greyhound, Otterhound, Irish Setter, Boxer, Pomeranian, Chow Chow, Dachshund, Bull Terrier, Boston Terrier, English Bulldog, Miniature			

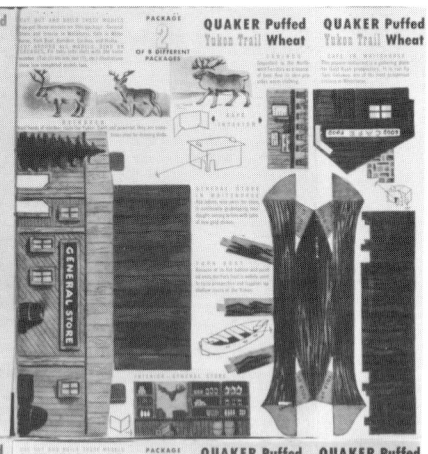

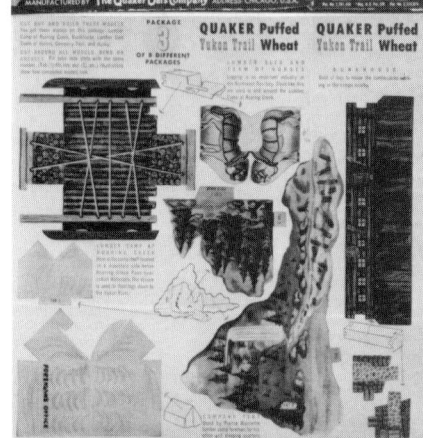

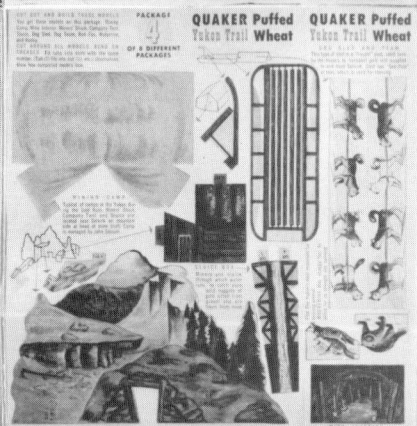

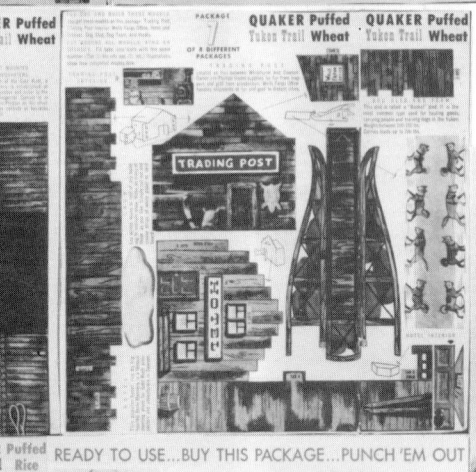

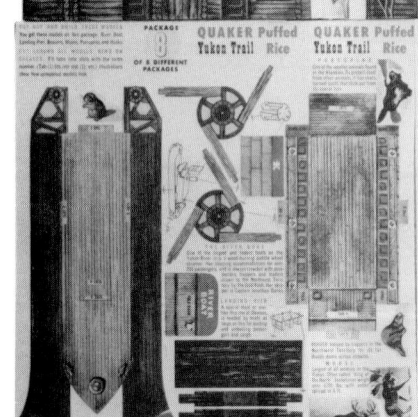

S151-158

S204

S180

S182

Schnauzer, Golden Retriever, German
Shepherd, Scottish Terrier, Kerry Blue
Terrier, American Foxhound, each   50¢ to $1.00

1950

S175	Yukon Adventure Picture Cards, 36 to set, each	25¢	to	$1.00
S180	Mounted Police Whistle w/cord	15	22	30
S181	Contest Postcard	10	15	20
S182	Contest Winner Poster	100	200	300

1952-54

S201-203	Pictures to Color Package, 3, each	7	13	20
S204	Trail Goggles Package Back	10	15	20
S205	Western Gun Collection, 5 *	10	15	20
S206	Movie Viewer *	15	18	22
S207	Western Wagons, 5 *	30	35	40
S208	Antique Car Set, 5 *	10	20	30
S210	Totem Pole Collection: Thunderbird, Fight w/Otters, Burial Pole, Killer Whale, Sun and Raven, complete set	25	40	55
	Records, 45 or 78 RPM (S255-S257)			
S255	Challenge of the Yukon/Maple Leaf Forever	1	2	3
S256	Case of the Orphan Dog	2	4	6
S257	Case of the Indian Rebellion	2	4	6
S259	Gold Ore Detector	35	48	60
S260	Pedometer	15	20	25
S262	N. America Big Game Trophies, set	5	12	18
S263	Prospector's Camp Stove, unmarked	50	75	100
S264	Prospector's Camp Tent, unmakred	50	75	100

		Good	Fine	Mint

1955

S265	Yukon Square Inch Land Deed	4	8	12
S266	Klondike Land Pouch	25	35	50
S267	Map of Yukon Territory, in color	15	22	30
S269	Distance Finder	30	40	50

1956

S270	Membership Button	100	250	400
S271	Ten-in-One Trail Kit	75	150	250
	Pocket Comics, 4, 2 sizes: 5" or 7" (S272-S275)			

113

S272	How He Became a Mountie	8	12	18
S273	How Yukon King Saved Him From The Wolves	8	12	18
S274	How He Became a Sergeant	8	12	18
S275	How He Found Yukon King	8	12	18
S278	Color Photo of TV Preston, Richard Simmons	8	12	16
S280	Yukon Adventure Story Cards, set of 36 (same as S150, but copyrighted in 1956), each		25¢ to $1.00	
S281	T-Shirt	10	25	50

SHADOW, THE

In 1930 the announcer/narrator for mystery broadcasts based on stories from Street and Smith's Detective Story Magazine was characterized as the Shadow. So successful was the character that S & S started the Shadow Magazine in 1931. In 1934 the character was featured in roles within the program. However, it wasn't until 1936-37's season that the classic Lamond Cranston, Margo Lane, the "ability to cloud men's minds" and the rest of the package was developed. The Shadow Club items were premiums offered by the magazine. The others were radio related. Blue Coal was the sponsor during most of this period and until the late 40's. Various other companies picked up the program through the end of 1954 when it left the air. In addition to the items listed below, sample copies of the Shadow Magazine of 9/38 were also offered on the air, as were several booklets on coal and home heating. The Dec 15, 1940 issue showed Shadow store items which could also be ordered through the mail. Included were the Shadow pencil lite, disguise kit, mask, Tec-To-Lite flashlight, "Shadow Knows" stationery, game, official hat and cape.

		Good	Fine	Mint
S350	Shadow Photo	20	40	60
S352	Shadow Club Stud or Pin	75	120	145
S353	Shadow Club Rubber Stamp	25	35	50
S355	Blue Coal, Glo-in-the-Dark Plastic Ring, 1941	100	200	350
S356	Blue Coal Ink Blotter, four-color, many versions	5	8	12

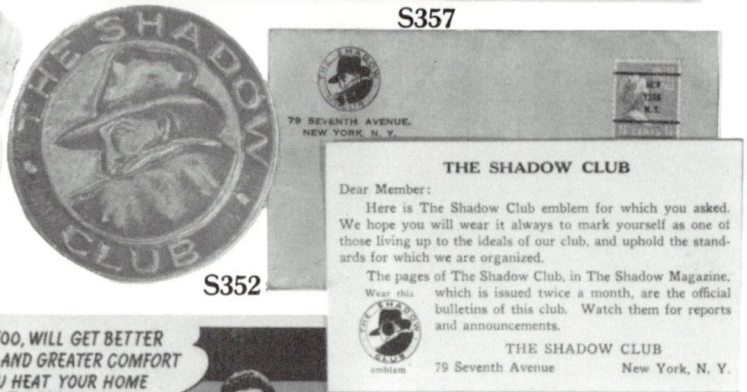

114

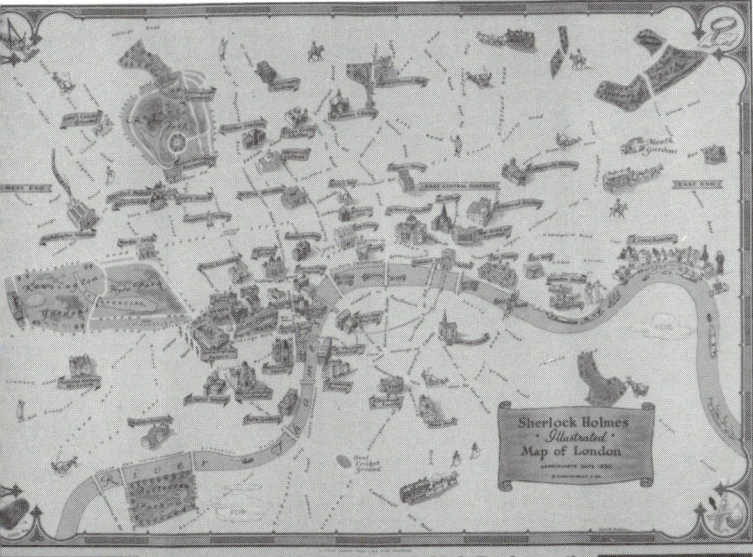

S357	Envelope Stickers, each		5	10	15
S370	Blue Coal Match Book, 3 versions, each		10	20	45
S375	Crocodile Plastic Ring, black stone, 1947 (Carey Salt)		50	150	250

SHERLOCK HOLMES

Sir Arthur Conon Doyle's master of deduction seems to work well in just about every medium. The show first aired on Oct 20, 1930 and was broadcast almost weekly (save the 1937-38 period) until 1950. In 1939 Basil Rathbone and Nigel Bruce recreated their movie roles on the airwaves and the popularity of the program climbed until 1946. In early years the show had many sponsors. George Washington Coffee offered the two books in 1933. The Household Finance map is copyrighted 1936.

S401	Collection of Sherlock Holmes Stories, Vol. 1	5	15	25
S402	Collection of Sherlock Holmes Stories, Vol. 2	5	15	25
S405	Map	20	40	70

SINGING LADY, THE

Irene Wicker as the Kellogg's Singing Story Lady was first heard on NBC Blue in 1932. She assumed a fairy princess type role as she read and acted the voices of classic fairy tales and other children's stories. Occasional songs were worked into the format. The program remained popular into the 40's. Artist Vernon Grant designed most of the premiums.

		Good	Fine	Mint
1932-34				
S442	Mother Goose Story Book	8	12	16
S444	Nursery Song and Rhyme Book	4	6	10
S445	Mother Goose Package Backs, each	2	4	6
1935				
	Mother Goose Film Booklet:			
S450	The Old Woman in the Shoe	3	5	8
S451	Tommy Tucker's Birthday Party	3	5	8
S452	Old King Cole	3	5	8
S453	Little Bo-Peep	3	5	8
S454	Song Book	5	10	15
1936				
S460	Party Kit Booklet	3	6	10
S465	Punch-out Circus	20	35	50

SKIPPY

The "Skippy" radio program was loosely based on the comic strip of the same name by Percy Crosby. It was broadcast from 1931 to 1934, sponsored the first two seasons by Wheaties and the final one by Phillips' Dental Magnesia Toothpaste. In the radio version, Skippy was an often misunderstood boy who got in and out of trouble with ease and agility. His friends were called Sooky and Carol. It aired daily from 5:00 to 5:15 PM on NBC.

		Good	Fine	Mint
S468	Picture	10	20	30
S469	Christmas Card	8	15	25
S470	S.S.S.S. Cello Pinback	3	4	5
S471	Secret Code Folder	10	18	25
S472	Life Membership Certificate	8	12	16
S473	Secret Pledge	10	15	20
S474	Wheaties Score Card & Captain Application	10	15	20
S475	Captain's Badge	10	30	50

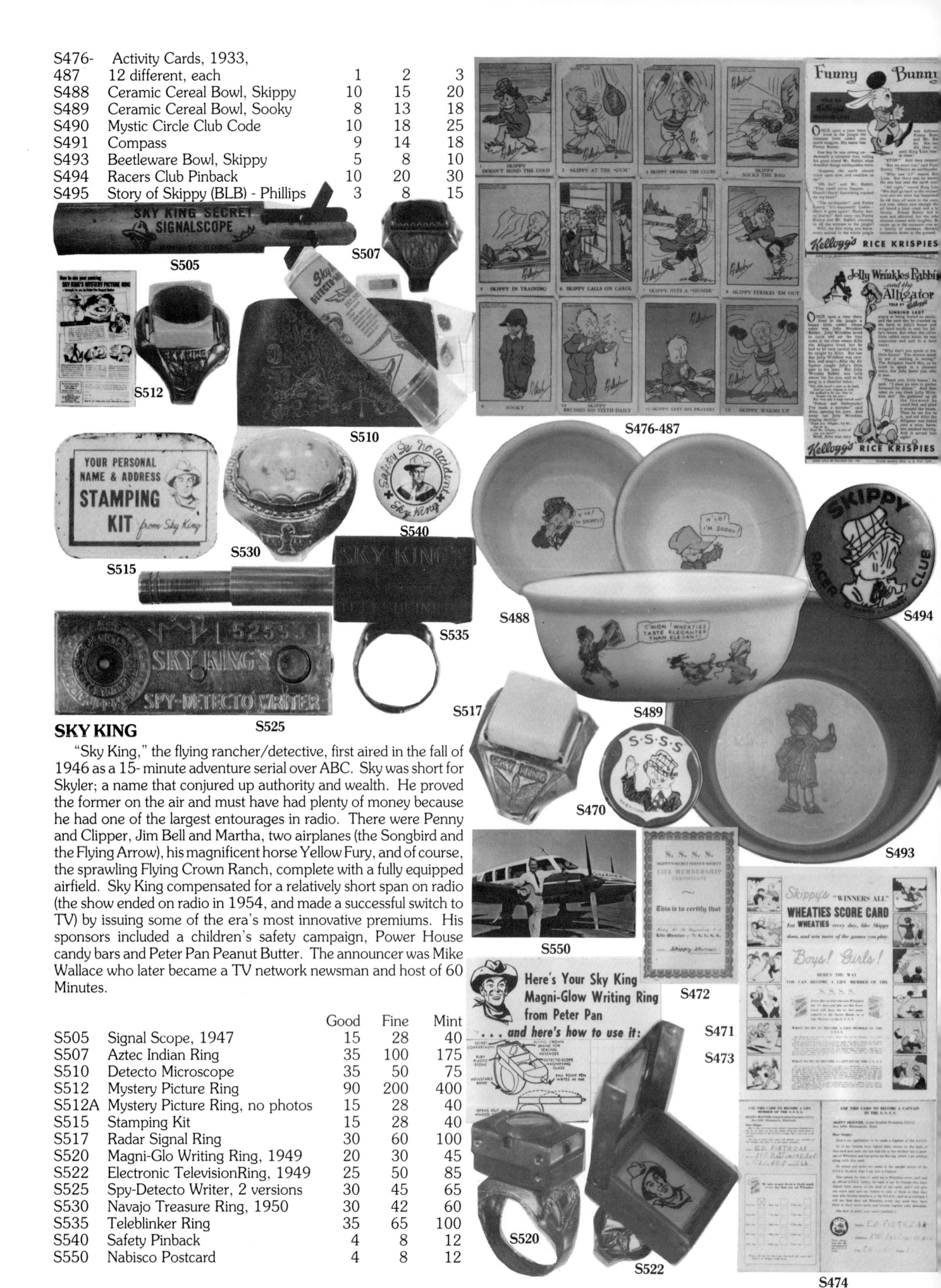

S476-487	Activity Cards, 1933, 12 different, each		1	2	3
S488	Ceramic Cereal Bowl, Skippy		10	15	20
S489	Ceramic Cereal Bowl, Sooky		8	13	18
S490	Mystic Circle Club Code		10	18	25
S491	Compass		9	14	18
S493	Beetleware Bowl, Skippy		5	8	10
S494	Racers Club Pinback		10	20	30
S495	Story of Skippy (BLB) - Phillips		3	8	15

SKY KING

"Sky King," the flying rancher/detective, first aired in the fall of 1946 as a 15- minute adventure serial over ABC. Sky was short for Skyler; a name that conjured up authority and wealth. He proved the former on the air and must have had plenty of money because he had one of the largest entourages in radio. There were Penny and Clipper, Jim Bell and Martha, two airplanes (the Songbird and the Flying Arrow), his magnificent horse Yellow Fury, and of course, the sprawling Flying Crown Ranch, complete with a fully equipped airfield. Sky King compensated for a relatively short span on radio (the show ended on radio in 1954, and made a successful switch to TV) by issuing some of the era's most innovative premiums. His sponsors included a children's safety campaign, Power House candy bars and Peter Pan Peanut Butter. The announcer was Mike Wallace who later became a TV network newsman and host of 60 Minutes.

		Good	Fine	Mint
S505	Signal Scope, 1947	15	28	40
S507	Aztec Indian Ring	35	100	175
S510	Detecto Microscope	35	50	75
S512	Mystery Picture Ring	90	200	400
S512A	Mystery Picture Ring, no photos	15	28	40
S515	Stamping Kit	15	28	40
S517	Radar Signal Ring	30	60	100
S520	Magni-Glo Writing Ring, 1949	20	30	45
S522	Electronic TelevisionRing, 1949	25	50	85
S525	Spy-Detecto Writer, 2 versions	30	45	65
S530	Navajo Treasure Ring, 1950	30	42	60
S535	Teleblinker Ring	35	65	100
S540	Safety Pinback	4	8	12
S550	Nabisco Postcard	4	8	12

116

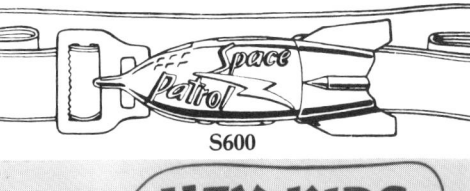

SPACE PATROL

Commander Buzz Corey's first Space Patrol mission for the United Planets of the Universe was heard on ABC in 1950. Eventually the programs were simulcast on ABC-TV under the sponsorship of Ralston, the greatest premium believer in orbit. A high spot on the run was the discovery of "Planet X." It became the focus of a contest and subject of premiums. The laughs were provided by Cadet Happy . . . female interest by Carol (Buzz's girlfriend) and Tonga (a converted villainess). Dr. Rylard Scarno and Prince Bacharatti were the evil masterminds that surfaced most often in the 30-minute strip of continuous adventures. Their modest ambition, as usual, was to dominate the entire 30th Century universe. Terra, a man-made planet slightly larger than Earth, was the headquarter base for the Space Patrol. The last season, 1954-55, was co-presented by Nestle's Chocolate and Weather Bird Shoes.

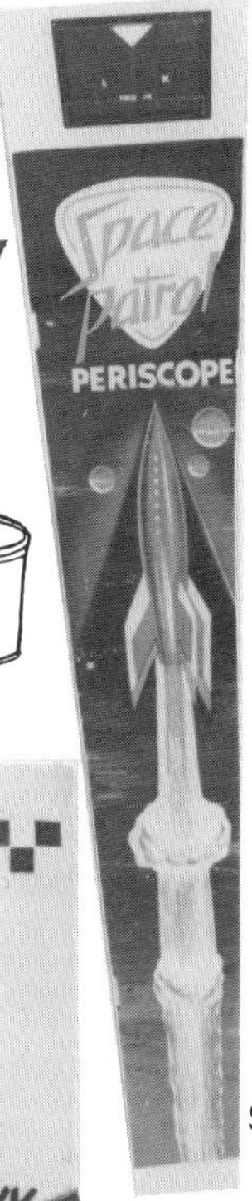

Most Ralston equipment was offered for sale in grocery stores as an immediate purchase incentive as well as the normal box top approach through the mail. Plastic premiums distributed in this manner are available in different color versions. In some cases there was even a subtle design change.

Grand prize in the "Name the Planet" contest was a 35-foot, 1000 pound clubhouse shaped like the Terra V rocketship, including a motor truck to pull it, plus $1,500 cash. First prizes included 250 each: Space Patrol wristwatches, autosonic space rifles, outer space helmets, and Space Patrol emergency kits. The second prize group consisted of 750 Schwinn Varsity bicycles.

		Good	Fine	Mint
S595	Membership Card	10	20	30
S596	Handbook	25	45	80
S597	Handbook, reprint	3	5	6
S598	Badge, plastic	30	100	150
S599	Photo	5	10	15
S600	Decoder Buckle & Belt	50	75	135
S601	Cosmic Smoke Gun, green, long barrel	70	125	180
S602	Cosmic Smoke Gun, red, short barrel	70	125	180
S603	Ring, plastic	200	325	450
S604	Rocket Ship Balloon, in envelope	50	100	150

117

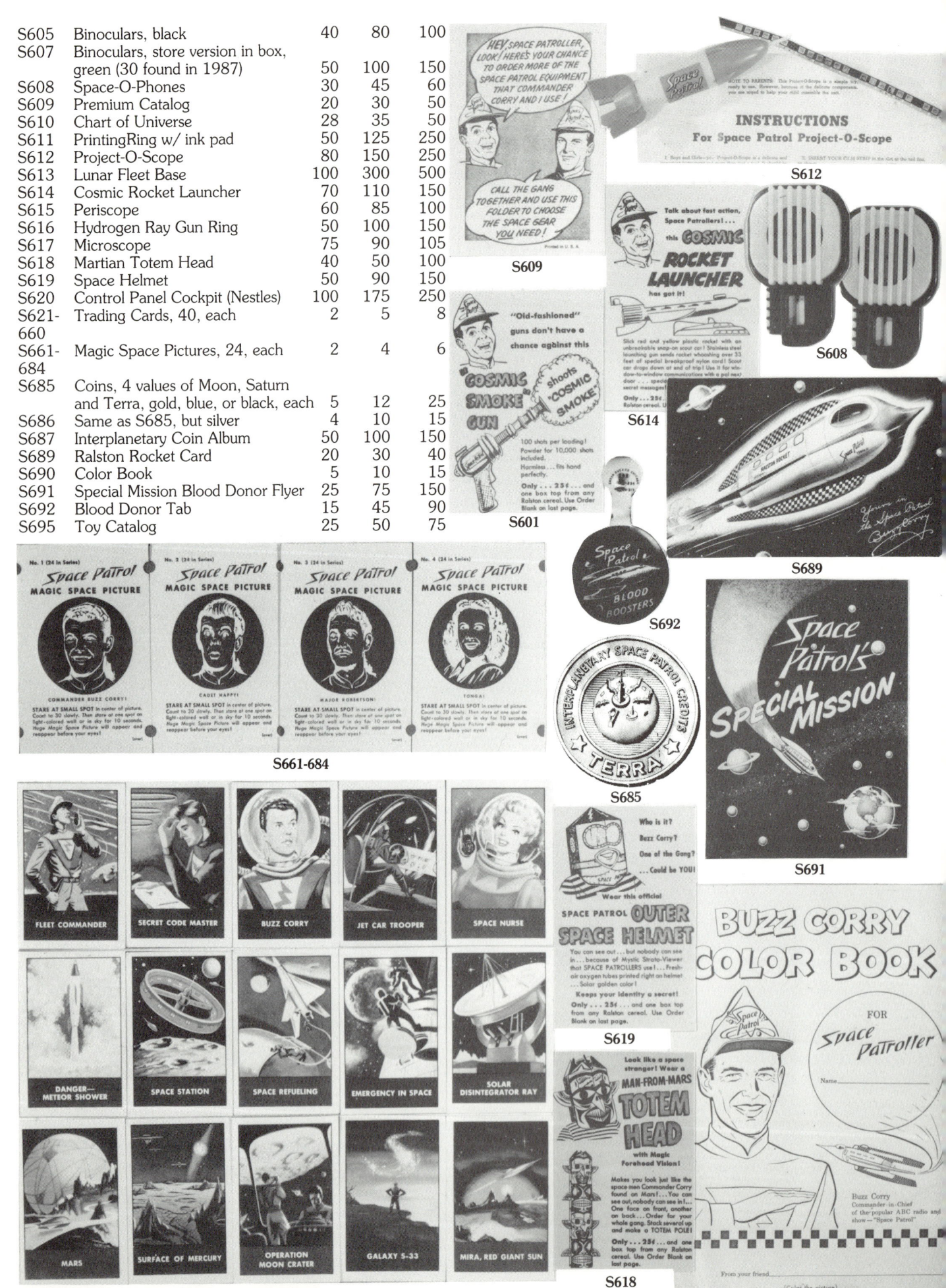

#	Item			
S605	Binoculars, black	40	80	100
S607	Binoculars, store version in box, green (30 found in 1987)	50	100	150
S608	Space-O-Phones	30	45	60
S609	Premium Catalog	20	30	50
S610	Chart of Universe	28	35	50
S611	PrintingRing w/ ink pad	50	125	250
S612	Project-O-Scope	80	150	250
S613	Lunar Fleet Base	100	300	500
S614	Cosmic Rocket Launcher	70	110	150
S615	Periscope	60	85	100
S616	Hydrogen Ray Gun Ring	50	100	150
S617	Microscope	75	90	105
S618	Martian Totem Head	40	50	100
S619	Space Helmet	50	90	150
S620	Control Panel Cockpit (Nestles)	100	175	250
S621-660	Trading Cards, 40, each	2	5	8
S661-684	Magic Space Pictures, 24, each	2	4	6
S685	Coins, 4 values of Moon, Saturn and Terra, gold, blue, or black, each	5	12	25
S686	Same as S685, but silver	4	10	15
S687	Interplanetary Coin Album	50	100	150
S689	Ralston Rocket Card	20	30	40
S690	Color Book	5	10	15
S691	Special Mission Blood Donor Flyer	25	75	150
S692	Blood Donor Tab	15	45	90
S695	Toy Catalog	25	50	75

118

SPEED GIBSON OF THE INTERNATIONAL SECRET POLICE

Straight from the mold of Jimmie Allen, 15-year-old Speed Gibson and his pilot buddy, Barney Dunlap, circled the globe in hot pursuit of the Octopus, an elusive arch criminal. Speed's uncle, Clint Barlow, was described as the best agent I.S.P. ever had and wherever Clint went Speed and Barney were sure to follow. Premiums, however, were uninspired. The show began syndication in 1937, but was short-lived.

		Good	Fine	Mint
S704	Code Book	10	20	30
S705	Flying Police Shield	8	12	16
S710	WINGS Newspaper	10	20	30
S715	Secret Police Badge, green	5	7	9
S717	Plezol Member Badge, red	3	5	8
S725	Shooting Rocket Gyro	5	10	15
S726	Great Clue Hunt Map Game	10	20	30

SPIDER, THE

The Spider, beginning with the Oct 1933 issue, became one of the most popular pulp crime fighters of the 30's lasting 118 issues through the Dec 1943 number. The Spider was the concealed identity of young millionaire, Richard Wentworth. His mission was dealing with criminals who lived comfortably outside the law. Criminals feared his swift and lethal justice. Each victim was left with a crimson spider mark on their foreheads . . . the same mark found on his club ring.

		Good	Fine	Mint
S750	Ring	150	300	500
S751	Membership Card	30	50	70

SPIRIT, THE

Created by Will Eisner, The Spirit is one of the all time classic comic heroes and the subject of an unusual premium promotion. The format of the comic book was firmly established around 1938 and the kids were buying them like wild. Newspapers had included color comic sections for over 20 years, but the idea to include a free "comic book" seemed like a winner. Thus The Spirit comic section first appeared in 1940. It was printed on one full-size page, but designed to fold down to comic book size. These special sections are premiums unto themselves, but at least one premium was created to promote the sections and sent out by the newspapers.

| S755 | Spirit Paper Mask | 50 | 110 | 200 |

SPY SMASHER

Spy Smasher was a comic book hero that came and went with the Second World War. He was around long enough, however, to establish a club and mail out a few premiums.

		Good	Fine	Mint
S760	Victory Battalion Membership Card	4	8	10
S761	Member's Pinback	8	12	15
S762	Photo	20	30	40

STRAIGHT ARROW

Straight Arrow was in reality rancher Steve Adams, who materialized in 1948 and was around until 1954. Unfortunately, the strength of radio was already beginning to fade. It was a strange show to last as many years as it did. None of his adventures, however, could measure up to the point in each broadcast when Steve went to the secret cave to put on the garb of Straight Arrow. He would bolt to the bareback Palomino Fury and thunder from his gold-laden hideaway calling his Comanche war cry "Ken-nah" to right the wrongs of mankind. He was assisted by Packy McCloud, the only other human who knew the true identity of Straight Arrow. Nabisco owned the character and thus the Nabisco copyright appears on many non-premium store items. Some items made by Advertizers Service Division, Inc. were used both as premiums and sold in stores. One contest was held with a Palomino colt as the grand prize.

1949		Good	Fine	Mint
S800	Injun-Nuity Cards - Book 1, 36 cards	10	17	24
S802	Comanche Headband w/Tribe Card and Instructions for Sign Language and Indian Trail Sign	20	25	35
S803	Tom-Tom & Beater	35	70	150
S804	Gold Arrow Ring	20	27	35
S805	Bandana	15	25	40
S810-821	Puzzles (probably not premiums), 12 different, each	3	6	10

1950				
S824	Face Ring	15	28	35
S825	Mystic Wrist Kit, plastic bracelet w/gold arrowhead & cowry shell	30	80	135
S830	Injun-Nuity Cards - Book 2, 36 cards	10	17	24
S833	Tribal Shoulder Patch	20	30	40
S835	Golden Nugget Picture Ring (cave ring) w/pciture	25	65	125
S836	Arrow Tie Clip	10	20	30
S837	Secrets of Indian Lore Manual (Injun-Nuity cards - Books 1 & 2 reproduced in book form)	12	20	30

1951				
S840	Injun-Nuity Cards - Book 3, 36 cards	10	17	25
S843	Rite-A-Lite Arrowhead	30	60	90

1952				
S846	Injun-Nuity Card - Book 4, 36 cards	10	17	25
S847	Puppets, props and scripts for Straight Arrow show	8	13	20

SUPER CIRCUS

ABC-TV first presented "Super Circus" in 1948. The format was sort of a circus-burlesque for kids. It aired to a live audience each Sunday afternoon from the Civic Theater Studios in Chicago. Claude Kirchner was the ringmaster, Mary Hartline led the band and performed in skits with clowns Cliffy, Nicky, and the 12-year-old Scampy. Early sponsors were Canada Dry, Peter Pan Peanut Butter, Curity Bandages, Mars Candies and Weather Bird Shoes. There were animal and other circus acts, but the clown skits and beautiful Mary bouncing as she led the band captured the most attention. Kids sometimes got to join in and were rewarded with the opportunity to dig into penny bowls usually sweetened "with a big half dollar."

		Good	Fine	Mint
S850	Fourth Anniversary Book	10	20	30
S851	Mary Hartline Doll	20	40	60
S852	Mary & Cliffy Puppets	10	20	30
S853	Side Show	15	30	45
S854	Snicker Shack	8	15	22
S855	Postcard size Fan Photo w/ Autographs on the Reverse	5	10	15
S856	Mary Hartline Button	5	10	15

SUPERMAN, THE ADVENTURES OF

After a false start in syndication, Superman took to the Mutual airwaves in 1940. The opening had to be one of the radio's best!(Rifle shot and ricochet) "Faster than a speeding bullet . . ."(Steam locomotive at full throttle) "More powerful than a locomotive . . ."(Rush of wind) "Able to leap tall buildings at a single bound . . ."(Man says) "Look!. . . Up in the sky!It's a bird! . . . It's a plane! . . ."(Announcer) "It's Superman!"

Mild-mannered Clark Kent (played for many years by even milder-mannered Bud Collyer remembered by most as the TV host of "Beat the Clock" and other game shows) brought the man of steel to life on radio with a simple voice change. But Clark and Superman were familiar from comic books and the listener's mind was the best stage for Superman's more outstanding feats. Lois Lane, Editor Perry White and Jimmy Olson were an integral part of the broadcasts. The show strictly adhered to the comic book characterizations. Our imagination still had a part to play when characters such as Poco, a small visitor from outerspace, became a factor in the program. Batman and Robin even appeared on the show from time to time.

Most of the episodes surviving on tape pit Superman against the Nazis and tout Kellogg's PEP (the super delicious cereal), warplanes and military buttons. Actual character premiums were few. The two airplane rings were not actually Superman premiums, but are so widely publicized as such they are listed below. The silver metal airplane (brass ring base) was offered by PEP, but sometime after it dropped Superman sponsorship. The black plastic airplane ring (silver ring base) was offered by Kellogg's Corn Flakes. A 1945 contest awarded War Bonds as prizes.

Superman-Tim premiums began appearing in 1942 and had no connection with the radio show at first. This was a department and clothing store promotion to build monthly traffic. However, when the program went to participating sponsorship, local spots became available and many stores tied the two promotions together. The Superman-Tim promotion ended in 1950. The last Superman radio show, which converted to complete 30 minute adventures on ABC in 1949, aired in 1951.

Other Superman premiums were offered in comic books and by gum and candy companies.

		Good	Fine	Mint
1938-42				
S858	Superman of America Ring	300	600	900
S859	Action Comics Button	30	60	90
S860	Action Comics Button	20	40	60
S861	Code Card	5	10	15
S862	Membership Certificate	10	20	30
S863	Cello Button	8	16	24
S864	Secret Compartment Initial Ring - Version One - paper picture inside	300	700	1200
S865	Same as S864, but with Superman stamped in metal where the eye appears on S864	300	700	1100
S866	Crusaders Ring	40	55	75
S869	Junior Defense League Pin	25	60	100
S870	Superman American Pin	20	50	85
	Superman of America:			
S875	Certificate	10	14	18
S876	Button	12	20	28
S877	Code Card	4	8	12

1942-50

Military Pins (see PEP Cereal Pins):

		Good	Fine	Mint
S880	Balsa Wood Airplanes, 33, each	3	5	7
S885	Cardboard Airplanes, 40, each	3	5	7
S890	Walky Talky	25	45	65
S893	Buckle and Belt	35	65	120
S894	Press Card for Stamps	8	14	20
S898	PEP Airplane Ring, 1948	35	70	150
S899	Corn Flakes F-87 Airplane Ring, 1948	55	110	175

The two preceding rings have no connection with Superman, but are listed here due to widespread information to the contrary.

		Good	Fine	Mint
	Superman-Tim Premiums:			
S900	Membership Button, profile	12	17	22
S901	Membership Button, Tim's head insert in circle	10	15	20
S902	Membership Card(s), each	5	8	12
S905	Superman-Tim Ring	35	70	150
S908	Monthly Manuals, 1942	8	15	25
S920	Monthly Manuals, 1943	6	14	22
S932	Superman Good Stuff Sweatshirt	20	40	60
S934	Birthday Postcard(s), each	6	12	20
S935	Puzzle Cards	10	12	15
S936	Patch	30	60	90
S939	Stamps, 1942-44, each	4	8	12
S940	Monthly Manuals, 1944	6	12	20
S952	Stamp Albums, each	12	24	36
S955	Superman Red Backs	4	6	10

(Red Backs first appeared in 1944 in 1, 5, and 10 denominations and were redeemed for toys and other prizes of non-premium nature.)

S960	Monthly Manuals, 1945	5	9	12
S961	Christmas Play Book	15	30	50
S962	Monthly Manuals, 1946	6	12	18
S963	Monthly Manuals, 1947	6	12	18
S964	Monthly Manuals, 1948	6	12	18
S965	Monthly Manuals, 1949	6	12	18
S966	Monthly Manuals, 1950	6	12	18
S970	Stamps, 1945-50, each	5	10	15
S972	Badge (Fo-Lee Gum)	50	100	150

1950-59

S980	Flying Superman	30	45	60
S981	T-Shirt	10	25	40
S985	Krypton Rocket (red) & Launcher	20	45	70
S986	Extra Rockets, blue and green, set	15	30	50
S988	Dangle Dandy	5	12	20
S990	Ring (Nestles)	4	10	15

TARZAN

"Tarzan" first aired on a syndicated basis in 1932. Sponsors varied; noodles, milk, and coffee show up on premiums. The initial series starred Edgar Rice Burroughs' daughter, Joan, and son-in-law, James Pierce, in a three-times-a-week serial based faithfully on the popular Burroughs' books. As networks strengthened, syndicated episodes diminished and were withdrawn in 1935 or 1936. A second syndication was revived in 1951 and CBS took over the show for its final year in 1952. No premiums from the second go-around have been identified.

		Good	Fine	Mint
T205	Jungle Map and Treasure Hunt, Kolynos & other sponsors, 1933	30	70	125
	Radio Club Buttons and Badges:			
T210	Drink More Milk	30	70	100
T211	Bursley Coffees	30	75	120
T212	Signal	15	25	35
T213	Nielen	50	75	120
T214	Running Tarzan	50	75	120
T215	KSL Royal Bakers	60	95	150
T216	Vita Hearts	65	100	160
T225	Radio Club Girl's Bracelet, 1934	50	110	150
	Statue Set (Fould's Products):			
T240	Offer Folder	15	28	40
T241	Tarzan	10	15	20
T242	Kala (Ape Mother)	5	10	15
T243	Numa (Lion)	5	8	12
T244	Jane Porter	5	10	15
T245	Cheetah (Panther)	5	8	12
T246	Witch Doctor	5	10	20
T247	Set of Three Monkeys	5	10	20
T248	D'Arnot Fr. Lieut.	5	10	15
T249	Pirate	5	10	20
T250	Cannibal	5	10	20
T251	Water Color Set	8	12	25
T252	Instruction Sheets for figures, each	20	35	50
T265	Masks, each	10	20	30

TENNESSEE JED

Tennessee Jed Sloan was a Civil War era mountain man type sharp-shooter. A Davy Crockett like do-gooder who could always hit his target "dead center." "Tennessee Jed" was heard on ABC from 1945 to 1947. Tip Top Bread was the sponsor.

		Good	Fine	Mint
T310	Magic Tricks Booklet	15	20	25
T311	Paper Mask	10	15	20
T312	Blotter	5	12	18
T315	Look-Around Ring	30	40	60
T319	Atom Gun	15	20	25
T320	Paper Gun	15	19	23
T321	Pocket Puzzle	10	15	18

TERRY AND TED (UNCLE DON)

This 1933 adventure daily serial resembled the popular Hardy Boys book series. The sponsor was Bond Bakers. In this case the two boys, Terry, nine years old, and Ted, eleven, were assisted by their guardian, Major Campbell, in solving mysteries and combating international spies. They traveled in a unique, motor home type vehicle invented by the Major called a "land cruiser." It could "go along regular roads, across country like a tank, or over water like a speed boat." Enemies were always trying to steal the plans. Uncle Don, also famous for reading the comics on the radio, served as narrator for the program.

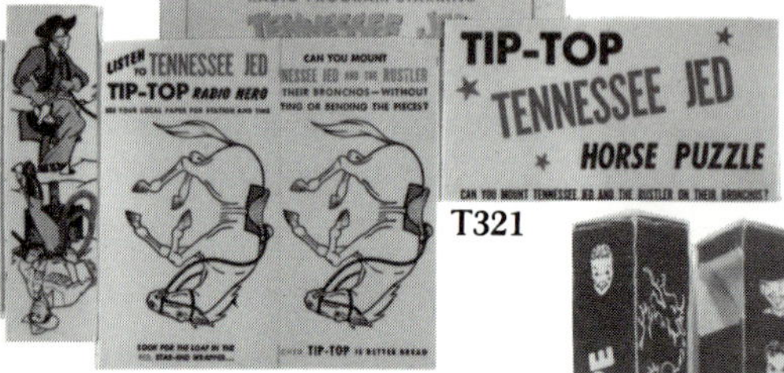

		Good	Fine	Mint
T340	On the Trail of the Secret Formula	10	17	25
T341	A Letter to Boys and Girls from Uncle Don	5	12	20
T345	Map	20	30	40

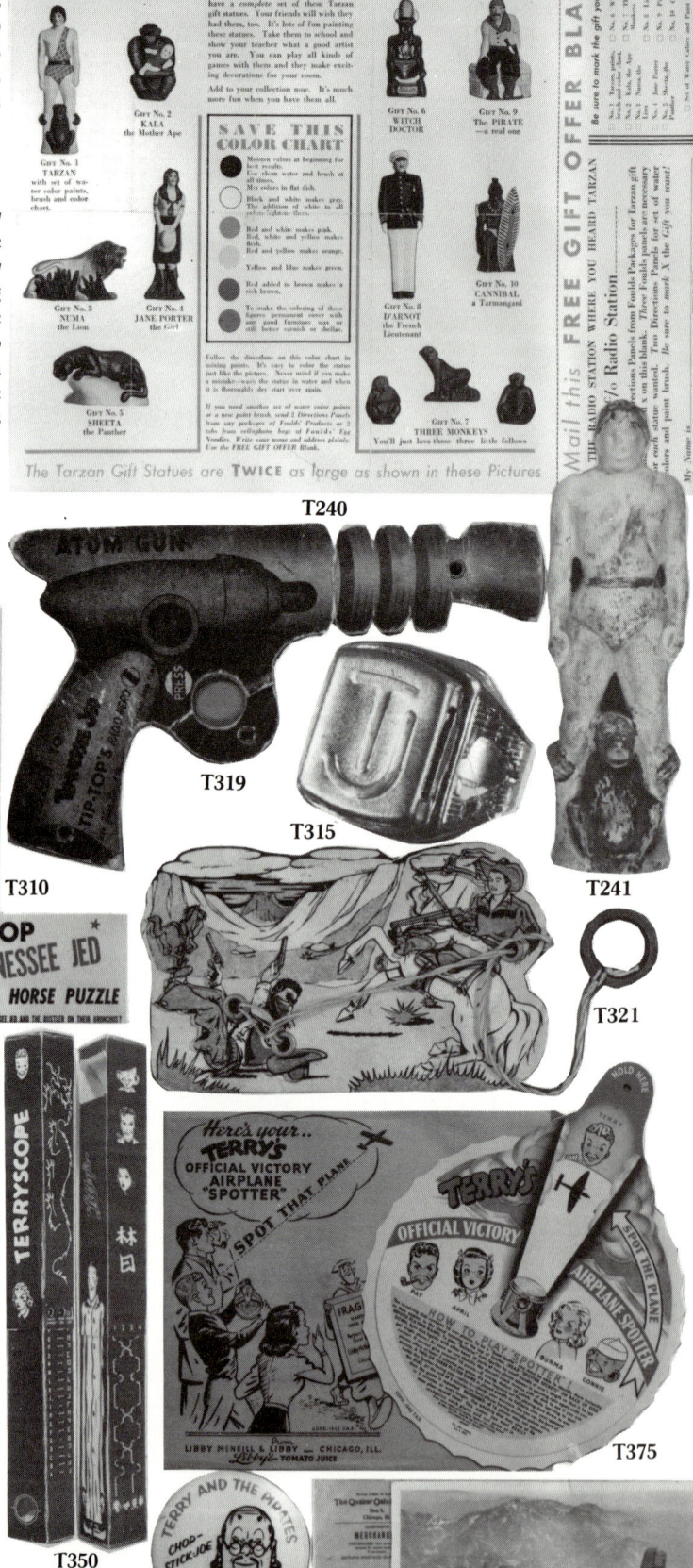

TERRY AND THE PIRATES

The radio version of "Terry and the Pirates" was faithful to the comic strip concept created by Milton Caniff. The program featured all the leading characters - Terry, Burma, Hotshot Charlie, Pat Ryan, Connie and the Dragon Lady. It began as a three-times-a-week serial in 1937, with Dari-Rich as sponsor, and probably aired continuously until 1948. Premiums prove that Libby, McNeil, Libby sponsored the show in the years 1941 and 1942 with Quaker Oats taking over in 1943. Terry supported the war effort in several premiums. In 1943 you received a "mascot" photo of a B-25 as evidence your name appeared on a role of microfilm urging the B-25 pilot to "Drop one on the Japs and Nazis for me." Pilots accepted the microfilm as a good luck piece. When World War II ended, the show's popularity seemed to drop sharply. During the Korean Conflict, Terry and the Gang were revived on TV with Canada Dry Ginger Ale as sponsor.

		Good	Fine	Mint
1941				
T350	Terryscope	25	40	55
1942				
T375	Victory Airplane Spotter	20	30	40
T378	"Ruby of Genghis Khan" Game Book	25	35	45

124

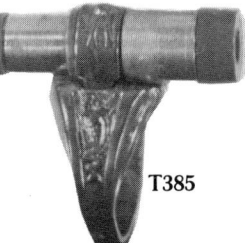

1943-48

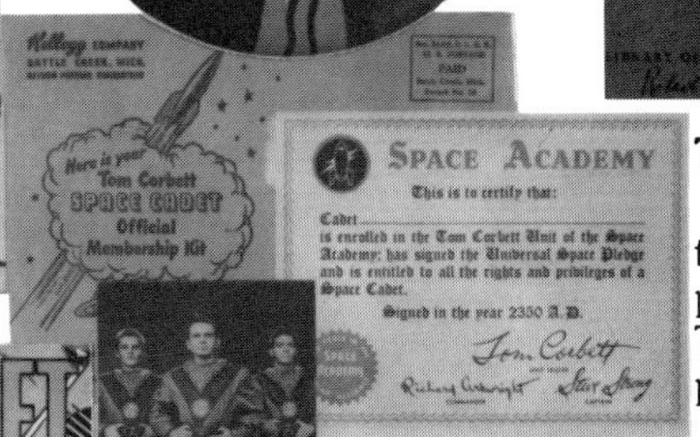

		Good	Fine	Mint
T380	Comic Strip Cast Drawings, set of 6, 1944	30	55	80
T381	Mascot Plane Photo	10	20	30
T383	Terry Jingle Contest Ad, 1945	5	10	15
T385	Gold Detector Ring	25	32	38

1953

Canada Dry Pocket Size Comics - 36 pages:

T390	Hotshot Charlie Flies Gain	3	6	10
T391	Forced Landing	3	6	10
T392	Dragon Lady in Distress	3	6	10
T393	Canada Dry Buttons, set of 5, including Terry, Burma, Dragon Lady, Hotshot Charlie and Chop-Stick Joe, each	5	12	20

THURSTON, THE MAGICIAN

Howard Thurston was one of the top performing magicians in the 20's and one of radio's earliest issuers of premiums. The program was sponsored by Swift and Company out of Chicago. The premiums indicate it aired in 1928-29. NBC also carried the program in 1932.

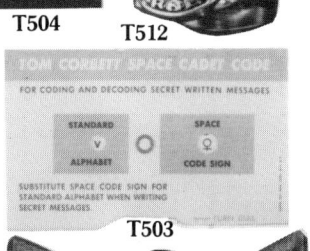

		Good	Fine	Mint
T400	1928 Coin	10	20	30
T401	1929 Coin	10	20	30
T402	Library of Magic, 5 volumes, each	2	4	8

TOM CORBETT, SPACE CADET

"Tom Corbett, Space Cadet" began on ABC radio in Jan 1952 and ended the same year. However, the show went on to have a successful TV run. The program was sponsored by Kellogg's. The action centered around young boys (Space Cadets) learning under the dedicated leadership of Captain Strong at the Space Academy located on the planet Luna. Tom's friends in battling space pirates and other futuristic rogues were Roger Manning (the wise guy of the crowd) and Astro (the strong guy). There was some overlap of radio and TV premiums.

		Good	Fine	Mint
	Membership Kit:			
T500	Space Academy Certificate	10	15	20
T501	Membership Pinback	8	12	16
T502	Patch	15	22	30
T503	Cardboard Decoder	20	26	35
T504	Cadet Cast Photo	8	12	16
T505	Space Cadet News, Vol. 1, No. 1	15	20	25
T510	Package Back w/Space Cadet Equipment, 4 different, each	10	15	20

T512	Face Ring		20	40	60
T520-531	Plastic Rings, 12, each,		6	10	15
T550	Decoder		25	35	45
T560	Rocketship Flashlight Pin (plastic store item) w/card		4	7	10
T570	Rocket Ring w/expansion band		15	35	75
T571	Bread End Label Album I		10	20	35

TOM MIX

"Tom Mix" aired as a 15-minute NBC Blue and later Mutual Network serial (and eventually complete half-hour episodes) from 1933-1950. It was one of the longest running kids' programs and offered the most premiums. Ralston of Checkerboard Square was the sponsor from beginning to end.

In 1934 the National Chicle Company did a series of 48 Tom Mix 8-page booklets which were similar to gum cards. Each was like a chapter of a book. The first 24 comprised a story called "Tom Mix and Tony at the Bar-Diamond Ranch." A cover was published for these booklets. On it was advertised the Tom Mix deputy ring which was given for gum wrappers or a combination of wrappers and coins.

Except for lending his name and posing for advertising stills, Tom Mix had nothing to do with the radio show. On the program and in premiums much was made of his experience as a movie stunt man, his wounds in the Spanish-American War, the Boxer Rebellion and the Boer War.

As the story went, Mix also served as a Western sheriff, a U.S. Marshal and a Texas Ranger. It's no wonder he didn't have time to do the daily radio show because he was also the "World's Champion Cowboy" of the rodeo circuit, trained Tony the "Wonder Horse", "made more Hollywood movies than anyone on the screen", formed his own circus and played command performances before the crown heads of Europe. Throughout all of these exploits he found time to recover from 12 gunshot wounds, 47 movie stunt injuries, 22 knife wounds and a four square inch hole in his back suffered in a dynamite explosion.

Actually, most of what has become known as the "Tom Mix legend" has been discounted as pure press agentry. The most likely hazards in his life were fast cars, fast motorcycles, and fast women. Mix died in an auto accident in 1940, but the show continued just as it always had.

The characters were described as Radio's Tom Mix, the Old Wrangler, Sheriff Mike Shaw, Wash the cook, Pecos Williams, Jimmy and Jane, and the man who repossessed the T-M Bar ranch, miserly Amos Q. Snood. But the Tom Mix phenomenon that served so well in the Depression and survived near character destruction during the Second World War could not compete in the age of television. It was Hoppy's turn.

		Good	Fine	Mint
1933				
T600	Life of Tom Mix Manual	30	38	50
T601	Life of Tom Mix Manual and Premiums Catalog, enlarged edition	28	35	45
T602	Horseshoe Nail Ring, no markings(No way to tell if original)			
T603	Premium Photo 4" x 6"	7	10	15
T604	Straight Shooters Sweater Patch	20	28	35
T605	Bandana	22	32	45
T606	Wooden Gun, opens and cylinder spins - rubber stamp markings on handle	45	55	100
T607	Western Lariat	20	32	40
T608	Good Luck Spinner	12	20	30
T609	Genuine Leather Cuffs w/ Tom imprint	25	50	80
T610	Lario	25	30	35
T611	Spinning Rope, red, white, and blue twine w/TM logo on wooden handle	25	40	55

T612	Cowboy Hat	30	45	60
T613	Spurs w/leather TM strap	35	60	90
T615	Rodeorope (store-item also offered as premium)	35	60	85

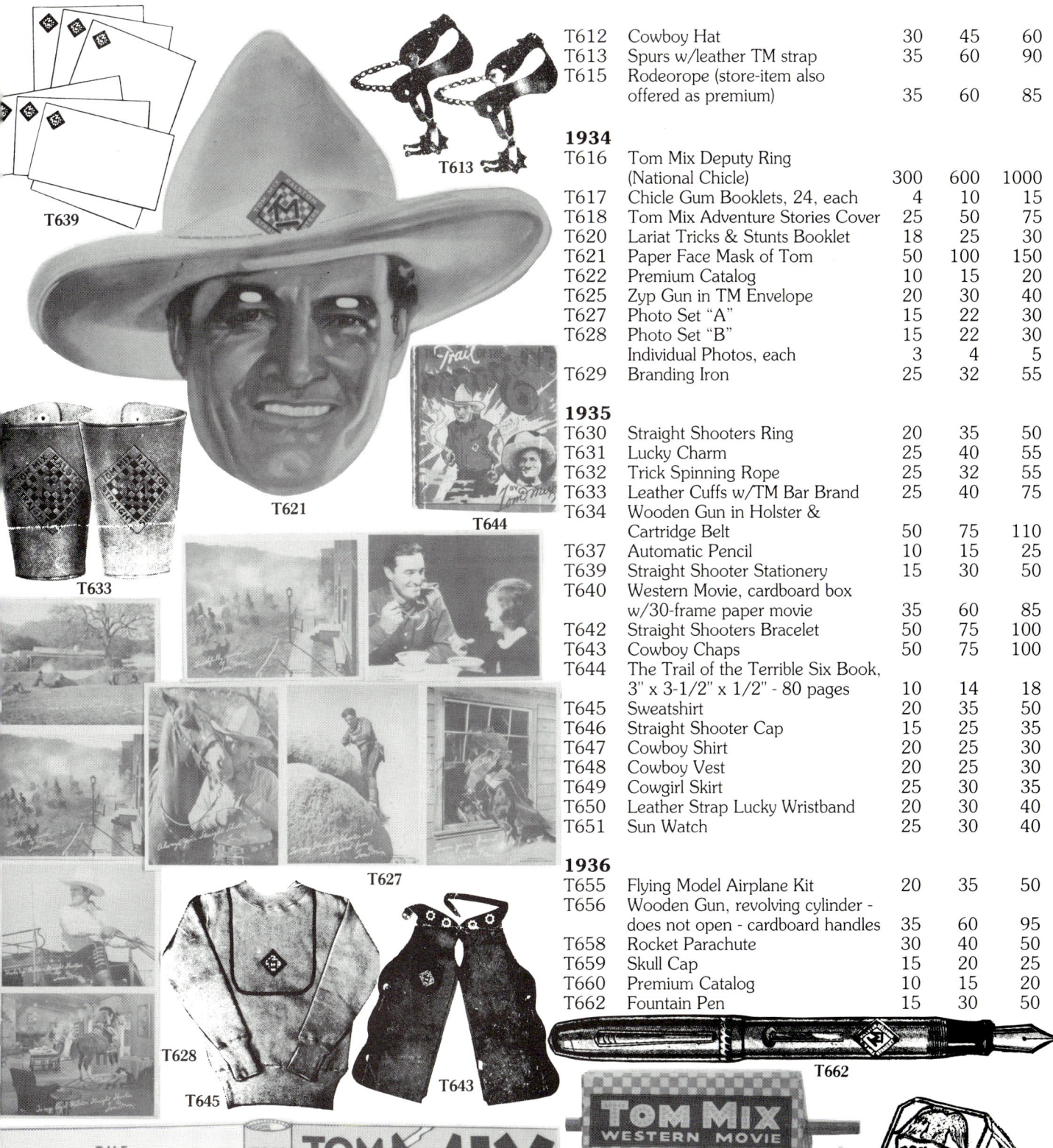

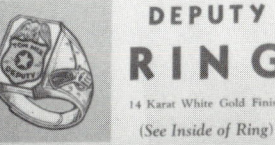

1934

T616	Tom Mix Deputy Ring (National Chicle)	300	600	1000
T617	Chicle Gum Booklets, 24, each	4	10	15
T618	Tom Mix Adventure Stories Cover	25	50	75
T620	Lariat Tricks & Stunts Booklet	18	25	30
T621	Paper Face Mask of Tom	50	100	150
T622	Premium Catalog	10	15	20
T625	Zyp Gun in TM Envelope	20	30	40
T627	Photo Set "A"	15	22	30
T628	Photo Set "B"	15	22	30
	Individual Photos, each	3	4	5
T629	Branding Iron	25	32	55

1935

T630	Straight Shooters Ring	20	35	50
T631	Lucky Charm	25	40	55
T632	Trick Spinning Rope	25	32	55
T633	Leather Cuffs w/TM Bar Brand	25	40	75
T634	Wooden Gun in Holster & Cartridge Belt	50	75	110
T637	Automatic Pencil	10	15	25
T639	Straight Shooter Stationery	15	30	50
T640	Western Movie, cardboard box w/30-frame paper movie	35	60	85
T642	Straight Shooters Bracelet	50	75	100
T643	Cowboy Chaps	50	75	100
T644	The Trail of the Terrible Six Book, 3" x 3-1/2" x 1/2" - 80 pages	10	14	18
T645	Sweatshirt	20	35	50
T646	Straight Shooter Cap	15	25	35
T647	Cowboy Shirt	20	25	30
T648	Cowboy Vest	20	25	30
T649	Cowgirl Skirt	25	30	35
T650	Leather Strap Lucky Wristband	20	30	40
T651	Sun Watch	25	30	40

1936

T655	Flying Model Airplane Kit	20	35	50
T656	Wooden Gun, revolving cylinder - does not open - cardboard handles	35	60	95
T658	Rocket Parachute	30	40	50
T659	Skull Cap	15	20	25
T660	Premium Catalog	10	15	20
T662	Fountain Pen	15	30	50

		Good	Fine	Mint
T663	Girl's Dangle Bracelet w/four charms - TM Brand, Tom on Tony, Steer Head and Six Gun	50	75	100
T664	Championship Belt (red & black checkerboard) & Buckle	25	50	75
T664A	Buckle only	14	20	30
T666	Signet (initial) Ring	30	65	100
T667	Straight Shooter's News, Vol. 1, No. 1	20	25	35
T668	Unmarked Compass Magnifier, silver	8	14	20

		Good	Fine	Mint
1937				
T670	Premium Catalog	10	15	20
T675	Gold Straight Shooter's Badge	15	28	40
T676	Silver Straight Shooter's Badge	15	28	40
T678	Care Instructions for Live Baby Turtle (Branded live turtles now extinct)	10	25	35
T678A	Live Turtle Newspaper Ad	10	15	20
T679	Movie Make-up Kit, first version	24	35	50
T679A	Make-up Kit Tins Only, unprinted TM brand & w/character type embossed in lid	4	6	8
T680	Telescope	18	28	50
T681	Straight Shooter's News, Vol.1, No.2	18	22	30
T682	Telephone Set	20	30	45
T684	Target Ring (Marlin Firearms Co.)	70	150	250
1938				
T690	Premium Catalog	8	12	16
T691	Postal Telegraph Signal Set, blue	22	28	38
T692	Photo in Silver Frame	27	35	50
T692A	Frame only	10	12	15
T693	Secret Ink Writing Set - manual, ink developer & cardboard decoder	25	32	50
T695	Wrangler's Badge	20	35	50
T696	Ranch Boss Badge	30	50	70
T700	Mystery Ring, look-in picture ring w/picture	90	150	250
T702	Bullet Flashlight, nickel plated brass w/paper decal	20	30	40

128

1939

T710	Premium Catalog	7	12	15
T711	Periscope	18	25	35
T712	Pen and Pencil Set	15	28	40
T714	Wooden Gun, no moving parts	25	50	75
T715	Three-color Flashlight	20	35	55
T716	Streamline Parachute Plane	30	50	100
T718	Pocket Knife	22	27	32
T720	Stars of Radio Program Postcard	10	20	30

1940

T730	Premium Catalog	7	12	15
T731	Gold Ore Charm	20	55	75
T732	Gold Ore Watch Fob	15	22	30
T733	Gold Ore Assayer's Certificate	8	15	20
T734	Indian Blow Gun & Target, complete w/4 darts	50	85	125
T735	Brass Compass & Magnifier	22	32	40
T736	Electric Telegraph Set, red, w/instructions	25	35	50
T737	Elephant Hair Range w/instructions, unmarked	50	125	200
T738	Tom Mix Comics #1	35	70	100
T739	Movie Make-up Kit, second version	20	30	45
T739A	Black & Red Tins, each	3	6	8
T740	Tom Mix Comics #2	28	45	75

		Good	Fine	Mint

1941

T750	Tom Mix Comics #3	20	35	50
T751	Tom Mix Comics #4	20	35	50
T752	Tom Mix Comics #5	20	35	50
T753	Tom Mix Comics #6	20	35	50
T754	Tom Mix Comics #7	20	35	50
T755	Six Gun Decoder	22	35	50
T756	Manual, 16 pages	40	60	100
T758	Captain Spur Medal	50	85	125

1942

T770	Signature Ring	60	125	200
T771	Tom Mix Comics #8	25	35	50
T772	Tom Mix Comics #9	20	35	50
T773	Tom Mix Commandos Comics #10	25	40	50
T774	Tom Mix Commandos Comics #11	25	45	60

1944

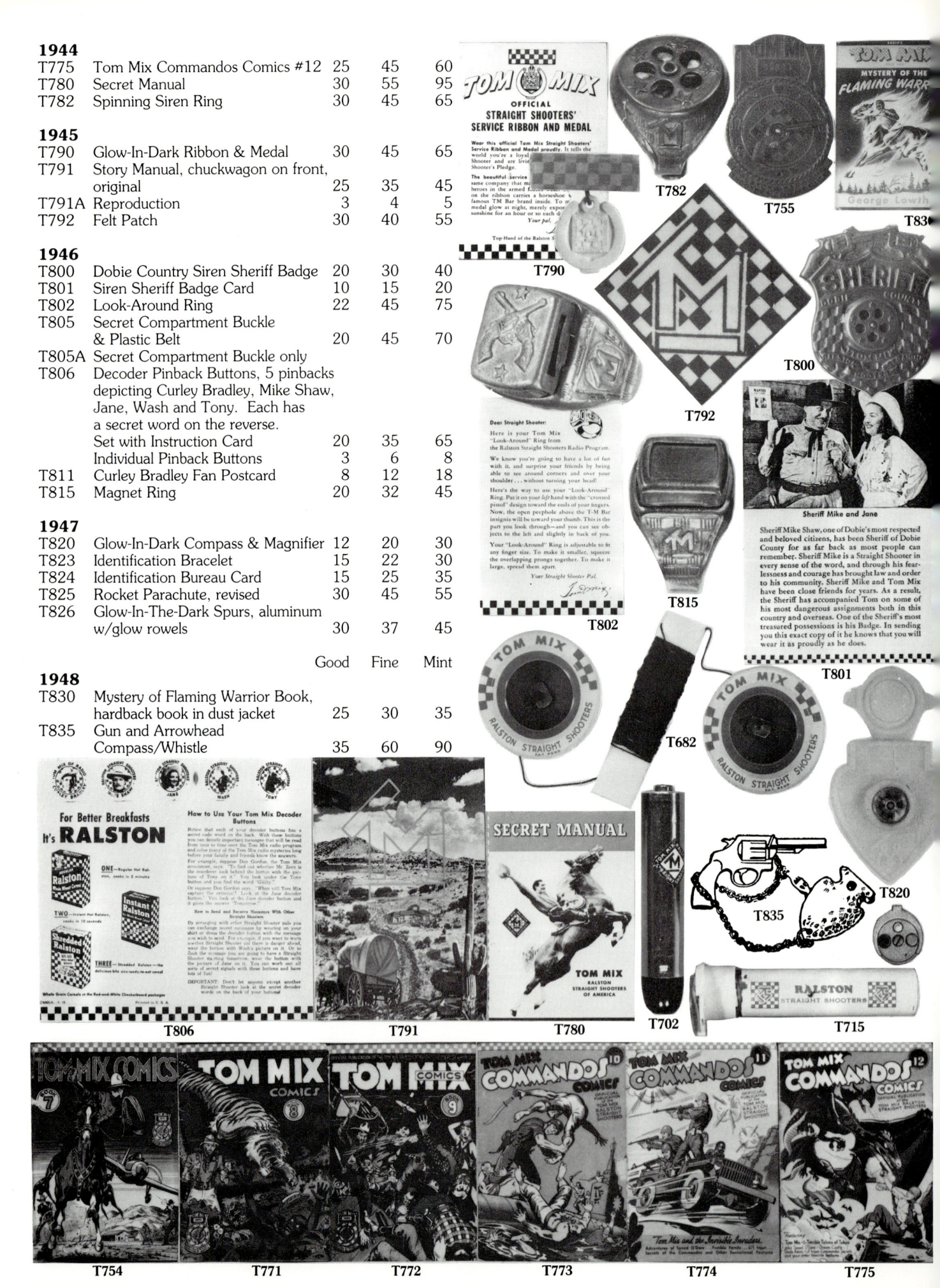

		Good	Fine	Mint
T775	Tom Mix Commandos Comics #12	25	45	60
T780	Secret Manual	30	55	95
T782	Spinning Siren Ring	30	45	65

1945

T790	Glow-In-Dark Ribbon & Medal	30	45	65
T791	Story Manual, chuckwagon on front, original	25	35	45
T791A	Reproduction	3	4	5
T792	Felt Patch	30	40	55

1946

T800	Dobie Country Siren Sheriff Badge	20	30	40
T801	Siren Sheriff Badge Card	10	15	20
T802	Look-Around Ring	22	45	75
T805	Secret Compartment Buckle & Plastic Belt	20	45	70
T805A	Secret Compartment Buckle only			
T806	Decoder Pinback Buttons, 5 pinbacks depicting Curley Bradley, Mike Shaw, Jane, Wash and Tony. Each has a secret word on the reverse.			
	Set with Instruction Card	20	35	65
	Individual Pinback Buttons	3	6	8
T811	Curley Bradley Fan Postcard	8	12	18
T815	Magnet Ring	20	32	45

1947

T820	Glow-In-Dark Compass & Magnifier	12	20	30
T823	Identification Bracelet	15	22	30
T824	Identification Bureau Card	15	25	35
T825	Rocket Parachute, revised	30	45	55
T826	Glow-In-The-Dark Spurs, aluminum w/glow rowels	30	37	45

1948

		Good	Fine	Mint
T830	Mystery of Flaming Warrior Book, hardback book in dust jacket	25	30	35
T835	Gun and Arrowhead Compass/Whistle	35	60	90

T782 T755 T830 T790 T792 T800 T801 T802 T815 T806 T791 T780 T702 T682 T835 T820 T715 T754 T771 T772 T773 T774 T775

1949

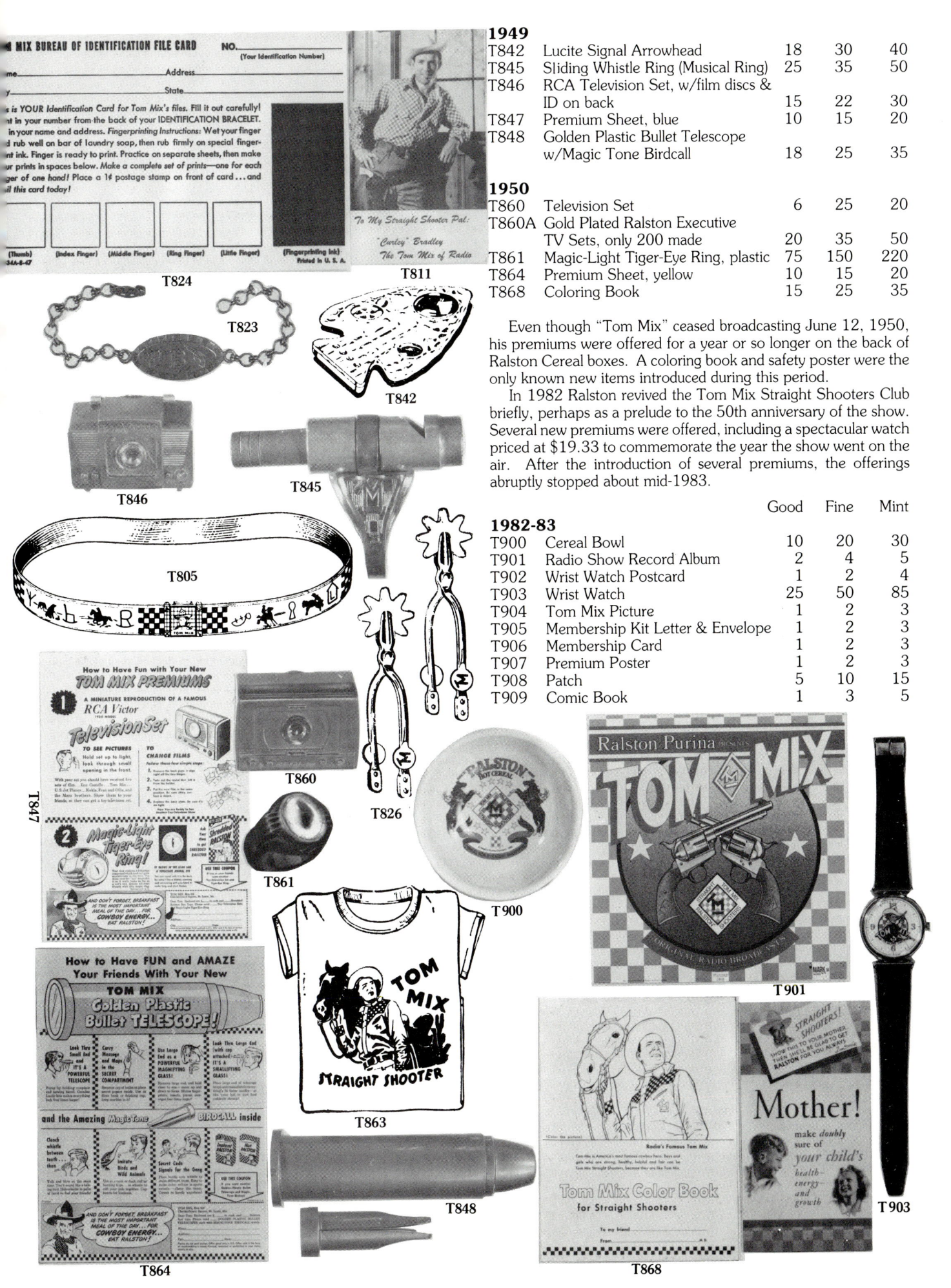

T842	Lucite Signal Arrowhead	18	30	40
T845	Sliding Whistle Ring (Musical Ring)	25	35	50
T846	RCA Television Set, w/film discs & ID on back	15	22	30
T847	Premium Sheet, blue	10	15	20
T848	Golden Plastic Bullet Telescope w/Magic Tone Birdcall	18	25	35

1950

T860	Television Set	6	25	20
T860A	Gold Plated Ralston Executive TV Sets, only 200 made	20	35	50
T861	Magic-Light Tiger-Eye Ring, plastic	75	150	220
T864	Premium Sheet, yellow	10	15	20
T868	Coloring Book	15	25	35

Even though "Tom Mix" ceased broadcasting June 12, 1950, his premiums were offered for a year or so longer on the back of Ralston Cereal boxes. A coloring book and safety poster were the only known new items introduced during this period.

In 1982 Ralston revived the Tom Mix Straight Shooters Club briefly, perhaps as a prelude to the 50th anniversary of the show. Several new premiums were offered, including a spectacular watch priced at $19.33 to commemorate the year the show went on the air. After the introduction of several premiums, the offerings abruptly stopped about mid-1983.

		Good	Fine	Mint

1982-83

T900	Cereal Bowl	10	20	30
T901	Radio Show Record Album	2	4	5
T902	Wrist Watch Postcard	1	2	4
T903	Wrist Watch	25	50	85
T904	Tom Mix Picture	1	2	3
T905	Membership Kit Letter & Envelope	1	2	3
T906	Membership Card	1	2	3
T907	Premium Poster	1	2	3
T908	Patch	5	10	15
T909	Comic Book	1	3	5

131

VIC AND SADE

A small budget soap opera beginning in 1932, "Vic and Sade" succeeded on some of the best writing in early radio. Paul Rhymer, their creator and writer, could produce 30 pages on the simplest happening around the house. The show aired for over 8 years with only 3 actors. A few more were added before it left the air in 1944 when P&G found a new vehicle for its Crisco brand. Only one map on thick cardboard has been found. It may have been part of a store display.

V400	Map		10	25	40

WILD BILL HICKOK, THE ADVENTURES OF

Guy Madison (Wild Bill) and Andy Devine (Jingles) appeared on radio 1951-54 and TV from 1952 to 1958 as first a syndicated and then an ABC network program. Kellogg's Sugar Corn Pops sponsored the show and featured the characters on cereal boxes. Most of the money must have gone into the well produced programs. The premiums were very cheap and only the Secret Treasure Map and Guide are worthy of collecting. There were paper thin tin stars and plastic gun model kits of various types, but all were disappointing when you received them. The Western Bunkhouse Kit was a $2.95 mail order item and is not a premium (as is often advertised).

1952-54

		Good	Fine	Mint
W300	Secret Treasure Map w/envelope	20	30	40
W301	Secret Treasure Guide	5	12	20
W304	Breakfast Game Score Card	3	6	10
W305	In-Pack Tin Star Badges, Junior Ranger, Deputy Sheriff, Deputy Marshall, Jingle's Deputy, Sheriff or Special Deputy, each	2	3	5
W315	Old Time Plastic Gun Kits, Colt Peacemaker, Derringer or Pepper Box, each	3	6	9
W320	Colt Six Shooter	5	10	15
W322	Rifle Model	5	10	15
W330	Bond Bread Trading Cards, each	2	4	6

WIZARD OF OZ

Several years before the movie and for one brief season (1933-34) the famous L. Frank Baum Oz stories were dramatized on radio in three-times-a-week 15-minute episodes: 5:45-6:00

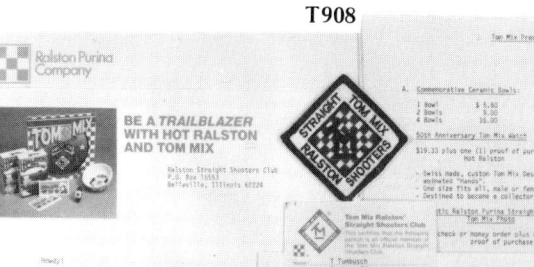

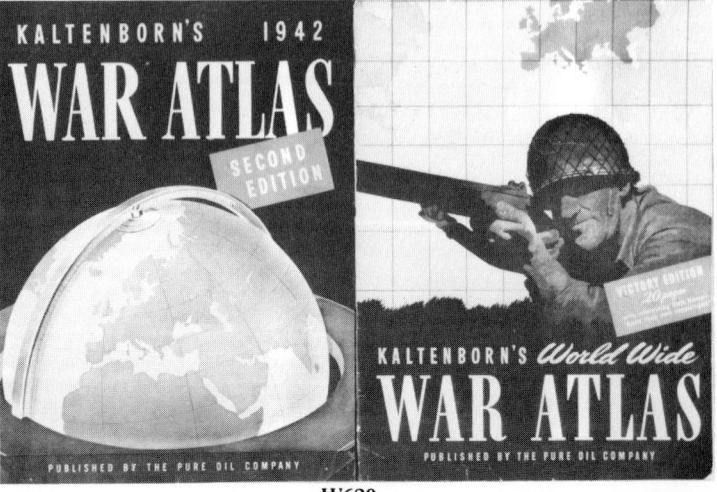

132

PM. The sponsor was Jell-O gelatin desserts. A series of four special condensed stories were offered as premiums. Hardback store versions of these books also exist. The premiums are paper bound with a Jell-O ad on the back cover.

		Good	Fine	Mint
W400	Ozma and the Little Wizard (A)	15	20	25
W401	Tiktok and the Nome King (B)	15	20	25
W402	Jackpumpkinhead and the Sawhorse (C)	15	20	25
W403	The Scarecrow and the Tin Woodman (D)	15	20	25

WORLD WAR II

The biggest news event during the golden age of radio was the Second World War. Listeners depended on radio 7 days a week to bring them up to the minute news of victories, defeats, invasions, and the chance of some news regarding friends, family, and loved ones. Shortwave hook-ups, first used in the second Byrd expedition to the South Pole, had been perfected for everyday use by the time the war was brewing in the late 30's. War correspondents of the air became a link to the action after the latest newspaper was published.

Men like Lowell Thomas, H.V. Kaltenborn, Edward R. Murrow, Drew Pearson, and Gabriel Heather were all first rate newscasters, but the War made them even more important as interpreters of what was happening and the possible outcome. Thousands of Americans became so close to the radio voices they asked for photos and printed materials so they could better follow the programs. Color maps and atlases of recent battles became a popular premium for sponsors of news programs.

W301

		Good	Fine	Mint
W600	Photos	4	6	10
W610	Map	5	10	15
W620	Atlas	5	12	20
W630	Other	5	and	up

133

CHILDREN'S RADIO PROGRAMS BROADCAST BY WEAF, WJZ, WABC, AND WOR, NEW YORK CITY, 1928-34
from Children and Radio Programs, a study published in 1936

Name of Program	Product	Station	Years	Type of Program	Typical Offers
Albert Payson Terhune Dog Drama	Dog Food	WJZ	1934	Dramatic dog stories by Albert Payson Terhune	Sample of dog food
Amateur Astronomer's Association	Sustaining	WOR	1932	Informal presentations of interesting facts about the heavens and how to locate the individual stars	
Adventures of Dr. Doolittle	Sustaining	WEAF	1933	Describing adventures from war letters of Dr. Doolittle	
Adventures of Helen and Mary; name changed to "In the Land of Let's Pretend"	Sustaining	WABC	1931-34	Dramatization of fairy tales; musical interludes and interpretations	Dramatization of favorite story requested by children
Adventures of Tom Mix and His Ralston Straight Shooters	Cereal	WEAF	1933-34	Adventures from the life of Tom Mix, famous film star and former cowpuncher	Bandana for top of box
Billy Batchelor	Cereal	WEAF	1933-34		
Bobby Benson	Cereal	WABC	1932-34	A dramatized serial laid in Western Colorado	Membership in H-Bar-O Rangers for box top
Borrah Minnevitch and His Harmonica Rascals	Ice cream	WOR	1934	Famous harmonica band who made mouth organs sound like symphony orchestras	Harmonica and instruction book on harmonica playing
Betty Boop	Sustaining	WEAF	1932	Antics of Betty Boop, the cartoon character, and her pals	
Babe Ruth Boys' Club	Gasoline	WOR	1934	Babe's stories about baseball and advice to the stars of tomorrow	Baseball bats; tickets to ball games
Babe Ruth Boys' Club	Cereal	WJZ	1934	Dramatized baseball stories	Membership in Babe Ruth's ball club; contests with prizes of baseballs, bats, and trips to Chicago World's Fair
Buck Rogers in the 25th Century	Food drink	WABC	1932-34	Fantastic adventures of boy in the year 2433-34	Planetary map, illustrated book of Buck Rogers' adventures
Capt. Jack	Dessert	WABC	1932	Dramatic show; adventure stories of Capt. Jack, aviator and soldier of fortune	Membership in Good Luck Flying Corps, button, secrets of aviation, toy cut-out airplanes; leather aviators jackets for 100 longest lists of words from "chocolatine"
Champion Skaters	Roller skates	WABC	1931	Songs; also talks to children on how to become champion roller skaters	Booklet on roller skating and skating cap
Chandu	Breakfast food	WOR	1932-33	Occult drama in serial form concerning adventures of Chandu the Magician, and the	Magic tricks

				Regent family	
Chick-Chick Fun	Egg dyes	WABC	1931-33	Musical program of appeal to children	
Chinaberry Children's Program	General merchandise	WOR	1934	Stories for small children	
Cowboy Tom and Indian Chief	Type-writers	WABC	1932-33	Songs and stories of ranch life	Membership in Cowboy Tom's Round-up and photo of gang List of Indian words
Cranky Crocodile	Sustaining	WOR	1933	Adventures of the Cranky Crocodile; musical background	Paper crocodile sent free
Children's Hour	Food products	WABC	1931-34	Variety program; vaudeville show composed mostly of amateur children performers; songs, recitations, and other specialties	Voting for most popular performer
Cooking School for Children	Groceries	WJZ	1933	Cooking lessons for children	Simple recipes for children
Children's Hour	Sustaining	WOR	1933-34	A "review" type of program in which talented juvenile amateurs take part; singing and sketches	
Don Carney - Dog Chats	Dog food	WJZ	1933	Stories of dogs	
Damrosch Hour	Talking machines	NBC	1929	Music appreciation hour conducted by Walter Damrosch	Manual for school children
Dick Daring, a Boy of Today	Breakfast food	NBC	1933	A script show for children	Books and puzzles
Dancing Class of the Air	Sustaining	WOR	1929-34	Dancing teacher, describes new steps, such as Carioca, Rhumba, Continental, etc.	Charts illustrating routines of dance steps
Detectives Black and Blue	Toothpaste	WOR	1932-34	Comic sketches concerning antics of amateur dectectives	Detective badges and caps
Devil Bird	Food drink	WABC	1933	Dramatized adventures based on the experiences of Bob Becker, author and explorer	Prizes for names of dog puzzles, and cowboy lassos
Dixie Circus	Drinking cups	WJZ	1929-31	Circus band; dialogue portraying two people at the circus	Rubber balloon to child who sent in name of local storekeeper who used cups
Dog Tales	Sustaining	WOR	1932-34	Stories of dog heroism	
Dogs	Household medicine	WOR	1934	Stories about dogs	
Durant Heroes of the World	Motor cars	WEAF	1929-30	Stories of heroes	Pictures of world heroes
Don Lang - True Animal Stories	Dessert	WABC	1932-33	True animal stories	Word building contests; membership in club Painting book, and recipe book, free
Erector Buddies	Construction game	WABC	1929	Sport talks by famous figures in world of sports	Kaleidescope to look at colored pictures
Fairy Tales	Sustaining	WEAF	1933-34	Dramatization of popular fairy tales	

135

Program	Sponsor	Station	Years	Description	Premium
Fu Manchu	Hand lotion	WABC	1932-33	Dramatization of mystery stories of Sax Rohmer's famous character	Membership button
Flying Family - The Hutchinsons	Sustaining	WOR		Serial based on the experiences of the famous Hutchinson family who made aeroplane flights some few years ago	Membership pins and puzzle
Girl Scout Program	Sustaining	WOR	1932-34	Girl Scout news	
Girls and Boys of Many Lands	Sustaining	WOR	1933-34	Foreign travel discussed from children's angle	
Gus Van	Rubber goods	WJZ	1931	Van and Schenk in comedy sketch; orchestra	Contest; prize, a fox terrier puppy
Happy Landing and Mitzi Green	Bread	WOR	1933	Adventure serial starring the juvenile actress and her pals	Jigsaw puzzle, which child was to cut out and reassemble, returning it to company making him eligible for cash prize
Ivory Stamp Club	Soap	WJZ	1934	Stories of stamps	Stamp album and stamps
Indian Powwow with Chief Lone Bear	Sustaining	WOR	1933-34	Indian tales and folklore	
Iodent Big Brother Club (later changed to Iodent Club)	Toothpaste	WEAF	1930-32	Eight piece orchestra; novelty songs with guitar	Membership in club; receipt of the club newspaper and membership badge; a trip to New York City occasionally awarded to a magazine contributor
Jack Armstrong, All American Boy	Breakfast food	WABC	1933-34	Serial dramatization of life of American Boy	Autographed picture of Johnny Weismuller (swimming champion) for package tops; plane models; cash-prize contests for name of Jack's horse and dog
Jeddo Dramatic Program	Coal	WJZ	1933-34	Dramatization of classical children's stories	Robin Hood hat
Jolly Bill and Jane	Sustaining	WOR	1929-34	Dramatized adventures and fables	Membership in Hot Cereal Breakfast Club; "Rastus" doll, patterned after trade-marked figure
Just Dogs	Dog remedies	WOR	1933-34	Stories about dogs	
Jolly Junketeers	Dessert	WJZ	1931	Singing and dialogue	Membership offered to all children who wrote affirming use of product
Junior Bugle-replaced by "Sunday Morning at Aunt Suzanne" (similar program)	Sustaining	WABC	1933-34	Newspaper of air for children; story by each columnist; musical selections, travel stories, children's stories, etc.	Free copies of some of poems and articles presented over air
Junior Detective	Dairy products	WJZ	1931	Dramatic sketch by children for children	Membership badge
John Martin's Story Hour	Sustaining	WEAF	1933-34	Children's stories	
Kaltenmeyer Kindergarten	Sustaining	NBC		Comedy dramatization of a kindergarten class Songs, music, etc.	

Program	Sponsor	Network	Years	Description	Premium/Offer
Kiddies Cooking Class	Sustaining	WOR	1933-34	Instruction to young children in simple cookery	
Just Willie	Rubber goods	NBC	1931-32	Children's program	
Lonely Cowboy	Sustaining	WOR	1932	Guitar and cowboy songs	
Lady Next Door	Sustaining	WEAF	1929-34	Dramatic sketch, children taking the principal roles	Invitation to join the "Magic Circle"
Little Buster Circus Parade	Popcorn	WJZ	1931-32	Description of circus parade	
Little Orphan Annie	Food drink	WJZ	1931-34	Dramatic story based on Little Orphan Annie cartoon strip	Cash prizes with secret prize for all entries Beetleware mug; picture of Annie; word contest
Lone Ranger	Bread	WOR	1934	Melodramatic sketches of the West in which the Lone Ranger and his famous horse "Silver" bests the outlaws and thieves	Free theater parties, admission to aviation meets, visits to U.S. Battleships, etc. Occasional offers of theater tickets to the first fifty non-members who apply for membership
Lone Wolf Tribe	Gum	WABC	1931-33	Dramatization of American Indian life with emphasis on Indian virtues and ideals	Membership in "Lone Wolf Tribe"; saddle blanket Various equipment
Lucky Kids	Cod liver oil	WABC	1932	Dramatization of nautical adventure stories	Enrollment in Deep Sea Scouts; emblem and creed
My Bookhouse Story Time	Books	WABC	1929-31	Dramatization of Junior Literary Guild books	Tiny story book
Macy-Bamberger Boys' Club	General merchandise	WOR	1932-34	A club conducted for boys; subjects of interest that help to build character discussed	
Maltine Story Program	Malt	WJZ	1930-32	Dramatized children's stories and a short address by child-health specialists	Booklet for parents: Feeding Your Child from Crib to College
Maud and Cousin Bill	Grocery products	WJZ	1932-33	A Booth Tarkington comedy depicting the life of a typical American boy or girl	
Maverick Jim	Grocery products	WOR	1933-34	Melodramatic sketches of episodes of the old Southwest; lots of gun play and "tough hombres"	Horse race game
NBC Children's Hour	Sustaining	WJZ	1931-33	Recitations, talks, music and song; encouragement to children to develop talent by participating in program	
NBC Music Appreciation	Sustaining	NBC	1929-34	Dr. Walter Damrosch and a symphony orchestra broadcasting a regular course of classical music during the winter months	
Nursery Rhymes	Sustaining	WEAF	1933-34	Songs	
Once Upon a Time	Milk	WOR	1934	Fairy stories for the kiddies	

Program	Sponsor	Station	Years	Description	Premium
Old King Cole	Refrigerators	WEAF	1929	Stories, jokes, and music	Booklet containing stories of Old King Cole
Phil Cook, The Quaker Man	Breakfast food	WJZ	1930-32	Songs, piano numbers, and humorous monologues	Doll; tudor teaspoon for the weight measures of two packages
Paul Wing, the Story Man	Cereal	WEAF	1932-33	Dramatized stories of two children in a mystic land	Jigsaw puzzle
Pollyanna, the Glad Girl	Shoes	WABC	1932	Song and children's stories	Prizes for best handwriting & best letter
Poet of the Birds	Sustaining	WOR		Bird calls and imitations	
Quaker Early Birds - Gene and Glen	Cereal	WEAF	1931-32	Dialogue dramatizing the lives of a married couple "Jake and Lean"	Tudor plate teaspoon; marbles for boys, bracelets for girls, kites, airplanes, pearl beads, gliders, etc.
	Gasoline		1934		Jigsaw puzzles
Rex Cole Mountaineers	Refrigerators	WEAF	1930-31	Mountaineer orchestra and songs	Various booklets
Raising Junior	Cereal	WJZ	1930-32	Playlet - advice on raising children	
Rin Tin Tin	Dog food	WJZ		Adventures of the movie dog, Rin Tin Tin	Sample of dog biscuit
Rin Tin Tin Thrillers	Dog food	WABC	1933-34	Adventures of the German police dog; dramas based on feats of a heroic dog and other famous dogs in fact or fiction	Identification locket attachable to dog's collar; Book of dog biographies, picture of Rin Tin Tin, and information regarding care and feeding of dogs
Red Goose Adventures	Shoes	WABC	1931	Indian stories told to two children by an old Indian Chief	Prizes for essay contest
Ray Perkins	Food products	WOR	1934	A program of nonsense, songs, and chatter	
Story Teller's House	Sustaining	WOR	1933-34	Entertains children with fairy tales, legends, songs, and stories	
Salty Sam	Sustaining	WJZ	1934	Story and song	
Seckatary Hawkins	Food drink and cereal	WEAF	1932-33	Dramatic sketch	Club membership and button
Shadow	Magazine	WABC	1930-31	Dramatized tale of mystery	Cash prize for best description of the Shadow; Choice of 1 of 14 magazines, free
Salty Sam the Sailor	Toothpaste	WABC	1931-32	Songs and sea' yarns	Bicycle and cash prizes to answers in word contest
Sheffield Scrap Book Club	Dairy products	WEAF	1933	Discussions of the filling of a scrapbook with songs, stories, poems, etc.	Scrapbook (to be filled and returned to sponsor for distribution to children in hospitals); prizes for best scrapbook

Program	Sponsor	Station	Years	Description	Premiums/Features
Singing Lady	Breakfast foods	WJZ	1932-34	Songs and stories by The Singing Lady	Nursery and rhyme book; birthday present consisting of small chest filled with samples of various packages
Skippy	Cereal and toothpaste	WABC	1932-34	Dramatization of comic strip by same name	Membership in secret society; code, badge, secret directions for handshake; cash and other prizes for word-building contests
Stamp Club	Sustaining	WOR	1932-34	The values and methods of collecting stamps	
Stamp Adventurers Club	Dog food	WABC	1933-34	Authentic dramatic, historical, episodes behind stamp issues	Prizes of stamps or radio for best snapshot, drawing, or picture of dog; prizes for two-line jingle in doggie tunes; pin with picture of dog and printed description of breed
Tastyeast Jesters	Yeast	WJZ	1930-33	Pep, Vin, and Vigor - three men singers; dialogue appeal to children and adults	Sample of yeast
The Tattered Man	Sustaining	WEAF	1933-34	Experiences of Tattered man	
True Stories of the Sea	Canned food	WOR	1934	Yarns of adventures on the high seas narrated by a retired skipper of sailing ship days; music by a rollicking quartette	
Tarzan	Chocolate milk beverage	WOR	1934	Adventure serial of Edgar Rice Burroughs' famous character	Club membership
Terry and Ted	Bread	WOR	1933	Serial adventures of two boys and their uncle who get into company of international spies; Uncle Don performed as narrator	Map of adventures of Terry and Ted
Uncle Don Reads the Comics	Vitamins	WOR	1933-34	Uncle Don reads the Sunday News comics for young children	Picture book
Uncle Ollie and His Kremel Gang	Dessert	WABC	1931-32	Stories, partially dramatized, and music	Prizes for greatest number of package fronts
Vass Family	Sustaining	WEAF	1932	Comedy sketch; Southern songs, comedy tunes, ballads, etc; typical Southern family	
Winnie the Pooh	Sustaining	WEAF	1933-34	Dramatization of A.A. Milne's book	
Wizard of Oz	Dessert	WEAF	1933-34	Dramatization of children's book by the same name	Story books
Ye Happy Minstrels and Tiny Band	Cereal	WABC	1933-34		Song requests and letters solicited from children; Ye Happy Minstrels' Memory Book containing songs, stories, and games

THE NUMBER OF PREMIUMS GIVEN AWAY 1931 TO 1960

Rarity is one element of value. Many collectors have often wondered just how many of each premium were sent out in response to these tempting radio commercials and the ads found in newspaper comic sections, magazines and comic books.

This listing is the first attempt to answer the questions about "how many premiums were given away?" The information compiled here came from many sources. Several of the offering companies have provided records over the years to a number of collectors and to the author. Tapes of old radio broadcasts, Sunday Funnies and comic books provided many dates. Historical data from designer, manufacture or fulfillment company files provided quantities in some cases. All currently known data has been collected and presented with knowledge of limitations and observations as follow:

- There are often conflicting records and none are complete.
- Companies often hired outside fulfillment companies which further confused record keeping.
- Rarely is there any information on bounce-back premiums. A quantity of these were made up and shipped to a fulfillment operation to be used as necessary. Companies were mainly interested in tracking the original offers to gauge the success of their advertising and promotion programs.
- Offers of a single premium outperformed membership clubs or ads where many premiums were offered.
- The number of premiums mailed has only a passing relationship with rarity or value. Leftover premiums may have been stored, distributed in some other way, or offered later under another name. Successful premiums such as the Atomic Bomb Ring were offered again and again in different ways nearly doubling the distribution of the initial offering listed here.
- Beginning in the War years manufacturers discovered the idea of buying a limited number of premiums. When the supply was gone it was gone. Only in rare cases was an additional order placed. "While the supply lasts" is abbreviated in the following list as "WSL".
- Start dates reflect the date of an offering company, newspaper, comic, or one recorded on an old radio tape or disc. End dates refer to deadline dates shown in ads, announced in commercials, or company information. Dates from printed material may be off somewhat, but are in the ballpark.
- Quantities come from a variety of sources. Manufacturing data available were for recorded manufacturing runs. In some cases more than one manufacturer was involved. The number given is accurate only to the extent of the data collected and may not include lowest cost bids from another company on reruns.
- Where there is a void of old shows on tape, company cooperation, or any advertising it was impossible to list an item.

In each case the number listed is for the total number given away between the offer period listed. Initial testing results were combined with the national roll-out quantity wherever possible. Some items were offered more than once in distinctively different promotions, sometimes with a design change. These have been listed separately.

In the month's we dealt with the various results some reasonably projectable patterns developed. The information was programmed into the computer and projections were run for premiums where we had exact information. The system proved reliable enough to attempt estimating distribution of items where the data was lost. These estimates are identified with an asterisk (*). Undoubtedly these are sometimes far from actual, but are presented for whatever interest they may hold. The process was complicated enough to limit its use to the most collectible premiums. Where multiple items were offered separately in the same ad or catalog the validity was questionable and therefor no attempt was made to estimate distribution in these situations. Where we were able to pin down reasonably accurate offer dates, but failed to find the quantity offered or generate a reasonable estimate, the dates are still presented for the reader's guidance.

One of the results of this research has been to discover some correct names and dates not previously known. Accordingly some code numbers had to change as a few things were rearranged.

The process of reconstructing the past is complicated and not without fault. Any reader caring to provide information of help to the effort is eagerly encouraged to contact the author c/o Tomart Publications, P.O. Box 292192, Dayton, OH 45429

CHARACTER	STARTING PREMIUM	EXPIRATION OFFERING BRAND	NUMBER DATE	DATE	DISTRIBUTED
Orphan Annie	Shake-up Mug	Ovaltine	6/26/31	8/29/34	110.000 *
Skippy	Picture of Skippy	Wheaties	8/28/31	11/6/31	14.222
Skippy	Christmas Card	Wheaties	11/12/31	12/15/31	14.500
Inspector Post	Jr. Detective Corp.	Post Toasties	5/21/32	10/15/33	56.000 *
Skippy	Skippy Cards	Wheaties	1/2/33	in-pack	2.000.000
Skippy	Skippy Bowl	Wheaties	3/1/33	in store	300.000
Dick Daring	Magic Trick Book	Quaker Puffed	3/1/33	12/31/33	150.000 *
Orphan Annie	Mug	Ovaltine	3/6/33	7/31/33	1.580.000 *
Jack Armstrong	Babe Ruth Movie Book	Wheaties	7/7/33	4/21/34	106.538
Jack Armstrong	Johnny Weismuller Photo	Wheaties	8/15/33	12/18/34	30.213
Jack Armstrong	Shooting Planes	Wheaties	9/7/33	12/28/34	424.441
Tom Mix	Straight Shooter Membership	Ralston	10/8/33	9/30/34	
Tom Mix	Life Story Manual	Ralston	10/8/33	9/30/34	
Tom Mix	Picture of Tom Mix & Tony	Ralston	10/8/33	9/30/34	1.222.046
Tom Mix	Straight Shooters Sweater Patch	Ralston	10/8/33	9/30/34	
Tom Mix	Lucky Horseshoe Nail Ring	Ralston	10/8/33	9/30/34	
Tom Mix	Wooden Gun, opens	Ralston	10/23/33	9/30/34	856.771
Jack Armstrong	Grip Developer	Wheaties	11/7/33	1/27/36	100.736
Tom Mix	Bandana	Ralston	12/3/33	9/30/34	186.434
Tom Mix	Lucky Spinner	Ralston	12/14/33	12/31/34	600.000 *
Jack Armstrong	Photos, set of 3	Wheaties	1/7/34	7/31/35	110.377
Tom Mix	Action Photos - Set "A"	Ralston	1/25/34	6/1/34	87.435
Dick Daring	New Bag of Tricks	Quaker	3/1/34	12/31/34	250.000 *
Jack Armstrong	J. Armstrong Picture Offer	Wheaties	3/13/34	5/29/36	12.056
Jack Armstrong	B. Fairfield Picture Offer	Wheaties	3/13/34	5/29/36	2.406
Jack Armstrong	Wee Gyro	Wheaties	3/19/34	9/13/35	99.462
Jack Armstrong	Horse Naming Contest	Wheaties	6/10/34	8/24/34	62.976
Frank Buck	Jungle Game	Black Flag	6/17/34	8/17/34	8.000 *
Babe Ruth	Book, Scorekeeper, Membership Pin	Quaker	7/15/34	—	—
Jack Armstrong	J.A. on his Horse - Picture	Wheaties	7/18/34	10/5/35	64.212
Joe E. Brown	Bike Contest - Bike Club Button & Funny Bike Book	Quaker Oats	9/9/34	10/31/34	50.000 *
Jack Armstrong	Stamp Offers	Wheaties	11/10/34	4/15/36	452.787
Tom Mix	Zyp Gun	Ralston	11/11/34	12/28/34	3.000 *
Tom Mix	Branding Iron	Quaker	12/2/34	2/28/35	46.204
Babe Ruth	Big Book of Baseball	Quaker	12/2/34	—	115.000 *
Tom Mix	Theater & Western Movie "Rustler's Roundup"	Ralston	1/13/35	3/13/35	275.718
Amos 'n Andy	Weber City Map	Pepsodent	1/27/35	4/3/35	400.000 *
Tom Mix	"Trail of the Terrible Six"	Ralston	2/16/35	4/17/35	292.294
Devil Dogs	Ring and other premiums	Quaker	2/16/35	—	—
Jack Armstrong	Bernie Bierman Picture	Wheaties	2/27/35	3/29/35	351
China Clipper Movie	China Clipper Ship Kit	Quaker Oats	3/16/35	11/16/36	—
China Clipper Movie	Pilot's Cap	Quaker Oats	3/16/35	11/16/36	—
China Clipper Movie	Aviation Goggles	Quaker Oats	3/16/35	11/16/36	—
China Clipper Movie	Gold Plated Aviation Ring	Quaker Oats	3/16/35	11/16/36	—
China Clipper Movie	Gold Plated Bracelet	Quaker Oats	3/16/35	11/16/36	—
China Clipper Movie	Wing Emblem Pin	Quaker Oats	3/16/35	11/16/36	—
Tom Mix	Trick Spinning Rope	Ralston	3/23/35	5/24/35	44.318
Babe Ruth	Baseball Ring	Muffets	4/22/35	11/30/36	—
Babe Ruth	Girl's Baseball Bracelet	Muffets	4/22/35	11/30/36	—
Babe Ruth	Professional League Baseball	Muffets	4/22/35	11/30/36	—
Babe Ruth	Umpire's Scorekeeper	Muffets	4/22/35	11/30/36	—
Babe Ruth	Baseball Cap	Muffets	4/22/35	11/30/36	—
Babe Ruth	Girl's Beret	Muffets	4/22/35	11/30/36	—
Babe Ruth	Toe Plates	Muffets	4/22/35	11/30/36	—
Babe Ruth	Heel Plates	Muffets	4/22/35	11/30/36	—
Orphan Annie	Mug w/ROA & Sandy Running	Ovaltine	4/22/35	—	900.000 *
Jack Armstrong	Sloop (Test)	Wheaties	5/13/35	12/16/37	30

* Rounded or estimated number

Show	Premium	Sponsor	Start	End	Quantity
Orphan Annie	2nd Shake-up Mug	Ovaltine	6/9/35	8/31/36	1,747,000*
Dizzy Dean	Membership Pin	Grape-Nuts	7/14/35	12/31/35	21,313
Dizzy Dean	Lucky Piece	Grape-Nuts	7/14/35	12/31/35	8,496
Tom Mix	Lucky Wrist Band	Ralston	9/29/35	11/29/35	34,216
Tom Mix	Sun Watch	Ralston	12/1/35	2/1/36	58,818
Amos 'n Andy	Free toothpaste sample	Pepsodent	1/12/36	2/17/36	—
Scoop Ward	Reporter's Badge	Ward's Bread	1/12/36	4/30/36	26,000*
Tom Mix	Rocket Parachute	Ralston	1/12/36	3/12/36	186,423
Joe E. Brown	Membership Pin & Club Manual	Grape Nuts	3/1/36	12/31/36	28,525
Tom Mix	Wooden Gun	Ralston	3/8/36	6/8/36	155,688
Melvin Purvis	Jr. G-Man Corp Membership Badge & Instruction Manual	Post Toasties	3/8/36	12/31/36	185,789
Melvin Purvis	Jr. G-Man Corp Girls' Division	Post Toasties	3/8/36	12/31/36	7,902
Frank Hawks	Sky Patrol Membership Pin & Manual	Post Bran Flakes	3/14/36	12/31/36	78,000*
Dizzy Dean	Membership Pin	Grape-Nuts	3/15/36	12/31/36	82,493
Dizzy Dean	Winners Ring	Grape-Nuts	3/15/36	12/31/36	55,662
Frank Hawks	Air Hawks Membership Wing Badge	Post 40% Bran	4/12/36	12/31/36	42,943
Joe E. Brown	Membership Ring	Grape Nuts	4/19/36	12/31/36	92,000*
Joe E. Brown	Diamond Squirt Ring	Grape Nuts	4/19/36	12/31/36	9,400*
Joe E. Brown	Periscope	Grape Nuts	4/19/36	12/31/36	—
Fibber McGee & Molly	Spinning Tops	Johnson Wax	4/22/36	5/30/36	—
Betty & Bob	Pic. Offer for Betty & Bob Program	Bisquick	4/30/36	5/6/36	11,201
Radio Orphan Annie	Birthstone Ring	Ovaltine	6/7/36	2/10/37	342,278
Jack Armstrong	J.A. Map - Talismans	Wheaties	9/19/36	4/29/37	156,036
Jim Babcock	Buckaroo Book & Range Rider's Compass	Log Cabin Syrup	9/20/36	6/30/37	—
Tom Mix	Championship Cowboy Belt & Buckle	Ralston	9/27/36	12/27/36	83,447
Tom Mix	Championship Cowgirl Bracelet	Ralston	9/27/36	12/27/36	2,318
Jack Armstrong	J.A. Oriental Stamp Offer	Wheaties	9/30/36	4/1/37	19,992
Orphan Annie	Circus	Ovaltine	9/30/36	11/4/36	618,949
Bobby & Betty	Huskie Club Pin	Huskies	11/1/36	4/30/37	—
Bobby & Betty	Lucky Rabbit Foot	Huskies	11/1/36	4/30/37	—
Tom Mix	Signet Initial Ring with Straight Shooter newspaper & TM Bar Sweater Emblem	Ralston	11/1/36	2/1/37	852,418
Jack Armstrong	Bernie Bierman Picture	Wheaties	11/3/36	—	215
Jack Armstrong	Big 10 Football Game	Wheaties	11/24/36	2/15/37	6,378
Tom Mix	Compass & Magnifying Glass	Ralston	11/30/36	3/6/37	20,739
Tom Mix	Movie Make-Up Kit	Ralston	1/10/37	4/10/37	48,600
Tom Mix	Target Ring	Marlin Guns	1/17/37	7/15/37	—
Bobby Benson	2-1/2¢ Bobby Benson Money	Force	2/7/37	—	—
Jack Armstrong	Moviescopes - African film	Wheaties	2/8/37	3/5/38	228,129
Radio Orphan Annie	2 Initial Signet Ring	Ovaltine	3/4/37	4/14/37	168,000*
Tom Mix	Straight Shooter Gold Badge	Ralston	3/14/37	6/7/37	156,222
Buck Jones	Membership Pin & Manual	Grape Nuts	3/21/37	12/31/37	98,275
Buck Jones	Membership Ring	Grape Nuts	3/21/37	12/31/37	124,400
Jack Armstrong	Cereal Bowl	Wheaties	4/8/37	in-store	several million
Orphan Annie	Foreign Coin Folder	Ovaltine	6/14/37	8/14/37	38,628
Fibber McGee & Molly	Trailer Contest	Johnson Wax	7/11/37	—	—
Jack Armstrong	Big 10 Football Games	Wheaties	8/7/37	5/31/40	176,446
Tom Mix	Live Baby Turtle	Ralston	9/26/37	12/26/37	135,000*
Tom Mix	Telescope	Ralston	11/21/37	2/21/38	110,000*
Jack Armstrong	Stationery	Wheaties	11/27/37	1/20/39	95,396
Tom Mix	Secret Telephone	Ralston	11/28/37	2/28/38	263,829
Radio Orphan Annie	Gold Plated School Pin	Ovaltine	1/17/38	3/27/38	37,337
Jack Armstrong	J.A. Whistling Rings	Wheaties	1/17/38	5/20/40	817,313
Tom Mix	Signal Sets	Ralston	2/20/38	5/20/38	418,450
Dick Tracy	Secret Compartment Ring	Quaker Puffed	2/27/38	12/31/38	447,367
Dick Tracy	Lucky Bangle Bracelet	Quaker Puffed	2/27/38	12/31/38	7,458
Dick Tracy	Secret Service Patrol Membership Badge & Secret Code Book	Quaker Puffed	2/27/38	12/31/38	810,108
Jack Armstrong	Explorer's Telescopes (in-store)	Wheaties	4/8/38	6/17/38	1,706,680
Dick Tracy	Secret Detecto-Kit	Quaker Puffed	5/15/38	6/30/38	79,500*
Orphan Annie	Shake-Up Mug	Ovaltine	5/15/38	—	152,000*

Character	Premium	Sponsor	Start	End	Quantity
Jack Armstrong	Wrist Compass (Test)	Wheaties	6/2/38	12/12/38	3,017
Jack Armstrong	Heliograph (Test)	Wheaties	7/11/38	10/13/39	1,389
Jack Armstrong	Wheaties Baseball Bat (Test)	Wheaties	7/18/38	6/6/39	266
Jack Armstrong	Baseball Rings	Corn Kix & Wheaties	7/27/38	10/28/38	46,501
Dick Tracy	Siren Plane	Quaker Puffed	8/14/38	—	—
Dick Tracy	Air Detective's Cap	Quaker Puffed	8/14/38	—	—
Dick Tracy	Flying Goggles	Quaker Puffed	8/14/38	—	—
Dick Tracy	Wing Bracelet	Quaker Puffed	8/14/38	—	—
Dick Tracy	Aviation Wings	Quaker Puffed	8/14/38	—	—
Dick Tracy	Training Ball	Quaker Puffed	8/14/38	—	—
Jack Armstrong	American Boy Subscriptions	Wheaties	9/12/38	4/15/41	6,137
Tom Mix	Fountain Pen (reoffer)	Ralston	9/12/38	1/31/39	44,528
Jack Armstrong	Wheaties Football Rings (Test)	Wheaties	10/17/38	1/6/39	629
Jack Armstrong	Grid-O-Scopes (Test)	Wheaties & Kix	10/18/38	1/6/39	1,043
Jack Armstrong	Hike-O-Meters	Wheaties	10/21/38	11/15/38	1,231,987
Tom Mix	Secret Ink Writing Set, Decoder, 8 pg Instruction Book	Ralston	11/5/38	5/9/38	62,118
Tom Mix	Pocket Size Flashlight	Ralston	11/20/38	2/28/39	113,711
Tom Mix	Mystery Ring	Ralston	12/5/38	1/31/39	942,477
Tom Mix	Pocket Knife	Ralston	1/15/39	3/8/39	1,124,368
Tom Mix	Periscope	Ralston	2/12/39	4/12/39	38,714
Jack Armstrong	Flashlight (in-store)	Wheaties	4/1/39	6/10/39	1,624,120
Orphan Annie	Goofy Circus	Ovaltine	4/2/39	5/2/39	75,000
Dick Tracy	Radio Adventure Book	Quaker Puffed	5/21/39	9/1/39	218,628
Dick Tracy	Siren Code Pencil	Quaker Puffed	5/21/39	9/1/39	7,914
Dick Tracy	Flashlight	Quaker Puffed	5/21/39	9/1/39	125,821
Dick Tracy	Aviation Cap	Quaker Puffed	5/21/39	9/1/39	—
Jack Armstrong	Pedometer	Wheaties	6/7/39	2/28/42	889,343
Jack Armstrong	Sentinel First Aid Kit - Billy & Betty and Rundia, the Magician	Corn Kix	6/27/39	11/14/39	22,351
Orphan Annie	Shake-up Mug, Annie jumping rope	Ovaltine	7/9/39	8/16/39	135,000 *
Frank Buck	Jungle Knife	Ivory Soap	8/13/39	9/30/39	10,000 *
Frank Buck	Ivory Ring	Ivory Soap	8/13/39	9/30/39	92,000 *
Buck Rogers	Whistling Rocket Ship	Muffets	9/17/39	WSL	250,000 *
Tom Mix	Wooden Six Shooter, solid	Ralston	9/24/39	11/24/39	178,918
Jack Armstrong	Rocket Chute (Test)	Wheaties	9/29/39	10/14/39	95
Jack Armstrong	J.A. Safety Signal Light Kits	Wheaties	10/9/39	9/30/40	162,520
Tom Mix	3-color Flashlight	Ralston	10/29/39	12/31/39	125,327
Jack Armstrong	Jr. Ace-First Aid Kit - Billy & Betty	Corn Kix	11/17/39	1/17/41	14,643
Tom Mix	Streamlined Parachute Plane	Ralston	11/26/39	1/28/40	26,917
Jack Armstrong	J.A. Magic Answer Box	Wheaties	1/5/40	12/31/40	606,203
Tom Mix	Telegraph Set w/Battery & Int'l Code	Ralston	1/7/40	3/10/40	64,510
Tom Mix	Movie Make-up Kit	Ralston	2/11/40	5/15/40	25,483
Jack Armstrong	Dragon Eye Ring	Wheaties	4/12/40	11/29/41	391,301
Jack Armstrong	Listening Squad Kit (Test)	Wheaties	4/13/40	6/10/40	417
Jack Armstrong	Sky Ranger Airplane	Wheaties	4/21/40	in-store	several million
Orphan Annie	Shake-up Mug, Annie jumping rope	Ovaltine	5/5/40	6/12/40	211,000 *
Jack Armstrong	Baseball Pencils – Luminous (Test)	Wheaties	6/22/40	7/30/40	735
Jack Armstrong	Cat's Eye Ring (Test)	Wheaties	7/13/40	7/25/40	410
Jack Armstrong	Luminous Pencil (Test)	Wheaties	7/13/40	7/30/40	253
Charlie McCarthy	Gold Plated Bust Ring	Chase & Sanborn	9/5/40	10/31/40	81,576
Tom Mix	Indian Blow Gun	Ralston	9/29/40	12/29/40	40,511
Jack Armstrong	Betty's Luminous Gardenia Bracelet (includes orders from soap opera)	Wheaties & Gold Medal	11/1/40	2/18/42	199,760
Orphan Annie	Secret Guard Membership Mysto-Snapper, Member Badge, Handbook & Slidomatic Decoder	Quaker Puffed	2/23/41	12/31/41	62,110
Tom Mix	Tom Mix Comic Book #5	Ralston	4/13/41	5/18/41	216,363
Orphan Annie	2 Orphan Annie Comic Books	Quaker Puffed	4/13/41	WSL	100,000

Show	Premium	Sponsor	Start	End	Quantity
Lone Ranger	Pre-Sponsorship Offer L. R. Photo	Corn Kix	4/23/41	10/11/43	97,654
Lone Ranger	Warning Sirens - L. R. Nat'l Defenders	Corn Kix	5/19/41	2/28/42	106,338
Jack Armstrong	Crocodile Whistle (Test)	Wheaties	5/23/41	6/19/41	809
Jack Armstrong	L.R. Blackout Safety Belts (Test)	Wheaties	5/23/41	7/26/41	2,081
Orphan Annie	Magnifying Ring	Quaker	6/18/41	8/15/42	50,000 *
Lone Ranger (Tests)	INSERT in Whistling Sirens Silver Bullet - Lone Ranger	Corn Kix	6/25/41	9/30/42	4,003
Lone Ranger in 41 states	- Whistling Jim		This was the original test		18
	Buckaroo Neck Scarf - Lone Ranger		to compare the pulling		388
Whistling Jim in 7 states around	- Whistling Jim		power of Whistling Jim		24
	First Aid Kit - Lone Ranger		in comparison with The		628
Atlanta, GA where	- Whistling Jim		Lone Ranger. It also		47
Merita Bread	Billfold & Play Money - Lone Ranger		tested several new pre-		408
controlled rights.	- Whistling Jim		miums at the same time.		21
The seven states not	Defenders Cap - Lone Ranger		The name Whistling Jim		576
included in General	- Whistling Jim		was later dropped. The		50
Mills Lone Ranger	Brooch & Earrings - Lone Ranger		same premium offered in		534
promotions were	- Whistling Jim		the non-Lone Ranger		65
Alabama, Florida,	Wrist Compass - Lone Ranger		territory was simply		866
Georgia, Louisiana,	- Whistling Jim		called a "Western" or		59
North Carolina,	Indian Headdress & Beads - Lone Ranger		"Cowboy" item.		330
South Carolina, and	- Whistling Jim				15
Virginia.	Concha Studded Cowboy Vest - Lone Ranger				65
	- Whistling Jim				5
	Cattleman's Belt - Lone Ranger				436
	- Whistling Jim				46
	Rough Rider's Polo Shirt - Lone Ranger				200
	- Whistling Jim				5
	Wild West Movie Viewer - Lone Ranger				654
	- Whistling Jim				38
Tom Mix	Comic #6	Ralston	6/28/41	8/30/41	220,432
Jack Armstrong premiums offered	INSERT in Warning Sirens Flashlight Pistol	Wheaties	7/17/41	9/2/41	367
in Lone Ranger	Congo Chess Game	Wheaties	7/17/41	9/25/41	91
premium mailings	Jungle Blow-Gun	Wheaties	7/17/41	11/17/41	138
Jack Armstrong	J.A. Picture Book (Test)	Wheaties	8/2/41	9/2/41	753
Tom Mix	Straight Shooters membership - Decoder Badge and Secret Manual	Ralston	9/28/41	11/30/41	234,821
Jack Armstrong	Sound Effect Kit	Wheaties	10/3/41	2/28/42	114,140
Lone Ranger	Lone Ranger Luminous Blackout Safety Belts	Corn Kix	10/21/41	10/16/42	566,585
Lone Ranger	Photo Ring (Test)	Corn Kix	10/31/41	11/6/41	463
Lone Ranger	Military Ring (Test)	Corn Kix	10/31/41	11/5/41	215
Lone Ranger	Military Pin	Corn Kix	10/31/41	11/5/41	77
Jack Armstrong	J.A. Bombsights	Wheaties	1/5/42	9/29/42	444,677
Lone Ranger	L.R.-200 Word Essay - "How I Earn Money to Buy Defense Stamps"		1/15/42	3/23/42	5,299
Orphan Annie	Training Cockpit & Manual	Quaker	1/15/42	3/31/42	46,233
Tom Mix	Western Signature Ring	Ralston	1/25/42	3/31/42	289,510
Lone Ranger	Military Pin	Corn Kix	2/5/42	4/26/42	19,542
Lone Ranger	Military Ring	Corn Kix	2/17/42	12/17/42	595,045
Lone Ranger	Lone Ranger Victory Corps	Kix/Cheerios	3/19/42	8/6/46	154,332
Lone Ranger	INSERT in Military Rings (Test)	Kix	4/7/42	in-pack	
	Military Stationery & 28 Army Insignia Stamps				65
	Football Dart Game				39
	Luminous Arm Band				135
	Meteorite Ring				85
	Ju Jitsu and Detective Book				62
Lone Ranger	Military Stationery (Test)	Corn Kix	4/24/42	5/29/42	116
Lone Ranger	Coat Emblem & Luminous Arm Band (Test)	Corn Kix	4/24/42	6/5/42	251
Lone Ranger	Coat Emblem & Semaphore Flags (Test)	Corn Kix	4/24/42	5/29/42	83
Lone Ranger	Semaphore Flags, Arm Band & Coat				

Character	Premium	Sponsor	Start	End	Quantity
	Emblem (Test)	Corn Kix	4/24/42	5/29/42	360
Lone Ranger	L.R. Defense Letters	Corn Kix	5/9/42	7/14/42	1,292
Lone Ranger	Plane Spotter plus Vic. Corps (Test)	Corn Kix	5/15/42	6/18/42	228
Lone Ranger	MacArthur Picture plus Victory Corps (Test)	Corn Kix	5/15/42	6/18/42	105
Lone Ranger	Set of Two Jigsaw Puzzles (Test)	Corn Kix	5/28/42	9/14/42	110
Lone Ranger	L.R. Scrap Rubber Campaign		7/1/42	8/27/42	1,383
Lone Ranger	L.R. Billfold	Corn Kix & Cheerioats	8/21/42	2/26/46	308,281
Lone Ranger	L.R. Blackout Kit Offer	Corn Kix	9/11/42	4/5/43	134,457
Tom Mix	Commandos Comic Book #10	Ralston	10/4/42	1/1/43	196,417
Jack Armstrong	Write a Fighter Corp Kit	Wheaties	10/9/42	1/8/45	149,407
Tom Mix	Commandos Comic Book #11	Ralston	11/22/42	2/11/43	175,349
Tom Mix	Commandos Comic Book #12	Ralston	1/10/43	3/17/43	134,239
Terry and the Pirates	"Mascot" Photo	Quaker Puffed	2/5/43	4/30/43	—
Jack Armstrong	Future Champions of America	Wheaties	10/6/43	8/8/46	113,719
Lone Ranger	L.R. Offers - Decals (Test)	Cheerioats	4/10/44	12/26/44	405
Lone Ranger	L.R. Offers - Masks (Test)	Cheerioats	4/10/44	12/26/44	422
Lone Ranger	L.R. Offers - Decoders (Test)	Cheerioats	4/10/44	12/26/44	343
Jack Armstrong	True-Flite Model Planes #1 P40 & Zero #2 Spitfire & Focke Wolf #3 Helcat & Nakajima #4 Fulmart-Heinkel #5 Thunderbolt - & Yak #6 Aircobra-Stormovik #7 Mustang - Jap Aichi Bargain Offer #1 #2	Wheaties	4/27/44	3/7/47	3,381,400
Lone Ranger	Regulation US Army Cavalry Spurs (Test)	Corn Kix	6/26/44	3/20/45	749
Lone Ranger	Tattoo Transfers	Corn Kix	9/7/44	10/30/45	237,414
Dick Tracy	Detective Kit, paper decoder, wall chart, suspect file, paper badge, certificate, tape, & manual	Tootsie Roll	12/12/44	2/28/45	149,722
Terry & the Pirates	Jingle Contest	Quaker Puffed	1/24/45	3/24/45	—
Lone Ranger	Military Poster Stamps & Album	Cheerioats	2/11/45	12/31/45	390,670
Lone Ranger	Secret Compartment Rings	Kix	2/11/45	6/30/46	503,738
Jack Armstrong	Cub Pilot Corps Pre-Flight Training Kit	Wheaties	4/6/45	2/28/46	399,798
Lone Ranger	Kix Airbase	Corn Kix	5/7/45	12/31/46	1,033,234
Jack Armstrong	Pre-Flight Training Kit	In Store with Wheaties purchase	2/2/46	12/1/47	2,000,000
Lone Ranger	Weather Ring	Breakfast Tray	5/7/46	12/1/47	603,483
Tom Mix	Magnet Ring	Ralston	10/5/46	2/15/47	462,950
Tom Mix	Name the Colt Contest	Ralston	1/12/47	2/15/47	—
Lone Ranger	Atomic Bomb Ring	Kix	1/19/47	WSL	3,400,000
none	Compass Ring	Nabisco	2/16/47	WSL	60,000 *
Tom Mix	Compass-Magnifying Glass	Ralston	4/6/47	12/31/47	174,287
Tom Mix	Rocket Parachute (revised)	Ralston	7/12/47	10/15/47	38,419
Terry & the Pirates	Pirate's Gold Detector Ring	Quaker Puffed	9/28/47	12/31/47	604,279
Lone Ranger	Silver Bullet	Cherrios	10/5/47	WSL	320,000 *
Capt. Midnight	Shake-Up Mug	Ovaltine	10/5/47	12/31/47	40,000 *
Tom Mix	Glow-In-The-Dark Spurs	Ralston	10/5/47	WSL	193,463
Lone Ranger	Six Shooter Ring	Kix	10/5/47	12/31/55	934,150
Green Hornet	Green Hornet Secret Seal Ring	Breakfast Tray	10/12/47	WSL	534,163
Tom Mix	ID Bracelet & Automatic Finger-printing Card	Ralston	11/3/47	1/15/48	73,478
Capt. Midnight	Spy-Scope	Ovaltine	11/10/47	2/28/48	276,000 *
Sky King	Secret Signalscope	Peter Pan PB	11/10/47	12/3/47	110,000 *
Sky King	Mystery Picture Ring (Test)	Peter Pan PB	12/10/47	2/15/48	139,765
Sky King	Stamping Kit (Test)	Peter Pan PB	12/10/47	2/15/48	29,462
Tom Mix	Name the Collie Contest	Ralston	1/7/48	2/15/48	—
Superman	Jet Plane Ring	PEP	2/27/48	6/30/48	315,000 *
Fireball Twigg	Explorer's Ring	Grape Nuts	2/28/48	11/20/48	84,000 *
Lone Ranger	Pedometer	Cheerios	2/29/48	6/30/48	894,681
Roger Wilco	Magni-Ray Ring	Power House	3/14/48	WSL	45,000 *

Character	Premium	Sponsor	Start	End	Quantity
Lone Ranger	Frontier Town	Cherrios	5/23/48	6/25/48	2,000,000 *
King Features	Metal Comic Rings, 12	Post's Raisin Bran	6/13/48	in-pack	several million
Superman	F-87 Super Jet Plane Ring	Kellogg Corn Flks	9/17/48	2/28/49	160,000
Roy Rogers	Name the Colt Contest	Quaker Oats	10/10/48	11/15/48	
Sky King	Name-a-Plane Contest	Peter Pan PB	11/3/48	12/04/48	
Lone Ranger	Flashlight Ring	Cheerios	11/3/48	3/18/49	666,190
Lone Ranger	Movie Film Ring	Cheerios	12/2/48	6/30/49	582,657
Ted Williams	Baseball Ring	Nabisco	9/19/48	12/1/48	75,000*
Sky King	Magna Glo Writing Ring	Powerhouse	1/12/49	6/30/49	753,345
Tom Mix	Musical Ring & Plastic TV Viewer	Ralston	1/19/49	WSL	437,918
Lone Ranger	Deputy Badge	Cheerios	1/20/49	12/31/49	320,000*
Roy Rogers	Microscope Ring	Quaker Oats	2/27/49	3/31/49	647,125
Jack Armstrong	Explorers Sun Watch	Wheaties	3/14/49	4/30/49	165,224
Frank Buck	Explorer Sun Watch	Wheaties	3/27/49	5/31/49	100,000*
Tom Mix	Signal Arrowhead & Secret Code	Ralston	4/17/49	WSL	47,771
Sky King	Electronic TV Picture Ring	Peter Pan PB	4/18/49	WSL	678,816
Sgt Preston	Dog Picture Cards	Quaker Puffed	5/15/49	in-pack & sets by mail	6-8 million
Lone Ranger	L.R. Mystery Deputy Contest	Cherrios	6/12/49	8/11/49	76,299
Andy Pafko	Scorekeepers Baseball Ring	Muffets	7/17/49	9/15/49	37,615
Roy Rogers	Picture Post Card - Contest	Quaker Oats	10/2/49	11/14/49	—
Sky King	Spy-Detecto Writer	Peter Pan PB	10/16/49	1/1/50	350,000*
Gene Autry	5 Comic Books	Quaker Puffed	10/10/49	WSL	—
Lone Ranger	Flashlight Pistol	Cheerios	11/2/49	2/26/50	424,601
Donald Duck	Donald Duck Living Toy Ring	Kellogg PEP	11/27/49	WSL	320,000*
Tom Mix	Golden Plastic Bullet Telescope & Magic Tone Birdcall	Ralston	12/5/49	WSL	135,214
David Harding	Counterspy Jr. Agent Badge	Pepsi	12/11/49	3/10/50	22,351
Lone Ranger	Bandana Offer	Betty Crocker Soups	2/1/50	12/31/50	48,347
Sgt Preston	Yukon Trail - 8 different packages	Quaker Puffed	2/5/50	on-pack - WSL	9 million
Roy Rogers	Deputy Sheriff's Badge	Quaker Oats	2/12/50	3/31/50	173,437
Tom Mix	Toy Television Set, 5 Films & Magic Tiger-Eye Ring	Ralston	4/9/50	WSL	122,817
Sky King	Navajo Treasure Ring	Peter Pan PB	5/1/50	6/30/50	500,000*
Lone Ranger	Luck Piece	Cheerios	5/1/50	7/31/50	34,402
Sgt Preston	Yukon Adventure Picture Cards, 36	Quaker Puffed	7/9/50	in-pack & mail	several millions
Lone Ranger	2 Gun Belt, Holster & Shirt	Cheerios	8/15/50	12/31/50	38,722
Lone Ranger	2 Guns & Belt	Cherrios	8/15/50	12/31/50	54,500
Space Patrol	First Membership Kit (no ring)	Ralston	10/16/50	12/31/51	397,418
Sgt Preston	Mounted Police Whistle	Quaker Puffed	10/22/50	12/31/50	211,365
Roy Rogers	Autographed Souvenir Cup	Quaker Oats	10/22/50	12/31/50	347,638
Lone Ranger	Saddle Ring	Cheerios	2/7/51	4/7/51	313,788
none	Rocket-to-the Moon Ring	Kix	3/11/51	4/20/51	57,117
Lone Ranger	Win a Horse Contest	Cheerios	3/28/51	5/28/51	—
Lone Ranger	Coloring Contest Postcards	Cherrios	4/13/51	6/8/51	431,591
none	Secret Compartment Boot Ring	Popsicle	5/1/51	WSL	175,000 *
Hopalong Cassidy	36 Wild West Trading Cards	Post	6/10/51	in-pack	several million
Roy Rogers	Humming Lariat	Carr Biscuits	7/1/51	WSL	—
Hopalong Cassidy	Why I like Grape Nuts Contest	Grape Nuts	7/8/51	8/15/51	80,000*
Gabby Hayes	"Peacemaker" Six-Shooter	Quaker Puffed	7/22/51	WSL	—
Gabby Hayes	5 Gene Autry Comic Books	Quaker Puffed	8/5/51	WSL	—
Hopalong Cassidy	Western Badges, 12	Post Raisin Bran	9/16/51	WSL	several million
Gabby Hayes	Shooting Cannon Ring	Quaker Puffed	10/16/51	WSL	289,472
Space Patrol	Jet-glow Code Belt	Ralston	10/20/51	12/31/55	177,235
Lone Ranger	Six Shooter Ring (reoffer)	Sugar Jets	1/10/52	1/30/59	350,000 *
Space Patrol	Cosmic Smoke Gun, red	Ralston	2/10/52	12/31/55	147,456
Sgt Preston	Totem Poles, 5	Quaker Puffed	3/23/52	WSL	48,000 *
Space Patrol	Lunar Fleet Base	Ralston	4/6/52	10/31/52	218,456
Roy Rogers	Riders Club Kits	Post	5/18/52	10/1/52	250,000 *
Major Mar's	Rocket Ring	Popsicle	6/1/52	WSL	125,000 *
Space Patrol	Second Membership Kit	Ralston	6/28/52	12/31/53	267,333
Gabby Hayes	Old Time Auto Collection, 5	Quaker Puffed	8/3/52	WSL	22,000 *
Wild Bill Hickok	Treasure Map	Kellogg's Corn Pops	9/14/52	none listed	185,000 *
Space Patrol	Space-O-Phones	Ralston	10/4/52	12/31/55	319,550

Show	Premium	Sponsor	Start	End	Quantity
Space Patrol	Binoculars, black	Ralston	1/3/53	12/31/55	168,718
Space Patrol	Magic Space Pictures	Ralston	3/14/53	7/15/53	several million
Capt. Midnight	Mug	Ovaltine	3/15/53	6/30/58	750,000*
Andy Devine	Rodeo Contest	Kellogg's Sugar Pops	3/15/53	4/15/53	—
Gabby Hayes/ Sgt. Preston	Western Wagon Kit	Quaker Puffed	3/22/53	WSL	15,000 *
Space Patrol	Project-O-Scope	Ralston	4/11/53	10/31/53	97,916
Terry & the Pirates	Comic Books, 3 different	Canada Dry	5/1/53	in cartons - WSL	1.5 million
Space Patrol	Microscope	Ralston	6/27/53	2/28/54	56,672
Space Patrol	Interplanetary Coins	Ralston	9/12/53	1/31/54	12-15 million
Space Patrol	Name the Planet Contest Folder	Ralston	10/1/53	12/1/53	several million
Space Patrol	Ralston Rocket Balloon	Ralston	10/1/53	12/1/53	several million
Capt Video	Space Men, 12	Post's Raisin Bran	10/4/53	in-pack	3,000,000
Space Patrol	Color Trading Cards	Ralston	12/12/53	3/31/54	several million
Space Patrol	Outer Space Helmet	Ralston	12/26/53	12/31/55	44,992
Space Patrol	Cosmic Rocket Launcher	Ralston	4/16/54	12/31/55	22,682
Andy Devine	Name an episode on Wild Bill Hickok's show	Kelloggs Sugar Pops & Smacks	5/23/54	6/15/54	—
Space Patrol	Man from Mars Totem Head	Ralston	6/5/54	12/31/55	32,681
Space Patrol	Periscope	Ralston	9/11/54	12/31/55	45,433
Space Patrol	Hydrogen Ray Gun Ring	Ralston	10/9/54	12/31/55	35,227
Space Patrol	Rocket Cockpit	Nestles	10/23/54	12/31/54	40,000 *
Lone Ranger	Masks, 8	Wheaties	11/24/54	on-pack	11,000,000
Lone Ranger	Comic Book	Cheerios	11/24/54	in-pack	5,000,000
Lone Ranger	Jr. Deputy Kit	Cereals	11/28/55	6/10/56	210,438
Lone Ranger	Secret Invisible Writing Clue (INSERT)	In-pack	11/28/55	2/15/56	24 million
Lone Ranger	Name the Pony Contest	Nestles	10/28/56	11/30/56	—
Lone Ranger	Tonto Injun Belt	Trix & Kix	12/10/56	6/30/57	56,918
Lone Ranger	Hike O Meter (Official)	Wheaties	12/10/56	6/30/57	142,333
Lone Ranger	Branding Iron Stamper	Kix	12/10/56	6/30/57	40,224
Lone Ranger	Fun Kit - LR Ranch Game Book, Photo, Crayons	Cheerios	1/3/57	7/15/57	184,416
Lone Ranger	Life Size Poster of Lone Ranger & Tonto		12/1/57	WSL	10,000 *
Lone Ranger	L.R. Wild West Town Plastic Figures, 22 pcs	Cheerios	1/12/58	1/31/59	95,061
Wyatt Earp	Marshall's Ring	Cheerios	4/10/58	2/28/60	193,466
Rin Tin Tin	Indian Totem Pole, 8	Nabisco	6/1/58	in-pack	—
Rin Tin Tin	Fort Apache	Cheerios, Kix & Frosty O's	1/4/60	6/30/60	38,815

WHERE TO BUY AND SELL

Thousands of radio and character premiums are found each year. Collectors find duplications or sometimes decide to sell their collections.

The best way to find items you're searching for is to contact as many dealers and collectors as possible. Ask what they have for sale or for specific items. Let them know your interest and get back in touch in a month or two.

Subscribe to the mail auctions. Watch the prices realized, where available, to determine the bids necessary to acquire items in a mail auction. Mailing a bid is usually not enough to capture a choice item. Call on the closing day to determine where your bid stands and decide if you wish to bid higher. A 10% raise over the highest bid is usually required.

The dealers and collectors listed have paid for the representation. They are some of the most active people in the buying and selling of premiums . . . probably involved in over 80% of all premium transactions.

Sellers are advised to contact the individual collectors if they wish to sell an individual items at "retail." Collections can best be turned without delay to a dealer. Naturally this would be at a price where the dealer could make money.

A substantial collection might also be sold through ads in Box Top Bonanza or at a show such as the Big D Dallas convention of radio premium collectors.

Collector and dealer advertisers are largely known to the author. The publication reserved the right to reject any individuals with a questionable reputation. This publication, however, cannot be responsible for any transactions between readers and advertisers. If a conflict arises, however, Tomart will contact the dealer or collector in an attempt to resolve the matter. Please contact Tomart Publications, P.O. Box 292102, Dayton, OH 45429 in the event of a problem.

HAKE'S AMERICANA & COLLECTIBLES
MAIL & PHONE BID AUCTIONS

Since 1967 we have specialized in the finest original collectibles (no reproductions) in these categories:

DISNEYANA • COMIC CHARACTER ITEMS • TOYS • RADIO PREMIUMS
WESTERN & SPACE HERO ITEMS • EARLY RADIO & TV ITEMS • ADVERTISING COLLECTIBLES
PRESIDENTIAL CAMPAIGN ITEMS • PINBACK BUTTONS OF ALL TYPES • SPORTS
MOVIE ITEMS • AVIATION • BICYCLES • AUTOMOTIVE • WORLD WAR I AND II
PATRIOTIC ITEMS, WORLD'S FAIRS • EPHEMERA • SHIRLEY TEMPLE &
RELATED DOLL ITEMS • GUM CARDS

Our bi-monthly catalogues offer a fascinating array of original collectibles. Each "Mail & Phone Bid Auction" catalogue pictures, describes, and gives an estimated value for some 3000 items in the above categories. Bidders participate by sending in a bid sheet and on the closing day of the auction, the status of bids may be checked by phone. We would like to show you what is available –

$3.00 Sample Copy — 1 Catalogue
$10.00 Subscription — 4 Catalogues
$20.00 Subscription — 8 Catalogues

Hake's

P.O. BOX 1444
YORK, PA 17405
(717) 848-1333

ILLUSTRATION BY BILL NELSON

Robert A. Brown, Box 1381, Edmond, OK 73083-1381. BOXES, CANS & SIGNS! 30's, 40's, 50's-cereal, Ovaltine-etc. premiums, character items, Quick YES/NO, will price. 405-341-4803 7-10 pm

Jerry & Mona Cook, 3288 White Cloud Dr., Hacienda Heights, CA 91745. (818) 333-7107. Collectors: Specializing in cereal boxes, radio & cereal premiums, Donald Duck, cap pistols, radio & TV heroes of the 40's & 50's.

Steve Dando, 4572 Mark Trail, Copley, OH 44321. Collector of antique radios and all radio & TV comic character premiums including Sky King, Tom Mix, Capt. Midnight, Capt. Video, Shadow, etc. Specialize in rings. (216) 666-7222

Robert De Cenzo, 18 Barber Rd., Framingham, MA 01701. 508-879-8541 after 6 PM. Radio premiums, games, and character related toys bought and sold.

Frank Della Vecchio, 125 Northfield St., Bridgeport, CT 06606. Collector of Captain Marvel Club items. Statues, buttons, anything related. Also Gene Autry pinbacks, etc. Area Code 203-374-3920.

John Dillinger Museum, P.O. BOX 869, Nashville, IN 47448 (812) 988-7381 Collector of Melvin Purvis premiums, G-Man items, 1930's crime related items.

DICK TRACY Collectibles wanted! Buying premiums, toys, books, ephemera, figures, anything. Many trade items - send LSASE. **Larry Doucet**, 2351 Sultana Dr., Yorktown Heights, NY 10598

JUST KIDS NOSTALGIA

5 GREEN ST.
HUNTINGTON, NY
11743

(516) 423-8449

Catalog Now Available !!!

Send $3.00 for 40 pages of
Toys! Premiums! Gum Cards! Figures!
Pinback Button! Watches! Posters!

These are just some of the characters you'll find

- Superman
- Batman
- Mickey Mouse
- Donald Duck
- Pinocchio
- Fantasia
- Roy Rogers
- Hopalong Cassidy
- Lone Ranger
- Flash Gordon
- Dark Shadows
- Munsters
- Star Trek
- Beatles
- Monkees
- Elvis
- James Bond

- Buck Rogers
- Tom Corbett
- Capt. Video
- Dick Tracy
- Joe Palooka
- Tarzan
- Frank Buck
- Dennis The Menace
- Howdy Doody
- Bonanza
- Man From U.N.C.L.E.
- Bullwinkle
- Sky King
- Tom Mix
- Capt. Marvel
- Capt. Midnight

- Davy Crockett
- Pinky Lee
- Winky Dink
- Jackie Gleason
- Dragnet
- Flintstones
- Casper
- Top Cat
- Mr. Magoo

COME VISIT
OUR SHOP
TUES. THRU SAT.
11:00 - 5:00

BIG-D COLLECTIBLE SHOWS

(FORMERLY CALLED CHILDHOOD TREASURES)

The most successful annual gathering of collectors in the U.S.. A show for collectors by collectors.

BIG-D has the largest gathering of premium dealers at any show! Radio and TV Give-aways, Box-Top Treasures, TV Toys, and more. BIG-D is the official National Association of Premium Collectors Show.

BIG-D also boasts of being named the official National Convention of Big Little Book Collectors. More mint BLB's than you have ever seen in one dealer's room.

Our huge Dealer Room also has the top dealers in the U.S., offering the very best in Pre-1966 Toys, Disneyana, Comics, Movie Posters, B-Western Items, Comic Characters Items, Toy Soldiers, Gum Cards and much, much more. The 1989 Show will be on July 21-23 at the Sheraton Park Central in North Dallas.

For a free information packet on the next show write: Don Maris, PO Box 111266-P, Arlington, Texas 76007, Tel (817) 261-8745.

OLD CEREAL BOXES WANTED

Collector paying excellent prices for nice condition boxes. Boxes should have front, back, and sides. Contact: Don Maris, PO Box 111266-P, Arlington, Texas 76007. Tel. (817) 261-8745

George Fahy, 15 Vividleaf Ln., Levittown, PA 19054. Private collector of radio & cereal premiums, books by Edgar Rice Burroughs. Special interest Capt. Marvel, Straight Arrow, Tarzan, comic character pinbacks, figures, rings, etc. 215-943-3985

Cereal boxes wanted! Top dollar for Kix's Atom Bomb Ring box, Cheerios' Disney and Lone Ranger boxes, all boxes advertising premiums. Also buying 1930's Disneyana. **John Fawcett**, RR 2, 720 Middl Tpk., Storrs, CT 06268

Superman Collectibles Wanted! I buy all Superman items from 1938-1960: toys, premiums, figurines, pinbacks, puzzles, coloring books, advertising material, novelties, anything! **Danny Fuchs**, 209-80T 18th Avenue, Apt. 4K, Bayside, NY 11360. "America's Foremost Superman Collector"

Gary Fugate, c/o Wilbur Fugate, 477 N. 16th St., Vale, Oregon 97918. Collector of radio premiums and viewmaster, especially Straight Arrow, Sky King, Sgt. Preston, and the Lone Ranger. See Box Top Bonanza for current address.

OLDEN RADIO
A Collector of Classic Old-Time Radio Programs

Relive the excitement of Radio's Golden Age...An Era in which Radio Reigned Supreme and truly was "The Theater of The Mind." **Olden Radio** presents three 60 minute cassette tapes to introduce you to the fascinating hobby of listening to and collecting old time Radio Programs... **Radio** as **Radio** was meant to be.

Tape one consists of Radio Premium Announcements of such treasures as Glow in The Dark Rings, Secret Decoders, and Autographed Pictures of your Heroes, which could have been purchased for a boxtop and a dime. Tapes two and three are made up of opening program themes, commercials, skits, routines, and a complete 30 minute mystery thriller from this bye gone era. 180 minutes of Classic Radio!!

This special package of 3 tapes can be yours for only $10.75 by making your check or money order payable to:

**Olden Radio
P.O. Box 8
Beech Grove, IN 46107**

Please allow 2-3 weeks for delivery.

Olden Radio is a Trader and Buyer of:

Old Radios...Especially Cathedrals, Mirror, Grandfather Clock, Novelty, Breadboard, Catalin, Crystal, Atwater Kent Electric Wooden Table Models. Also AK Advertising.

All Radio and Comic Collector Premiums and Related Toys. Favorite Characters: Captain Marvel, The Shadow, Buck Rogers, Sergeant Preston, Edgar Bergen/Charlie McCarthy, The Lone Ranger and Space Patrol.

Political Memorabilia. Especially Early Campaign Buttons. Charlie McCarthy, Shadow stud, Shadow picture.

Galaxy Patrol Fan Club, c/o Dale L. Ames, 22 Colton St., Worcester, MA 01610, Communication Specialist. Honors Tom Corbett, Captain Midnight, Space Patrol. Club publish 4 newsletters per year. (Also collect and trade)

John Hintz, P.O. Box 629, Burbank, CA 91501 Collector of all radio premiums. Buck Rogers, Capt. Midnight, Tom Mix, Orphan Annie, etc. Area Code 213-849-6304. 7-10 - 7 days (Pacific Time)

Debby & Marty Krim's

NEW ENGLAND AUCTION GALLERY

CATALOGS

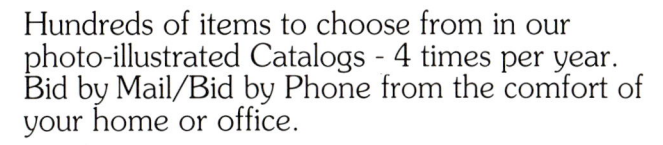

WHERE YOU CAN ALWAYS FIND:

PREMIUMS - WESTERN COLLECTIBLES - TOYS - GAMES - CHARACTER COLLECTIBLES - DISNEY - BASEBALL and MUCH MORE . . . .

Hundreds of items to choose from in our photo-illustrated Catalogs - 4 times per year. Bid by Mail/Bid by Phone from the comfort of your home or office.

! S U B S C R I B E   N O W !

SINGLE ISSUE: $5   ANNUAL (4 Issues): $15

Prices Realized Sheet included.

*** WE ARE MAJOR BUYERS OF MERCHANDISE***
From SINGLE ITEMS to LARGE COLLECTIONS
Call us when selling.

NEW ENGLAND AUCTION GALLERY
P.O. BOX 2273-P
WEST PEABODY, MA 01960
508-535-3140

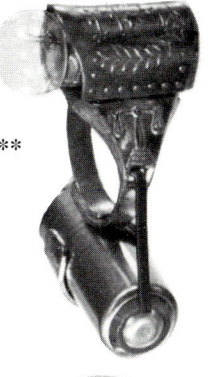

Martin Krim, P.O. Box 2273, West Peabody, MA 01960. Collector of comic strip cartoon games pre-1950 including Superman-Tracy-Mix etc. Area Code (508) 535-3140. Anytime.

Don Maris, Box 111266, Arlington, TX. 76007 Premium prices paid for pre-1970 cereal boxes and cookie boxes, radio premiums and older movie and comic characters advertising materials. Write or phone (817) 261-8745.

Jack Melcher, P.O. Box 14, Waukegan, IL 60087 Wants to buy radio premiums, games, toys, buttons, comic related items, Disney, political, gum wrappers BUY SELL TRADE 312-249-5626

DeWayne Nall, P.O. Box 555, Cleburne, TX 76031 Collector of Captain Midnight premiums and other related paraphernalia, i.e., radio and TV shows, advertising, comics, photos, books, and interesting facts and information. 817-641-5148 evenings.

Robert O'Connor, P.O. Box 29887, Los Angeles, CA 90027. Collector of radio & comic related premiums especially rings & decoders from Capt. Midnight, Tom Mix, Dick Tracy, Buck Rogers, Lone Ranger, etc. Also non-sport gum cards from 1930-1960.

William Osovsky, 2501 Ivy St., Chattanooga, TN 37404. Collector of Ralston Tom Mix premiums, green 20 Grand Ale bottles with neck and paper labels intact, Octagon soap premium kites, Alaga syrup tins.

BUYING
COMIC, CARTOON, TV, 7 MOVIE CHARACTER ITEMS: 1900-1980

Toys, games, books, radio/cereal premiums, dolls, model kits, tin windups, cereal boxes, gum card wrappers/boxes, decoders, rings, giveaways, catalogs, advertising dolls, etc. (Special interest in original boxes, mailers, etc.)

Action Boy	Disney (pre-1960)	Krazy Kat	Popeye
Addams Family	Dr. Evil	Little Nemo	Prince Valiant
Alien	Donald Duck	Lone Ranger	Robots
Gene Autry	Fantasia	Lost in Space	Buck Rogers
Batman	Felix the Cat	Matt Mason	Sci-Fi items
James Bond	Flash Gordon	Man from UNCLE	Shadow
Betty Boop	Flintstones	Jiggs & Maggie	Space Patrol
Beverly Hillbillies	Flip the Frog	Mego items	Spiderman
Bugs Bunny	Gasoline Alley	Mickey Mouse	Star Wars
Bullwinkle, etc.	GI Joe (pre-1970)	Tom Mix	Superman
Capt. Action	Green Hornet	Movie Monsters	Tarzan
Callisto	Henry	Munsters	3 Stooges
Capt. America	Hopalong Cassidy	Orphan Annie	Dick Tracy
Capt. Marvel	Invaders	Outer Limits	Wizard of Oz
Capt. Video	Jetsons	Phantom	and more!!
Tom Corbett	King Kong		
Comic books (pre-1955)			

P. David & Cynthia Welch
RR 2, Box 233, Murphysboro, IL 62966

ALL LETTERS ANSWERED!

BOX TOP BONANZA

SPECIAL OFFER!

Sample Copy $4.00
Annual subscription is $20.00.
For the collector of radio-TV premiums, comic, western and adventure character collectibles, is published six times a year.

Box Top Bonanza Magazine
Joel Smilgis, Publisher-Editor
153-1/2 - 15 Avenue   East Moline, IL 61244
309-752-9627

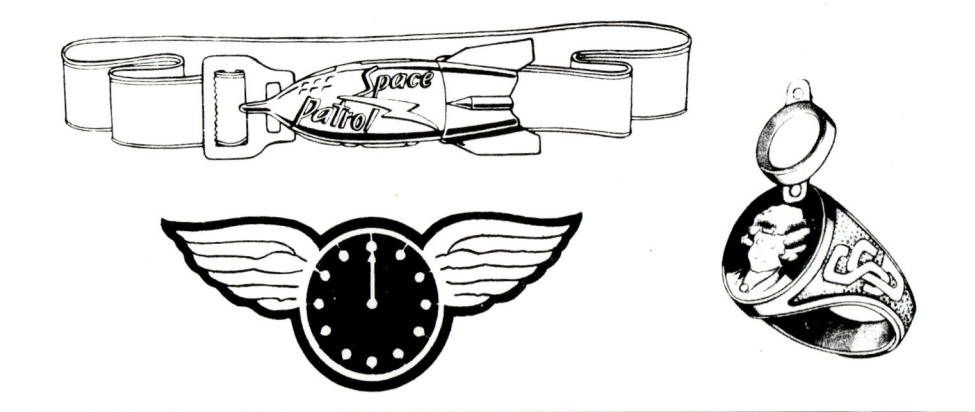

BOB HRITZ
P.O. BOX 1055
GLENDALE HEIGHTS, IL 60139
312-620-0156

WANTED TO BUY: I will pay top prices for items on this list in fine condition. I will pay a premium price for mint examples.

CAPTAIN MIDNIGHT
Mystic Sun God Ring
1957 Plastic Flight Commander Ring
1955-56 Manual
1955-56 Decoder
1957 Decoder (must be exc or better)
1955-56 Membership Card
1955-56 Flight Commander Certificate
1939 Skelly Photo of Patsy
1940 Skelly Flight Commander Pin
1941 Flight Commander Handbook
1942 Flight Commander Handbook
1942 Three Way Mystic Dog Whistle
1942 Orange Plastic Shake Up Mug with Blue Top (embossed design)
1943 Cloth Winged Clock Insignia
1944 Insignia Folder
1948 Iron On Transfer
1949 Insignia Transfer
Any chalk or styrocco figures of C.M. and crew (salt shakers, also original Ovaltine cans and jars with Captain Midnight ads)

PREMIUM RINGS
Captain Midnight Mystic Sun God
Captain Midnight 1957 Plastic Flight Commander
Sky King Aztec Indian Ring
Buck Rogers Repeller Ray Seal Ring
Superman Crusader Ring
Superman Secret Compartment Rings (both)
Green Hornet Secret Compartment Ring
Orphan Annie Altascope Ring
Kellogg's Snap Ring (yellow cap)
Kellogg's Pop Ring (white cap)
Kix Rocket to the Moon Ring with Rockets
Shadow Blue Coal Ring
PEP Airplane Rings (both)
Captain Video Picture Ring

PREMIUMS
Superman Belt and Buckle (Kellogg's)
Buck Rogers Sweater Patch
Buck Rogers Flight Commander and Chief Explorer Badges

TOYS
Japanese Tin Robots and original boxes for same
Corgi Green Hornet Black Beauty Car with Rocket and Spinner

HOPALONG CASSIDY COLLECTIBLES WANTED. Buying single item or your entire collection. **Ron Pieczkowski**, 1707 Orange Hill Dr., Brandon, FL 33511-2632. (813) 685-2338

Ed Pragler, Box 284-R Wharton, NJ 07885 WANTED: Radio premiums, boxtop and cereal giveaways, comic character toys. Also old Cracker Jack (none plastic), gum cards and wrappers, pinback buttons and other nostalgia items.

WANTED: Star Trek/Star Wars: large figures, ceramics, (radio-controlled/diecast toys), clocks, radios, watches, miscellaneous collectibles. **Jerry Randolph**, P.O. Box 8, Beech Grove, IN 46107

Jean Richmond, R.D. 4, Box 6, Wellsville, NY 14895 Collector of George "Gabby" Hayes memorabilia; also, W.C. Fields items wanted. Home telephone 716-593-4484 evenings.

Collecting all Buck Rogers memorabilia: premiums, radio, movies, television (1950-1981), newspaper strips, artwork, toys, games, merchandise, promos, boxes, advertisements, catalogs, posters, publicity, correspondence, biography, foreign. **Eugene R. Seger**, 16043 Bringard, Detroit, MI 48205 313-372-9133 evenings to 1 AM Eastern

Charles Sexton, 3245 Claydor Drive, Beavercreek, OH 45431. Collects radio premiums, comic collector items, radio programs and old movies and serials on video.

Sergeant Preston items, radio premiums, comic character, paper items and pinback buttons, cereal boxes, BLB's, non-sports gum cards, Disneyland souvenirs. Buy or trade. **Jim Silva**, 9562 Cerritos, Anaheim, CA 92804

WANTED: Kellogg's Pep comic, military and plane pins. Also Kix little plastic planes etc. from 1940's to complete personal collection.
Kenneth L. Taunton, 3105 Monroe, Joplin, MO 64804-1452

Tom Tumbusch, P.O. Box 292102, Dayton, OH 45429 Collector of all radio & comic collector premiums including Tom Mix, Sky King, Radio Orphan Annie, Capt. Midnight, etc. Area Code 513-294-2250 weekdays, 9-5.

Erik Turner, 1216 Briarcliff Rd., Reynoldsburg, OH 43068 Collector of radio, cereal and early TV premiums, including Capt. Midnight, Sky King, Tennessee Jed, Kellogg's Pep, Space Patrol, Tom Corbett, Capt. Video, etc. 614-864-1824

Collector of Capt. Midnight radio premiums & Pep cereal pins.
R. Weiss, 4519 Bela Way, Carmichael, CA 95608

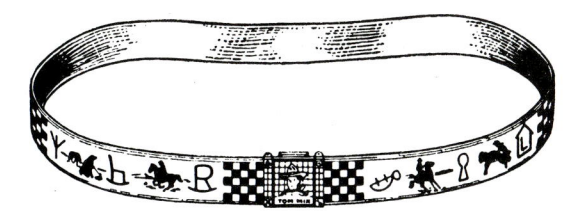

Larry Zdeb, 3031 Prairie, Royal Oak, MI 48072 Wanted - Captain Midnight 1955 Manual, Decoder, 1957 Decoder, Flight Commander items, Sun God/Sheeba rings. Also Space Patrol, Shadow, Jack Armstrong, etc. items. Phone 313-828-7173

WANTED

RADIO PREMIUMS, BOX TOP & CEREAL GIVEAWAYS, COMIC, CHARACTER TOYS

Amer. Eagle Defenders	Hop Harrigan	Sky King
Amos & Andy	Jack Armstrong	Space Patrol
Buck Rogers	Jimmie Allen	Straight Arrow
Captain America	Jr. Justice Society	Superman
Captain Battle	Lone Ranger	Tarzan
Captain Marvel	Mickey Mouse	The Flash
Captain Midnight	Orphan Annie	The Shield
Dick Tracy	Popeye	Tom Mix
Doc Savage	Sgt. Preston	U.S. Jones Cadets
Donald Duck	Shadow	Wonder Woman, etc.
Don Winslow		
Flash Gordon		
Green Hornet	Ralston Straight Shooter	

Items from above characters such as rings, badges, manuals, maps, pinback buttons, toys, banks, watches, clocks, gum cards & wrappers, dolls, books, comics, celluloids. Also want Cracker Jack (no plastic) and Checkers marked items, old Tootsietoys, Political, Automotive, Military Items, old cast iron and tin toys and banks, battery operated toys and lead soldiers. Trade items available.

ED PRAGLER
Box 284-R, Wharton, NJ 07885
Phone 201-875-8293

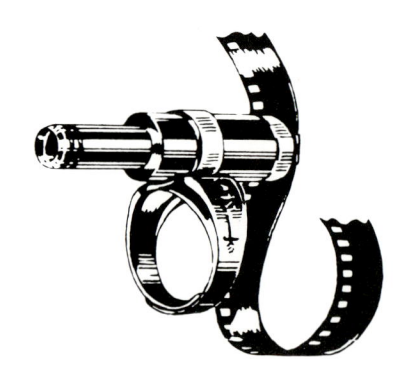

BIBLIOGRAPHY

Books

Lesser, Robert. *A Celebration of Comic Art and Memorabilia.* New York, NY: Hawthorn Books, Inc., 1974.

Eisenburg, Azriel C. *Children and Radio Programs.* New York, NY: Columbia University Press, 1936.

Lyons, Eugene. *David Sarnoff.* New York, NY: Harper and Row, 1966.

Dunning, John. *Tune In Yesterday.* Englewood Cliffs, NJ: Prentice-Hall, Inc., 1976.

Harmon, Jim. *Great Radio Heroes.* Garden City, NJ: Doubleday and Company, 1970.

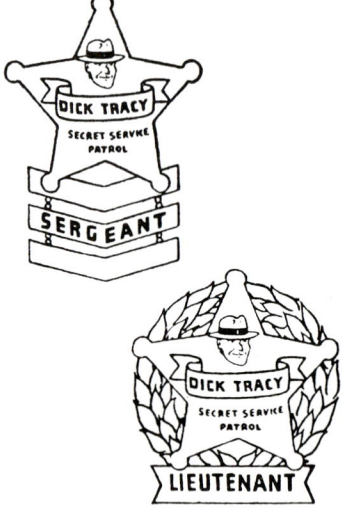

IF YOU COLLECT - - -

DISNEYANA ** COMIC CHARACTER ITEMS ** RADIO PREMIUMS ** POCKET MIRRORS ** WATCH FOBS ** CRACKER JACK ITEMS ** GUN POWDER ADVERTISING ** SPORTS MEMORABILIA ** COWBOY HERO ITEMS ** WORLD WAR I AND II PATRIOTIC ITEMS ** ADVERTISING PINBACK BUTTONS ** SMALL ADVERTISING COLLECTIBLES ** SHIRLEY TEMPLE ITEMS ** AUTOMOTIVE ** OTHER ITEMS OF POPULAR CULTURE . . . .
. . . .

Then HISTORICAL AUCTIONS are for you. Our tri-yearly, fully illustrated catalogues offer the finest in original collectible (no reproductions). Each issue contains a picture of the item, a description, and a guide value. Bidders can participate either by mailing or phone in their bids on any item offered. INTERESTED? One dollar will bring you a sample copy of the auction plus our current sales list.

Write: **HISTORICANA**
P.O. BOX 9007
LANCASTER, PA 17602
717-291-1037

Superman Items Wanted!

TOYS ∗ GAMES ∗ PREMIUMS
FIGURINES ∗ NOVELTIES ∗ ANYTHING!

DANNY FUCHS
209-80 18th Avenue Bayside, NY 11360

Since 1962 "America's Foremost Superman Collector"

© DC COMICS INC.

DeWayne Nall

P.O. Box 555

Cleburne, TX 76033

CAPTAIN MIDNIGHT COLLECTOR

"Mickey may be the leader of the club, but Tomart's Illustrated DISNEY-ANA Catalog & Price Guides are the leader of the definitive guidebooks on Disneyana" - Collector's Showcase Magazine

DISNEYANA

Tomart's DISNEYANA series is the only definitive price guide on Disney collectibles. If it's Disney there is a photo, value listing, or licensee listing in Tomart's Disneyana. No other Disneyana book is as complete or detailed.

Over 25,000 photos in color or b&w help you identify the most collectible Disney items licensed or sold in the U.S. Value estimates are listed for over 40,000 items. Included is a history of Walt Disney, his company and Disney merchandise from 1915 to the present. The four volumes in print will be price updated on a regular basis with additional volumes.

An easy to use classification system helps you locate an item of interest quickly. Each paper bound volume in the 576-page series is 8-1/2" x 11" with 80 pages in full color, including color, plastic laminated covers. Each volume is $24.95 plus $1.90 shipping. Buy the full set for $95 plus $4 shipping.

Below are a few highlights of each volume.

VOLUME ONE HIGHLIGHTS —
American on Parade
Christmas
American Pottery
Clocks
Animation Cels
Coins and Medallions
Banks
Cookie Jars
Books
Disneykins
Brayton's Laguna Pottery
Disneyland
Dolls
Chinaware

VOLUME TWO HIGHLIGHTS —
Donald Duck products
Figures - all types
Lunch boxes
Fisher Price Toys
Maps
Games
Mickey Mouse Clubs
Disney Goebel figurines
Mickey Mouse Magazines
Gum cards & wrappers
Model kits
Hagen-Renaker ceramics
Lamps & nightlights

VOLUME THREE HIGHLIGHTS —
Paint sets
Records
Pinback buttons, badges & tabs
Salt & Pepper shakers
Plates — collector
Sheet music
Postcards
Soap
Posters
Stamps
Puzzles & Puzzle sets
Toothbrush holders
Radios & Phonographs
Trains & handcars
Watches
Wind-up Toys

VOLUME FOUR HIGHLIGHTS —
Alphabetical listing of all recorded Disney Licensees.
Items not found in Volumes One through Three.

"On all matters pertaining to value on Disney items, the final word is Tomart's Illustrated Disneyana Catalog and Price Guides *by Tom Tumbusch"* - Danielle Arnet, syndicated antique columnist for USA Today *and the* Chicago Sun-Times